From Bourbon Street to the Twelfth Dimension

Finding Divine Love

Divine Love to You!

Rachel Otto

BALBOA.PRESS
A DIVISION OF HAY HOUSE

Balboa Press books may be ordered through booksellers or by contacting:

Balboa Press
A Division of Hay House
1663 Liberty Drive
Bloomington, IN 47403
www.balboapress.com
844-682-1282

Because of the dynamic nature of the Internet, any web addresses or links contained in
this book may have changed since publication and may no longer be valid. The views
expressed in this work are solely those of the author and do not necessarily reflect the
views of the publisher, and the publisher hereby disclaims any responsibility for them.

The author of this book does not dispense medical advice or prescribe the use of any
technique as a form of treatment for physical, emotional, or medical problems without the
advice of a physician, either directly or indirectly. The intent of the author is only to offer
information of a general nature to help you in your quest for emotional and spiritual well-
being. In the event you use any of the information in this book for yourself, which is your
constitutional right, the author and the publisher assume no responsibility for your actions.

Any people depicted in stock imagery provided by Getty Images are models,
and such images are being used for illustrative purposes only.
Certain stock imagery © Getty Images.

Print information available on the last page.

ISBN: 979-8-7652-4812-6 (sc)
ISBN: 979-8-7652-4814-0 (hc)
ISBN: 979-8-7652-4813-3 (e)

Library of Congress Control Number: 2023923758

Balboa Press rev. date: 01/18/2024

CONTENTS

PREFACE

Sparkles, star dust, my soul being is the lint of the Universe. After years of investing in myself with spiritual retreats, classes, workshops, and daily meditation this is the answer given to my personal question- who am I? I am a sparkle of love. Now that I know I am divine love, I wanted to let you know that you are divine love too. Not the love we have been taught. We are true divine love; an unlimited energy that makes up our bodies, our mind, our souls, our universe. I think you are the most perfect you. I am already in love with you.

The Universe laughed with me as confirmations soon came from other sources. All of them confirmed that we are just sparkles of love in the cosmos. Not as glamorous as being Cleopatra, Anastasia, or a reincarnated god. The deeper I went into the core of who I am, I knew if I understood myself, I could understand love. I thought this insight would teach me how to live a happy life. If I could find a happy life, so could you. I was right. I found how connected everything is and that love is the power of life. I found out that you really are the perfect you.

My quest for a happier me and a happier world began one drunken afternoon in New Orleans. Like a typical Friday we were meeting for drinks after work. Unlike most Fridays, this Friday was Mardi Gras weekend, which explained why we were wearing costumes. For fourteen days we have filmed all things Mardi Gras. The filming crew included: the VP of company, Myron, a fantastic cameraman; Marvin with his lovely wife; toss in three more of my friends and *the mayor of Bourbon Street*, Ernie Fruge.

We worked hard capturing the spirit of Mardi Gras on film. We met royalty of the krewes, painted with the artist of float making to riding in a parade. At six in the morning, we made king cakes at Swiss Bakery on

St. Charles Avenue. That evening we filmed a parade from the bakery's balcony. We experienced every nook and cranny of this beloved holiday.

As we crowded around an old wooden table on the edge of the sidewalk, Ernie led the drunken ruckus. Ernie started in on his normal buzzed lecture. He was dressed in all white as if he was ready for All Saint's Day at the bayou instead of Mardi Gras. In his drunken clarity, he said loudly, "I love Rachel!" Everyone cheered.

"Rachel has taught me stuff about love I never understood. I don't want to have sex with her. She's my best friend. Yet," he said with a Cheshire cat grin, "she is freaking hot, and I tell all the NOPD officers I am doing her."

The crowd cheered louder as Ernie continued, "Rachel has brought us all together, so let's drink to her and get us all some Rachel love."

The group of friends went wild cheering for me. "Three cheers for Rachel!" With that, everyone poured out into the street with excitement hugging and dancing around.

I giggled and sent love back to them all. My happiness came when I made others happy, and they knew that. My happiness is your happiness. We were all in a feeling of love. It was an amazing feeling that was different, different than other drunken Fridays.

"I want to live in this state," I proclaimed to all. We became a crazy, heart-throbbing, giggling group of love.

We all hugged each other. Ernie started hugging other people on the street and in the bar. Soon others caught on to our happiness. They were calling it "Rachel love." People would ask what we were cheering about. Instead of telling them, we would ask their name and then called it "their love" and all cheered. The cheers kept going on for the next person. The rest of the evening was joyful as we cheered all night, not for me but for everyone we met. We wanted to spread our group love. For the rest of Mardi Gras, we found ourselves on a quest to spread love and cheer.

In that moment, I was in my element. I lived for the hospitality of New Orleans. I was at the top of my game. I loved the French Quarter and I lived on Bourbon Street. I rode my bike up and down its cracked streets for two decades. I was a true French Quarter character as awarded by Wyndham Hotel. Life was fun in New Orleans. It was a lot of work and took a lot of energy. I was friends with chefs, cooks, dishwashers, bellmen, burlesque performers, artisans, and the owners of many fine establishments. I had my own waiter at Antoine's. I have eaten at the chef's table with all the different Brennan's family owners. I loved New Orleans, and she loved me. Yet, I didn't know what love was.

The question is how to keep this joyful life going at the proper pace. How to feel complete and not have to go to every event. How could I live with joy and without drama in a healthy, safe place? What was this feeling I had when Ernie professed our love for each other, but in a way, we could not understand? It was a love not defined in movies or books or in songs. This unconditional feeling of love was toward a man I was not married to. I had no lustful feeling for him. He was not of my kin and he was much older than me. Was this balanced joy I felt when he was around, when I would do projects for him, or when I would just think of him? He couldn't explain it either, yet we had deep feelings for each other.

The more I thought about this "love," the more I realized it was how I felt about the whole crew of people I sat with. I did not want to have sex with any of them. I did not want to hurt myself to make them happy. I totally and unconditionally loved them. Then I wondered if it was just the alcohol I was drinking.

This strange fleeting feeling of love came over me when I was working on an event or function. I was conscious of what I was doing. I wanted this feeling all the time. I did not feel this way at my house in the Marigny neighborhood. It was only a feeling I had with Ernie or with the Super Bowl champion New Orleans Saints. It really bothered me that I couldn't feel this at home. I had horrible anxiety when I was at my house. I lived in fear of things I could not explain. I was depressed and became an alcoholic. I was at my breaking point. Finding my happiness was the only thing that mattered.

I decided to start a spiritual journey. Before I knew it, I was bombarded with "wonderment" intending to excite me into buying a program, a sacred trip, eat new super foods, or learn new ways to stand on my head. I was overwhelmed and wanted to do it all.

What I've come to find is that the average person does not care about sacred geometry or how creation works, only about religion, political affiliation, or what church one goes to. Spirituality typically shows up when people are knee-deep in flood waters, or the fires are coming near them as their lungs are tightening within their chests. For some reason, most of us only pray to a higher source when we are desperate. We pray when we are afraid or in need, or if our life is in danger, or those we love may be suffering. Learning how to keep a balance in life with love and gratitude means we don't need to go to the extreme praying, begging, or negotiating to stay happy on this planet.

I was just looking for divine love. Divine love and divine consciousness answered all my questions about energy, angels, guides, healing, community, and the future. I found all of this and more in divine love. The best part was that I always had the answers. Divine Love powers everything in the universe. It is what we are made of. Divine love is the purest form of self-love, without an ego.

These are the stories of my life from this and from other lifetimes. I've changed the names and details of the events. I have come to an understanding of my own personal life. The desire to understand life did start earlier for me. This was the calling I needed to change my life. As a child I was taught to pay attention to life's lessons but forgot as an adult living the party lifestyle.

I invite you to join me on an expedition of life and spirituality through the understanding of dimensions powered by divine love. I will keep it simple. Dimensions are sacred geometry at work, constantly creating life. They exist within you. Let's learn how to take an astral flight and find our own understanding of spirituality. We will look at twelve dimensions in each chapter. There are meditations to help you explore each dimension. Other meditations teach you how to connect to nature, your personal guides, beings of light, and otherworldly beings. Basically, it's a book about understanding how to live a happy life on planet Earth.

While reading this book you may experience a light feeling, happiness, joy, freedom, expansion, and other healing responses. There is no right or wrong way of living on Earth. It's your personal journey, your Earth walk is just the way you chose it to be.

There is plenty of room for your own interpretation of each dimension. At the end of each chapter will be a channeled message from myself and others. I would like to open the doors for all beings to be able to find their special gift. To know that we all are truly divine beings that are connected to the world.

This book was conceived thinking about you and your happiness, also called Unity Consciousness. I want you to have everything that makes you happy and brings you joy. After you've done a meditation or read a passage that stirs an emotion, I recommend writing down or expressing the thoughts and feelings as they come up. Doodle on the side of the book. Keep a journal, maybe even dance about your day.

The idea is for you to experience and create your own beliefs. Your Earth walk is a very personal experience living on Earth. The tricky part is we didn't get the rules or all the information. It has been hidden in caves and monasteries, out of reach for the average person for centuries. We have forgotten who we were. We have forgotten the lives we have lived. We have lost our meaning of life and turned it, instead, into clichés or the latest social media post.

Choosing divine love over fear will change your life and the planet forever. By knowing equality with all things, we can understand the bigger picture of life in terms of dimensions. Experience the most joy every morning when you wake up. The meaning of life is not found in church, a temple or resort; it is embedded in your heart. We are to live in love! We are to experience life, not be hurt by or scared of it. When you let go of the past it will change your perspective. When choosing divine love to guide us, we become conscious. It will change your world. You are worthy of unconditional love. It is possible to change. It's all up to you. It's worth the effort to change to love.

I would like you to feel your divinity as the most perfect creation you are. "You are enough", as they say in pop culture. We are here for each other. These are my thoughts on how we can understand love and energy in a different way and how to live a peaceful life. And yes, I do have my own desires for the world. I want to live in a free society, and I do believe this is how we can start it.

My desire for you is to find your own meaning of life, your own silvery golden cord that weaves your tapestry of life. I believe we are all equal, and that we all have the same capabilities to grow and expand. It is only by choice of love over fear that we can do this. It's your life, your free will. I want to help you find your truths through meditation.

IN THE BEGINNING

It was during an orgasm while pleasuring myself that I began to remember the beginning of the universe. It was the existence of one conscious love. It was a vibration of energy of pure, in an orgasmic space. This memory took me back to the beginning of *ALL*, to the first formation of the OM sound. OM is a feeling of prismatic infinite oneness, an expansion of all the senses, a perfect single atom vibration of *ALL*.

This was not my normal daily release, instead it was my exploration of self. I thought to myself I have just experienced perfect oneness. I did not have to have do any more research on understanding my soul being. After taking one course on how to work with angels I thought I knew everything. I understood the entire universe, I thought to myself. Boy was I wrong, it was only the first door of the universe opening.

My first interest in understanding what a soul is came around when I was eleven years old. Ms. Vee first taught our sixth-grade class how to "leave" our bodies when we were in pain or preparing to go to the dentist. She taught us how to calm ourselves down and let go of physical pain. She gave examples of being at the dentist's office and being nervous about dental work. She would leave the office because she was scared. To help her not be afraid, she learned how to meditate and mentally leave her body.

Ms. Vee was an awesome teacher and was one of the foundations of the path laid in front of me. Two years later, in an acting class taught by local college students in Iowa, I first learned of the hara. I was taught life skills in all my extra activities.

Oh, what's hara? The hara is a physical spiritual center point inside the body at the lower part of your belly. You may have heard of hara meditations or hara breathing when you breathe through your belly. The hara is where you store and build energy, your core of energy. This core of energy, your hara, is part of your connection to *ALL, God, Source, Creator of Everything,* called your Godspark.

In that eighth grade acting class, I did my first guided meditation based on Shirley MacLaine's book *Out on a Limb.* One of the college-age teachers was reading it, and he was really getting into it. He wanted to make us understand how to flow together naturally, and how we could come together in a scene with a specific feeling of unity. The musical we were doing was called *Peace Child.* It made sense because we were exploring new ways of thinking.

One of the meditations he taught us from MacLaine's book, was us projecting ourselves outside our bodies. You would imagine you were held to Earth by a silver cord of life. It was an amazing feeling, an experience I would repeat at home every night for years. It was an awesome way to spend my evening until boys came into my reality.

I tried meditation again in college but couldn't sit still. I almost flunked Tai Chi class because my attention span was dwindling. I could not focus; I could not sit down. I was so hyper that the only peace I could find was in cannabis or sex. I don't know if I started using cannabis because it really did calm me down or if it was because of the boys or if simply for my love of plants. The "bad boys" I fell in love with were all major cannabis smokers. I was in Nebraska, the state whose tagline is "Nebraska, it's not for everyone."

As "bad" as the motorcycle-riding, pot-smoking men, they all graduated with various master's degrees. Not to mention, cannabis is now legal in most of the states. As even as you read these words, federal regulations are changing. Funny how a change of perspective can change the way you see your own life.

I traveled away from Nebraska to find a new life. Living judgment free, I see these times differently than I used to. It was just the time for exploration and experiencing joy.

New Orleans answered the call of my imagination for twenty-two years. New Orleans is a true extreme lifestyle of whatever you are into. If you love food, it's not just award-winning cuisine that's available. There are also festivals for just one fruit or vegetable. There is a major event every month. No matter what your interest is, at some point, New Orleans will have a huge event or conference to celebrate it. I made no less than six original costumes per year most of the time I lived there. New Orleans is not like the rest of America.

While living in New Orleans, I lived on Bourbon Street for eight years. For those years, 1134 Bourbon Street or *hell* spelled upside on a calculator, was our home. Not a bar or an antique shop, as many visitors thought as they wandered into my apartment when I did spring cleaning. It was a lifestyle I am so grateful to have experienced. I came to understand more about the world and that I was just a bright light in a dark vortex of human misery.

I meditated. Well, let's be truthful, I was only actually meditating the last two years I lived there. I had only tried meditation because my lovely girlfriend Ariel knew it would help me. I just could not do it. I could not let go of all the thoughts running through my head. Thoughts of planning for the next Mardi Gras party, hurricane worries, making budgets at work, politics and what was for dinner. I would be so wrapped up in anxiety that I could not see up from down. All I knew was go! Go! *Go!*

Go where? You may ask. Go to work, go to the bar, go to the meeting, go to the store. Go to bed, go to work, go to the bar, go to the store. Go to see friends, go to a meeting, go to bed, go to the store. Go to the Saints game, go to work, go to a party, go to a parade, go to a meeting, go to the bar, go to the store, go to bed. Go, go, go!

Do you know that feeling? For more than twenty years I could not sit down or calm down. For half of my life, I was running as fast as I could to get nowhere. Something had to give. I was running against a mythical clock in my mind. I was working toward goals I'd set as a child. I was running up debt and making a lot of trash. It was not much of a spiritual journey.

It took almost twenty-five years for me to go back to the techniques I had learned from my sixth-grade teacher. Now, I was initiated into several different ways by other gurus, teachers, and shamans. Each had their own way of getting to the same places or doing healing. My intention was to understand life. But instead, it was a place to hide from reality and the stark reality my marriage was not right for me.

In 2011, I officially began my studies of Reiki or energy healing, after the same girlfriend threatened to end our friendship if I didn't find my personal path. It was the wake-up call I needed. I very much wanted to study spirituality, healing, and the mysteries of the world. It was time for me to step into my joy and understand more than what was on the surface. It was a dream of mine to be a healer. I'd loved the X-Men comic books and cartoons as a child. I always wanted a special power, something to make me special.

Energy work uses some form of healing modalities to help with physical, emotional, and spiritual issues, called integrated medicine. *Integrated medicine* is a broad term that includes healing modalities like Reiki, laying on of hands, pranic healing, reflexology, acupuncture, vibrational healing, crystal healing, sound baths, and much more. Depending on modalities, energy will flow through the body's subtle energy systems.

Energy systems can be found within your body as well as surrounding your body. They have names like meridians, auric bodies, and chakras. These invisible energy structures are where many believe disease can be found. It could be said that you are physically or emotionally not well, your body is at "dis-ease" with yourself. Meaning that your body is not in line with yourself, your community, or your life. By clearing out what no longer serves you, removing the toxins in your body, you can find balance and good health.

Energy healing of any kind can help you heal yourself both physically and mentally. Energy healing works with modern allopathic medicine. It is not to be used in replacement of going to the doctor.

Reiki practitioners and energy healers can feel where your body has pain. They should not replace medical doctors but, instead, should work with Western medicine. Or better yet, find yourself a holistic doctor, work with a certified naturopath, use functional medicine or a holistic nutritionist.

When I attended a conference with the Dalai Lama, he told us healers were needed and that the art of healing could no longer hide in secrecy and mystery. He gave me courage to step into my desires, my passion, myself. First, I had to learn to live my life in balance and to find peace and understand my body. A healthy mind and healthy body would be the first step.

At the time, the movie *The Secret* was big in spiritual communities. I was able to manifest my dreams into reality at the drop of a hat. Not knowing the whole power of the law of attraction, *The Secret*'s author gave us the first part but left the second part out until the next book was written. Luckily for me, I did not have to wait for the second book. I had already understood gratitude from my own experiences. The more grateful I was for my life; the faster things would manifest.

Since I did have a complete understanding of the law of attraction, I was able to get bonus money from my father during a downturn in the country's economy. Using the manifestation techniques, I was able to will everything from a dream job to getting small objects.

Who would have guessed that helping a stranger in the building where I worked would bring me my favorite brand name of makeup? I did just as the movie said to do. I asked the universe about it. I imagined myself using the new eyeshadows in the morning as I scraped the last bits from my old container. I imagined what I looked like with the new makeup and then said, "Thank you, Universe, for allowing me to be happy with my new makeup, as I love the way it makes me look and feel."

A week later, after helping a random stranger, she gave me a beautiful gift, a complete set of Urban Decay make-up. The random stranger was one of the most well-known makeup artists in Hollywood. She was in town doing a movie, and she just happened to be staying in the building where I worked. No coincidences.

At this same time, I received money from my father. The money from my dad was more than enough to finish remodeling the bathroom and start my journey of myself. I do have to thank my parents, as every major turning point in my life it was them who supported me. It wasn't a special time, nor did it feel like a hero's journey. It was just another divine love moment in my life that I had created on my Earth walk. My journey was started by my own desire for more happiness.

My first reiki classes in Metairie, Louisiana was just the right starting place for my Earth walk. My first reiki teacher introduced me to Walter Lübeck. It was his class for angelic healing that taught me how to meditate and introduced me to astral realms. I studied Rainbow Reiki for years. He helped me become the healer I wanted to be. He helped me achieve 1st Dan Master Rainbow Reiki, one of the titles I cherish the most.

In these first moments of guided meditation, where I would experience oneness, it was my own personal experience. Walter showed me how to open the doors. From there, I just followed the guides for the highest good. I felt for the first time the presence of the archangel Metatron with his sacred geometry known as Metatron's Cube. When I was doing this meditation with Walter, he passed by my chair and gently nudged the space around me. I could immediately feel the spinning of the astral space I was in.

Perfect meditation with answers did not happen at first. I was hiding in meditation when the doors first opened. It was such a different experience than I'd ever felt. Overall, I tend to be a happy person. But the truth was, I was not happy or balanced at the time I started studying reiki. I was looking for something.

In meditation I just loved to step away from reality into a space that was nothing but pleasure. One of these heavens is called a Place of Bliss or Zen. This became a meditation of choice for me, as I was at the end of a marriage and was looking for myself. Such a time of transformation is a typical time for many people to "start" a spiritual journey. What I realized later is that our entire life is a spiritual journey. I was trying to escape my reality, instead of embracing my life.

In this guided meditation, led by Archangel Raphael, I would feel only oneness of pure joy, peace, balance, knowing, and wisdom. It was perfect harmony as one would say. Even what looked like chaos was fantastic. In these meditations, I could smell the cardamom of the angelic dragons. I would be allowed into the highest goddess heavens, feeling the soft petals of the roses. I could even smell the roses as they uplifted me into divine love.

It wasn't just prismatic colors and smells but also feelings of vibration in every cell of my being. Brilliantly it would push my buttons and set me into minutes-long orgasms of ecstasy without any drugs, alcohol, or plant medicine.

This is the existence when we are one with *ALL*. *ALL* is known as Source, Creator of All, or God, depending on what your religion or culture is. This true, pure Source is unlimited and has no judgment. It is pure and totally awesome love and consciousness.

To be honest, for me, it was a heaven of pleasure. I guess this is where Aleister Crowley, the English occultists and philosopher, got lost in. I totally can understand why. Being in pure divine love with angels in all forms is an amazing feeling. It was also a safe place. I was being fulfilled in meditation like I never thought possible.

It was the most sexual experience at that point in my life. And yet it was all safely confined to my guest room, by myself. This new form of self-pleasure was unlike what I was previously used to. This was a full-body experience, with orgasms lasting for fifteen to twenty minutes, not a few moments.

The blissful feeling stayed with me. I was finally happy. I really thought this was all I needed, and I could continue my fast-paced life easily now. Every day for months after dinner, I would go lie in the guest bedroom, taking all my anxiety from the day and releasing it in a loud, orgasmic, cosmic scream.

One day after work, I went into my daily routine of private spiritual studies. Memories of the beginning of time came flooding back to me. I started tingling, this time it was different. Immediately, I closed my eyes to go back to the memory while diving deep into a meditative state.

What happened next took me years to overcome and understand. As I closed my eyes to go back to the feeling, I was immediately physically bopped on the top of my head. Physically, I could feel something tap me or give me a little pop of consciousness, saying, "Get out."

"What was that?" I said out loud.

Raphael, my guardian angel, blocked me! He said I could no longer enter because I was hiding and not dealing with my real-life issues. My marriage was an issue, and I was unhappy with what my life had become. Instead of being able to forget all my troubles like I had been doing every day for six months, I got kicked out of bliss and back into reality. That really sucked, and I was a bit embarrassed that it happened.

It was true. I was kicked out of the heaven, of bliss, of *Zen* because Archangel Raphael told me I had to stop hiding. He told me that, if I was truly going to complete a spiritual journey, I had to be present on Earth and stop hiding in other heavens. The knowledge I needed to learn from the heavens was inside me. I had learned. Now it was time for me to move on.

Really? I thought. *Did I just get kicked out of heaven?*

I did.

It was almost seven years until I went back to this specific place. I'd learned my lessons, and I took that knowledge to help others. Everything we need to know is within us, and we can use meditation to seek answers, but we cannot exist there or hide in bliss. Later it was explained to me that I was *spiritually bypassing.* A great term to make me wonder how many seekers have had to come to this understanding.

I finally found what meditation could really do for me, but instead of using it to better myself, I was using it to hide. I could have just as well been watching pornography or masturbating in the shower instead of going into a peaceful state. I learned I had to deal with life instead of hiding in meditation. I often wonder how many people use spiritual journeys as a crutch to not change their lives.

I used to think it was only wealthy or retired people who could take the "big trip" to a highly spiritual place. I know it is a thing for retired people to find themselves after a long career on spiritual vacations in Sedona, India, Tibet, Egypt, or Hawaii. For many it may be the right time to do a spiritual journey when you are retired.

Then there are some people who follow gurus around to wellness workshops like rock and roll groupies. Many feel like it is just a reunion of old friends sharing their experiences. Only once did I see permanent change in a community from these types of events. Many of the best gatherings happen organically with your own tribe of friends. When spiritual journeys become overly based on profit, with a lot of selling and parlor tricks or gurus leading people to give up everything to follow them, is when you need to pull out discernment.

For me, the first spiritual events I attended felt more like cults, acting no different than corporations. They only wanted money or your soul. Here, there were women fawning over yogis. I saw "spiritual" men misleading people. A running theme of people getting caught up in spiritual sex, instead of diving deep into real issues. No. I was not at a tantric event. That would have been awesome, and I would have been prepared.

What I began to understand is that I am not the only one who hides in spirituality or "metaphysical" worlds. I believe many people get caught up in the different modalities of healing and continue to look outside themselves. Many use practices like Tantra for sexual release instead of personal growth and use hierarchy in spiritual practice to drain your wallet. From online psychic readers to the new "loom" practices, which take their structure from pyramid schemes, there are several ways to get lost in spiritual practices financially. Even in the now moment, I have gotten caught up myself, again with a new spiritual group that was going to lead me to new clients and promises of grand futures. After a year with my $2000 investment, I still have no clients from the new program.

I got into rituals, months-long meditations, and mantras. I followed certain spiritual practices, some very ancient. I have come to understand that we cannot find divine love and divine consciousness in old paradigms. They have all been tainted at some point or monetized. Currently, very few practices are authentic. These events are a great way to learn and expand but they may include old fear or misleading information.

Spirituality, or the belief in the mysteries of life, comes from within and isn't at an external location. The spiritual journey is not one that can be purchased, no matter what anyone says. It is only a personal experience in life. There is no time travel back to undo your past. Only space to forgive and learn the lessons from the past.

I do believe many issues people are facing today are just being covered or hidden in medications and false hopes. Sprinkle in deep fake videos, and the latest trending reel, and fear is allowed to continue to expand. Capitalism is king. We are, in fact, addicted to fear and power.

Meditation offers amazing places to learn from, not to hide in. I have met people who have become hermits and traded real life for astral living. Not ideal. Nor is taking designer drugs to get to this state. I have come to understand that other realms are here to teach us and to enable us to experience places we may never go. They are not here for holidays or to hide in or to party in. They are places to expand our personal knowledge and understanding.

Side note, when you truly experience your joy and balance, you can achieve the same feelings as you do with designer drugs. The big difference is, with drugs, the lessons are fleeting. You may be able to instantly talk to the trees while you are on Ayahuasca. Integrating that feeling into your everyday life needs a clear experience. I have experimented with some designer drugs. At first it was just that awesome giddy feeling and loving everything. The next day was painful physically, but still I would journal what I experienced. After years of meditating and self-exploration, I could integrate lessons learned. Plant medicine no longer became a hiding place but, rather, a tool for me to calm down, sleep, or let go.

Not all plant medicine is meant for daily consumption or even needed to test human boundaries. I am not a fan of the abuse of ayahuasca, it has become another tool to escape from reality that only those with money can do. Unless you are a heroin addict, ayahuasca is not the answer. I would start with a cacao ceremony. The cacao ceremonies I have attended have all opened my heart. Each has changed me for my highest good.

People get caught in the web of micro-dosing psychedelics without professional supervision. They get stuck in a false reality. I call it the "ego cloud." This is a dark cloud of false greatness, a man-made heaven where you get to talk to trees and otherworldly beings. It's where self-proclaimed gurus of the current drug can show you how to connect to fear, connect to anxiety, connect to a space of greed and self-loathing. The biggest disappointment of the ego cloud is that none of the lessons you learned stay with you. They are passing experiences that make you want more but do not fully integrate into your being. Friends have taken their own lives after being stuck in the ego cloud of lies. It hurts seeing friends caught in harmful activities or cults. You want to help them, but you can't set them free from their desires. This is a hard lesson to learn, you can't always help others.

Some plant medicines are like tricksters. They will lead you to believe the only way to this place of bliss is with their drug of choice. They keep you in a cycle of addiction. Maybe not to the substance they give you but, instead, to the false feeling of connection. It is also found in sugar, coffee, alcohol and other legal products that disconnect us from ourselves. In this creates a "dream of separation" or the false disconnection from nature, or the world. Individuals deeply long for communion, a way to reconnect to themselves and to nature.

We have a long history of substance abuse. Just look at the name given to alcohol. It was called "spirits" because people felt it brought them closer to God. They could feel God's "spirit" when they drank the elixir the monks made. That's not much different than new designer drugs.

New, exciting research is being done with ketamine, psilocybin, cannabis, and CBD. With professional supervision, true shamans or doctors prescribing you medicine for addiction, depression, and other mental health issues. You can have life-changing results. We must show respect for these medicines and stop trying to escape from reality. Instead of hiding from reality, you can use them to help you experience true joy for living and heal past brain injuries and emotional states. Like I keep saying, this is best when done with professional guidance and not at a festival.

Life on Earth

When we are born, we are not handed a manual to tell us how to live. Nor is there one resource that can explain the mysteries of life. Trust me. I've looked in libraries, in art history, and online. No one path is perfect. Instead, the greatest gift given to us as humans on Earth is the experience of life itself with all its joy in the present moment. For us to experience life, the Source, the Creator, just wants us to live happily. We have all come to Earth to learn the same thing. We just don't know that until we do a spiritual walk or it's the end of our time here. I want you to know that spirituality is not outside of you, nor is it just meant for gurus and spiritual leaders. Living life is a spiritual journey or Earth walk.

Our great books have been tainted by the human ego or a need for suppression to gain power. The problem is that the people around us didn't know what they were doing either. They thought they knew what they were doing. They made mistakes and hid them deep down inside themselves or buried them in a closet. Many great lies are hidden away in basements and attics. Secrets are also hidden in the body, as examined by the book *The Body Keeps the Score* by Bessel van der Kolk, MD. The books discuss how past trauma is held in cells in our body. This book explains that some pain is not caused by bodily harm but may be from a memory or emotional trauma we have not released from the past.

Once, while getting a tattoo, the artist lifted the needle off my back, and I started crying in pain. The artist said, "I am not even touching you now. Why are you crying?" He got defensive. I could not stop weeping for my childhood traumas. The tattoo artist hit the place physically on my body where I was storing my sadness. It was not the pain of the needle. It was the pain of a situation I'd held onto for thirty years. He'd just freed the pain and tears from storage. I cried for days, releasing the trauma I held within my body.

"It's a Small World"

I vividly remember my first ride on Disney's "It's a Small World," which had automated dolls of different world cultures spinning around and popping up and down joyfully. Being a Nebraska girl, I'd only seen other cultures on TV, in books, or briefly experienced them at the state fair. It was on this Disney Land ride that it did feel like we were all just humans, the same exact makeup on the inside. We are different color varieties on the outsides, just like the farm eggs. Their shells came in different colors, but the insides were the same. The free-range chickens who lead happy lives gave bright orange yolks, yet those who were trapped in fear and cages produced basic white eggs with light yellow yokes. Neither is bad or evil, just formed from different circumstances. Once a guru told me we are all the same soul experiencing life. I could understand that when seeing the robotic children in the ride. We are all part of Source. We are each a drop of its soul.

From this experience in California, my eyes were open to a new understanding of being human. We are similar and not so different. It was on this trip at age thirteen that I fell in love with Southern California, and its lifestyle stuck with me. I was "California dreaming." It would take me thirty-some years to get back to the state and really experience my own understanding of life.

At thirteen, I first understood the concept of a *sentient being.* Which means one that has the ability to feel, perceive, and to experience life. By the end of this book, I do hope you will have an understanding that everything is just conscious energy. A plastic cup is made of conscious energy, just at a different vibrational level than animals or humans. As I understand it, every sentient being, well, everything, can simply be separated into two parts. We are all made up of two main factors that create our life, the material or the physical, and the soul or spirit. Your physical self is comprised of minerals, star dust, water, and atoms with your personal identification located in your DNA. As in the movie *Avatar,* though we may not appear to be blue and have a tail, we are directly connected to Earth and all her beings on it. The movie may have been just a glamorized version of Earth. We are all connected to the same tree of life, we just don't get to see it like you do in the movie.

The second part that creates your individual being is called your soul. It is your soul that carries all the history. It's your soul that preplanned your Earth walk and wrote its journey in the stars. It's your soul that's directly connected to the Creative Source or *ALL.* It is your soul that has history stored in the Akashic records. The Akashic Records are a collection of all universal events, thoughts, expressions, and emotions of all life forms: past through future.

In scientific terms we, and *ALL* of existence, are the product of Vesica Piscis. We are the sliver of life where conscious light (knowledge) meets divine love (energy). This place where two circles meet created the universe and our physical world. When the circle of conscious light collided with divine love, beings of light, planets, and everything was created. The Vesica Piscis is the simplest form of sacred geometry.

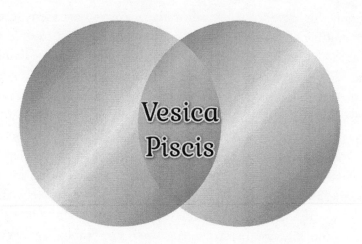

Vesica
Piscis

Beings of light come from stars, which is our true angelic state. Angels or *beings of light* give structure and harmony to all universes. After time unknown, beings of life felt mundane. *ALL*, the Creative Source or God, wanted to experience everything. Like a gigantic ocean, waves of droplets of souls expanded to feel everything. The energy of divine love gave creation a physical place to experience joy, pleasure, and honey lavender ice cream. Earth was this place where beings of light could physically experience everything God or *ALL* wanted.

Life is intended to be joyous! Life is not meant for suffering, pain, and fear as it has been taught for thousands of years. Ancient books tell of the twenty thousand years of pain and suffering, which we no longer need. *Now* is the time for you to experience a more joyful life through your connections, your beliefs, your truths between you and *ALL*.

I feel compelled to tell you about another understanding that I have gained on my journey. Titles are not always the correct description of the study. As I have struggled to decide what to call myself, my original thought was I am a "spiritualist." At the time, my thinking was that this meant I studied spirituality. I was told and shown differently at the oldest spiritualist center of North America, Lily Dale Assembly. Lily Dale is the real-life "Harry Potter Academy" of the USA. It has been in existence since 1879 in upstate New York. It has a magical healing aura and a feeling of oneness. It could be one of the greatest assemblies of people who study in spirituality. I am so honored to have studied and taught there. It, to me, is just wow!

I had some of my greatest experiences at Lily Dale, more than at any one location. Experiences that ranged from photographing past relatives, bending silver spoons with my mind to being blessed by a chartreus chrysanthemum. I learned how to commune with trees. I experienced all senses, from smelling the popcorn from the long past to seeing fairies and trolls. The plant people are marvelous there, as they each tell the stories of their dealing with humans.

The students, guests, teachers, speakers, the healing house and the grounds are all incredibly special. Exceptional beyond your imagination, it exists in the physical third dimension yet at times reaches far past the twelfth dimension. They too have third-dimensional issues that are to be embraced while there. The place is in its most original state. As in all places, some do feel that the energy has become stagnant, I think of it more as being timeless.

At Lily Dale, I was fortunate enough to take a class on mediumship called "To Touch the Soul: How to Become a Medium" by the brilliant instructor, Rev. Judith Rochester, PhD. Here, I learned how to communicate with human souls, as I had already been communicating with beings of light or angels. It was an awesome class. The staff was slightly taken aback by how easily I absorbed the knowledge. Instantly, I was able to commune with flowers and see ancestors arrive to pass messages on to me. I received channeled messages. I saw spirits and photographed them, as well as had the courage to give readings at Inspiration Stump as a student. It was incredible to have the courage to speak at the same place where the greatest spiritualists presented messages nightly. One of the members even told me that only once before had she seen someone who was able to receive all this new information so quickly.

I had been trained and initiated into healing with the Nine Choirs of Angels and Rainbow Reiki before my trip to Lily Dale. I was taught to leave human souls alone. "What knowledge could they (human souls) possibly have for us?" I was told.

To me, it was very logical. Why would I want to channel a human soul that was trapped on Earth or lived a hundred years ago? Such souls would have no understanding of modern issues. Nor would they have my highest good in mind if they had not gone to heaven. Only when my clients had human spirits around them, who had committed suicide or overdosed and wanted to be heard would I listen to human spirits. They would give beautiful messages of love for me to channel. These exceptions for me working with human souls were always an acknowledgement of the love they did have for their friends and family.

Once I was properly trained in mediumship, it was easy for me. I was taught in Rainbow Reiki how to free human souls from Earth, so they could feel the joy, peace, and healing of heaven. I was taught that ghosts and poltergeists are just human souls stuck on Earth because either they died instantly and do not understand they are dead. Another cause could be they died with a strong belief in hell and did not feel worthy of heaven. When they saw the light, they turned from it in fear, thinking they would be judged or that the bright light was the flames of hell.

I have been shown that hell as we know it, does not exist. It is a human creation of control or misunderstanding of the underworld and other forms of heaven. I have found a good understanding of the process of death in *The Tibetan Book of the Dead*. When I read the *Egyptian Book of the Dead*, I shuddered inside with memories of escorting people into the heavens. I felt sad when reading the human-influenced sections on judging their lives. I knew in my heart this was not true. This section was added to control humans' free will. This is similarly the case with so much of our culture today. That is what capitalism and marketing is all about; trying to get you to buy with a specific standard.

What Lily Dale really taught me was that I am not a spiritualist. A spiritualist is one who communicates with the dead only and belongs to a certain religious structure. I am connected to my family lineage and I use the guides of my ancestors. I work with them to learn about my past mistakes, to clear out family karma, to bring in abundance and the highest good. It is fun for me to connect to my grandmothers. I chat with them while cooking or baking. To me, connecting with past relatives is a personal thing, as I understand not everyone is open to hearing them. Spiritualists are to help those who can't hear information from past loves ones or need personal peace with physical death.

I am so grateful for my lessons at Lily Dale. The lessons came from every object, plant, animal and location. The land at the time was one of the few safe places for fairies and trolls. In fact, I saw my first real-life fairy there. I was utterly shocked. It looked just like a fairy I had seen in a cartoon. I also met my first troll there and not just any troll but the troll king! He allowed me to step out of my fears of monsters and into the understanding that just because it looks different, does not mean it is bad or evil. He pointed out that evil cloaks itself in beauty. Reminding me of the Bible story of the wolf in sheep's clothing, telling me to use discernment.

The channeling experience I had at Lily Dale was amazing for me. It started in meditation, a fuzzy buzzy feeling. I could feel the top of my head opening as the conscious light poured in. It was amazing and unreal at the same time. I picked up my journal and began to write in large script. I did not stop to read what I wrote. Nor did I even look at the paper. My head was being held straight. My back was straight, and I was in a trancelike state.

I always know I am connected to spirits or other guides when my eyes start watering. That day at Lily Dale tears randomly began to pour down my face. I could not feel them, I saw the drops of water on my hands. The energy flew through me—so quickly I didn't even know I could write that fast.

I was not able to sleep that night. I was tuned into the right frequency for Radio Wave beings. They sent information, downloads and healing. It was the most awesome feeling of oneness. I was truly in awe being connected to something higher and great that made me feel joyful. I have included this channeled message at the end of this chapter.

My personal beliefs do not go over well with some people. Some human souls have not elevated to heaven. There are those who would use lost souls as their scouts, their personal assistants. Unknowingly, I freed many souls from New Orleans, just by showing up.

I am not a psychic either. As I have been taught, we can only be given a glimpse of the next six months. Because of free will, anything can happen at any given minute. Not to say anything bad about psychics, as many of my friends are readers. People like Vanessa De Luna and Fatima Mbodj will not misguide you. I would say use discernment with any reader, even those on Jackson Square in New Orleans. Authenticity does exist in the psychic realm. You must use discernment before paying for any type of service, healer, psychic, or even a regular doctor. Always ask yourself, is this person for my highest good?

What I have come to understand about myself is that I am love. That does not translate easily in a third-dimension reality. In the third dimension, I call myself a healer, a spiritual coach. I have been trained in the healing arts. My astrological chart hints at me helping to elevate this world. My favorite name for what I do was given to me by a wonderful friend, D'ete. She said, "You're a mystic, Rachel." That resonates with me, as I do not follow anyone's healing modality. I am a *loveist*. I believe that love can be the answer to everything. I combine all religious beliefs, rather than subscribing to one. I follow the ways of the medicine women. I look to science for my oracles and guides. I feel the energy of chakras and see their colors. I hold space for those around me, knowingly and unknowingly. I read crystals and rocks. I talk to trees, birds, electronics and to the moon. I use sound to heal and know I still have much to learn.

My joke is that I can take you into the highest dimensions in meditation, and I know how to do taxes. What that means is I may be way out there on some topics, but I am grounded in reality. As long as money exists, I will play the game.

The rules I follow are natural law. Life is like a hoop or the medicine wheel that our ancestors tried to teach us. Just move forward with the experience of life, up and down, judgement-free. Like the seasons, we grow and change just like our Mother Earth does. Let's flow together. Accept that your life will always be full of learning. After all, Earth is called the learning planet.

The Meaning of the Journey

I believe the meaning of life can be summed up in a single line: You are a drop of the Creator's energetic soul, with your individual record, living on planet Earth as a being to experience free will and as much joy as possible.

For now, let's just agree that the meaning of life is to experience *Earth*. Earth is a learning planet. We are here to learn and experience, not to be controlled by others.

I believe everyone is capable of living a happy, sustainable life that suits their individual needs. As human beings, we as a collective have been tricked. Life before the year 2022 was a facade of what could be. The popular story of creation isn't how the original plan happened. Nor do the dates match up to the physical evidence of a world history of millions of years in the making. We have been living in untruths for so long that to feel divine love may feel awkward. You may have a healing response just by these few words, feelings of love.

The confusion comes when fear tries to control your happy life. Anxiety can overwhelm anyone's journey at any time. The key is to figure out how to take back control and stop the anxiety.

Meditation

All major religions have a form of meditation including Christianity, Judaism, Hinduism, Buddhism, and countless indigenous cultures. Anyone can feel the energy of religious beliefs and healing energies during a ceremony or at a sacred space. Meditations range from roseries to chants.

Through my own personal research, I have found meditation is the easiest healing connection and practice through which to live a life of balance. What I like best about meditation is that there are so many varieties. Everyone can find a way to meditate.

Meditation is key to our Earth walk and our individual experiences on this plane. It is about making a sacred space within yourself. It also puts you in alignment with yourself. The best thing about meditation is that they are free and not limited to only the wealthy. Meditation can be done anywhere at any time.

But, Rachel, I can't get the voices in my head to stop! I have too much to do. Or I can't find a place to be alone for twenty minutes. I can't meditate.

It is possible to find the time and learn how to be at peace with yourself. Meditation is a way of life. It took me until I was forty to finally learn how to meditate. Before I would dream of being a yogi in perfect lotus position and not moving for days. For me, this is how I saw meditation. It was something one had to achieve through great training. Strangely enough, meditation for me became a way of living, not just a practice.

The only common practice to meditation according to research is that your back is perfectly straight at some point. Research has shown that when each vertebra is aligned consciousness flows. Yet I can describe several meditations that don't even suggest that. Meditation is not limited or has any boundaries. Meditation is something everyone can learn and do with ease. I love meditation because there are no rules. No, you don't have to sit with your back perfectly aligned in lotus position.

A few tips for when first starting meditation is concentrating on your breath. This helps keep thoughts away. When you can't find the time, I used to recommend people try sitting quietly for one minute on the toilet. In the bathroom you can tune into your own physical space. I don't recommend doing this in the shower due to water waste. Locking your bathroom door for a few minutes of alignment might just change your outcome at work.

Just breathing in with your nose and "following" the breath through your body as you exhale is a great way to start. If you have never done that, do it right now! Close your eyes, breathe in through your nose. Imagine the air coming into your body. Follow each breath in and out. Concentrate on your own rhythm. See the breath making spirals into your diaphragm, into your lungs, into every organ of your body.

Once you can sit with yourself in silence for five minutes or longer, move to the next step of directing your meditations. A great next exercise is to reenergize your energy center or your hara, dan tain, ki, or chi point. In your belly area is where you store spiritual energy in your physical body. Here where your inner child lives is a point of connection. Feel your energy building here. Imagine as though your breath carries energy to this point and build it with each breath.

Another breathing meditation to try is to put your hand over your heart. Imagine that every breath is flowing to your heart. Feel as though your heart is doing the breathing and connecting you to all parts of your body. Do this for a few minutes to connect to your heart.

Another tool for meditation is using a mala or prayer beads to count your mantras or prayers. The number of "malas" or rounds of prayers depends on each individual or prayer. A mala is a necklace that has 108 beads or knots and it is used like a rosary. The largest bead or amulet is called the "god bead." This is achieved when you have said your mantra or prayer 108 times. One round is counting toward the "god bead," and then going in reverse and saying mantra 108 back to the start. One never crosses the "god bead" or count it. It symbolizes the start and the *ALL* point.

Once you've completed the number of rounds, you then can feel the songs or mantras connecting you with the healing energy. It's an awesome connection. The most malas I personally ever did was with Ganesh or a Hindu deities' mantra. I did it for three days in a row. I think I did hit ten thousand malas (full rounds of 108 prayers going to the end and back to the beginning). It did feel wonderful, and I do have a deeper connection to Ganesh.

I like silent meditations when I just float into all things. When I am expected to complicate it or to focus on one question or recite one prayer, I get lost in my own thoughts. Then my ego runs free. I become more of a philosopher, "I think, therefore I am." Then I can't stop thinking of what might happen. Like a gerbil on a hamster wheel, my mind begins to wander. When my mind starts buzzing with chat I have to stop and start all over. To prevent this from happening, I have made up my own mantra to help me. "I dream to create."

That's why I say it's OK if some types of meditation do not work or align for you. There are so many kinds. Try them all!

Types of Meditation

- Breath-Learning how to breathe properly is important. Doing yoga breath work is highly recommended and super helpful. An important lesson to learn is how to breathe toward your center point, your hara. Feeling your breath go deep into every cell. The idea is to truly *be—I am* with the breath.
- OM-OM is the first sound of all things. Just singing it or making a deep toning sound. I was taught it first starts with an "AH" sound then goes in to "OM". Play with the sound saying it three times, then try nine times.
- Mantras / Prayers
  o Rosery
  o Mantras can be of ancient roots or written daily.
  o Prayers are requests in many religions. These too can be ancient text or a personal wish.

- Sound
  - o Chanting
  - o Toning
  - o Delta Waves
  - o Music – playing an instrument or singing out loud.
  - o Sound Baths or listening to choirs.
- Transcendental meditation might be what you first think about when talking about meditations. It was made popular in the 1960s by artists and musicians exploring reality. This meditation is done silently contemplating the existence of life and exploring the void. Then publicized by celebrities with LSD or other hallucinogens to help extend the experience. We now know LSD is totally unnecessary for meditation.
- Somatic- I also love walking and dancing meditations or somatic meditations where you get your whole body into it. A simple shaking it out can do wonders for the whole body as a release. Once I laid on the floor and buzzed like a bee. I could feel that buzzing sound in every cell. I feel like doors open to new understandings of the world when I do somatic meditation. Examples are:
  - o Walking in nature- forest bathing is one type of outdoor meditation.
  - o Running, exercise- best practiced on an exercise machine of some kind indoors so you can zone out.
  - o Dancing
  - o Painting or sculpting
  - o Yoga/ Ti Chi / Stretching
  - o Getting a massage
- Guided meditations are guided by a person's voice or sound for healing and other desires.
- Element Meditations
  - o Gentle gazing into fire or a flame or listening to a fireplace.
  - o Grounding or rooting into the Earth. Feeling the grass or sand as you take each step. Consciously connecting as if roots were coming out of your feet.

o   Laying on the ground or a giant rock, whether you are under the stars or getting Vitamin D from the sunlight, this meditation couldn't be any easier.

o   Essential oil accessing healing powers of Mother Earth with scents. Essential oils have specific help or healing energy, use a good resource when finding the perfect smell. I have found a diffuser is ideal. I also like using it in humidifiers, depending on the area you live in.

o   Incenses- Used in many religions can be a type of meditation as well as use to set intentions. For example, sandalwood incense can invite Raphael. Other aromas like frankincense, palo santo, and myrrh can call in other guides. They are wonderful ways to set the mood for meditation.

o   Fresh water - Sitting under a waterfall or sitting next to a stream of moving water brings fluidity.

o   Ocean or gulf waters- Doing anything with the ocean can be meditative, just use common sense when picking a location.

o   Swimming or floating in water in a pool, spa, or your own bathtub.

o   Depravation tanks- These are closed in saltwater tanks that your body naturally floats in, giving a perfect place of no sound. Many large cities have these facilities.

o   Light therapy- Adding color light or just sitting with a color.

- Painting or drawing meditation- I hosted several watercolor and rock painting meditations. I also know artists who draw first thing in the morning to get their creativity flowing.

- Being mesmerized- I could spend hours looking at an MC Esher drawing in high school. His geometric drawings of balance and chaos are brilliant and very mesmerizing.

- Biofeedback - Biofeedback is a tool that can give you instant feedback on how to personally calm yourself down.

- BioMats- or rainbow mats are filled with amethyst or other quartz to amplify your meditation. There are meditation devices you can sit on, stand on and lay in. There are pods that project different colors, sounds, and use gemstones to increase your meditations to the highest potential.

After meditation is to give yourself time and be gentle on yourself. Drink extra water, as the experience was a spiritual detox. If possible, take a salt bath (any salt will do, like Epsom or Himalayan) or a sweet bath that is made with milk, mylks, honey with your favorite flower. Rest, relax, take a nap, go to bed early, and eat your favorite foods. Start with just one minute of being still and then extend the time till you can get to twenty minutes.

No matter how you meditate, what style you do, it always comes back completely into the *now* moment. Find a practice you feel comfortable with and bring that energy or healing into your daily life.

Healing Responses

I have mentioned healing reactions or rather healing responses. From unlimited potential with unconditional love, come all kinds of amazing outcomes. I am confident you will experience some form of healing response reading this book. Our human bodies may not be prepared for the new high energy of love and you may have a response. The most common response is falling asleep. Which is ideal because when we sleep the most healing to our bodies happens naturally.

Healing responses happen in many ways and form at different times in your life's journey on your Earth walk. Healing responses are unique to each individual and each situation. These responses are enjoyable experiences. You may have an unexpected experience in ways you may not consider when stepping into a higher consciousness. For example, clearing out energies in higher dimensions may have feelings of euphoria, a freedom you had been lacking. Some have no or little response. Some feel the energy working, others may see colors or symbols.

Some healing responses begin immediately. They can make you thirsty or hungry. In the evening while you are trying to sleep you may get a burst of energy. Or maybe all you can do is sleep. Healing responses come in all forms. There is no one right way to experience healing. From feeling lightheaded and fuzzy to just having the best deep sleep, healing is personal.

Crying is a healing response. It is a way of clearing out old ways, as is coughing or sneezing. These are all releases. Make sure to not to hold anything inside. Instead laugh, cough, or cry as needed. Don't try to hold in a sneeze or a cough. Release all that is no longer for your highest good. Once release is over, bring divine compassion into your heart.

There is talk about "ascension flu" or suffering to find peace. Luckily for us, living in the modern age, we know this is not true. We no longer need to suffer to find God within us. *ALL* has no desire for us to be in any kind of pain or suffering.

I do recognize that some issues or diseases cannot be fixed with mediation alone. The best is to work with Western medicine as well as Integrative medicine. Bones can mend quickly when a doctor sets them in place. Yet there are a few issues that are part of your contract with *ALL* to be healed. Only the person with the problem can heal themselves. Only they can change their habits.

No one can explain when or why something heals quickly and other issues may not. I know our minds, our bodies, and our spirits are very powerful. We need to treat ourselves with love and self-care. Without that self-love we may not be able to heal our problems. We all have some kind of wound to heal in our lifetime. There are various issues we were sent to Earth to work out.

Divine healing is for all beings, as it exists in everything with *ALL*. Step into yourself and step into everything! Most responses are giggling, extreme joy, fuzzy feelings, clarity and high waves of energy. Allow the healing to flow to you now with grace and ease.

My Story

I feel that my life is like a movie, Unbelievable events happen to me often. For example, once randomly selected to use my first husband's 1940's Ford truck in a Red Hot Chili Peppers video. I believe each person's life is constantly being recorded by the energy around you. Therefore, when you are in sync with your life, you can feel like you are the movie star, in your own life of course. I have had so many moments during which I felt I was watching my life like a live TV drama.

Like in a Quentin Tarantino movie, my thoughts suddenly turned to the unthinkable event that happened to New Orleans. I went from a gorgeous gypsy on Mardi Gras day 2005 to that summer when I was a Hurricane Katrina evacuee. It forever changed the landscape of the city and our souls. Escaping New Orleans changed me in ways I still don't fully understand. What should have been a five-hour drive to Houston took twenty-three and a half hours. I was able to make reservations at the last motel room available. I listened to my heart and not the guys in the bar. I packed my great grandmother's quilt, my cookbooks, photo albums, passports, and insurance papers. I spoke to hundreds of Katrina survivors, not one grabbed anything but clothes for an unplanned vacation.

The Houston motel had reviews of a half star out of five stars. I was surprised to learn upon arrival, that the rooms were rented out by the hour. We were in a prostitute's room. This was her income I was taking away. We sat in shock watching the news. The city was being washed away by floodwaters. The rest of the time we spent watching the free porn channels to help ease the pain. I watched my tears roll down my face while staring up at in the mirror above the bed. It made me giggle as I thought of the ladies with cum dripping down their face. As silly as the thought was, it gave me just a moment to take my mind off the loss of our lives, our city and our way of life.

The song "Wake Me Up When September Ends" by Green Day became the theme for that month. We traveled around the country waiting to see what was left of our home and art studio. From Houston, Texas, to Chandler, Arizona, to Denver, Colorado, we drove across the United States looking for shelter. My inspired actions of taking more than clothes allowed us to continue with our travel plans. I had the airline tickets, the passports, and all the information we needed to travel to Germany. The government was still not allowing the residents back into the city. This was time that we had planned for three years to go to Germany. I would have never dreamt that I would spend three weeks in the belly of the woman, Frauenau in Bavaria. What a great place to heal. A place where the name translates to in the womb of Mother Earth.

In my heart, I can still rewind every second of driving into New Orleans on September 22, 2005. I can feel the bumps of every crack on the Vieux Carre exit. Driving into the city was devastating. We were at ground zero for Hurricane Katrina. The stench that filled the air made me weep. We passed miles of debris stacked 20 feet high made of once beautiful houses and historic trees. They were all shoveled into one giant debris wall. Houses were spray-painted with a huge red "X," marking the date the house was searched and how many bodies were found inside.

I remember the sight of military trucks blockading the streets. We drove down Esplanade Avenue with not one car or person in sight, creeping at ten miles per hour. I can still feel the heart-sinking feeling of watching US Marines move barbed wire barricades so we could get to our home. This was not the community I loved. Instead, it felt like a war zone, with the stench of rotten food lingering in the air.

The house we owned at the time was built in 1835 in the Marigny district. It was a raised home. We were filled with joy and relief when we saw the house was still standing. A giant "X" and the numbers below signaled our house was searched on September 9 and zero bodies were found. Before we got out of the truck that was loaded up with supplies, Bob, my first husband, gave me a lecture in his best adult voice. "Hey, we don't know what is wrong with the house. There could be animals, even people hiding in the house. And don't go running in and getting hurt because there are no hospitals open."

His lecture made my heart sink back into the reality of Katrina. Any joy over being back home left me. We could see that a tree had crushed the roof of the porch. With great reverence, I acknowledged his warnings, for it was all true. We were really stepping into the unknown. With tears filling my eyes from the heart-wrenching drive into town, we cautiously made our way to the front door.

Unlike in the movies, I can still smell the rotting food in my refrigerator as the flies had taken over the kitchen. I see myself tiptoeing as we enter the house, calling out to animals or unwanted visitors to leave. The stench in the air still haunts me. I have worked for years to release the trauma of those months. This was the first of many experiences of feeling the law of correspondence and the law of cause and effect. Mother Earth was trying to get our attention. She wanted us to pay attention to what we have done to her.

Our house was built before the levees. It was raised three feet. The floodwater came right up to the door. It was wind damage and rainwater that hurt our historic shotgun home during the storm. As we both stepped into the kitchen, we took in the sight of blood pouring out of the refrigerator and into the living room. It was a bloody mess. An inconceivable smell and flies, worse than any horror movie because the sun was shining in. The deer my cousins sent me after their hunting trip had defrosted in the most horrifying way.

We tiptoed through the rest of the house, finding holes in the ceiling, rainwater damage, and more foul-smelling damage. A room full of rotted dead house plants and orchids that were meant to be planted was also full of bugs and bad smells. Finally, we reached the back door to see how the glass garden had fared in this horrific storm.

Suddenly, Bob went running past me and leaped like an Olympian over a fallen tree limb in the backyard. I can still hear the crack of his ribs as he tripped into a pit of storm trash with a loud whimper and thud. The image rewinds in my head in slow motion, as I watched his eyes enlarge with excitement. I watched him fly through the thick air as though he was a *Ninja Warrior*. A child like cry, "Yeah!" came out as he dashed into the unknown. Within one moment, his *joie de vivre* was smacked back to reality as the branch he leaped on cracked.

I saw red. No, not on the ground, no blood. It wasn't the first chakra of fight or flight red either. It wasn't fear that would make me run away. I saw red, like the cartoons when they get so pissed off their heads turn red and blow up. The red I saw was like the red blood that flowed in the old movie *The Shining*, pumping through my whole being. This was the first time I really believed I could levitate.

Instantly, it came to me. I was going to put him down right then and there. As if he was a wounded animal on a farm. One that had no way of going back to its normal life. Like a racehorse with a broken back, I was going to show him true compassion. I was going to just end his misery because there was nowhere to get help. The city had no police, no hospitals and very few residents. I heard bones crack; I saw the pain in his eyes. It was the compassionate thing, the right thing to do. I saw the stake that just missed his main artery by centimeters.

Suddenly, he became Superman and stood up. I can hear him saying to himself out loud, "Am I good? No." (Wince of pain.) "I am good."

With his inspired action, he sucked in his breath. A hard, sharp pain shot through his entire body, like it was in slow motion. He fell back down but not as hard. I could hear him thinking out loud, so hard, so many thoughts running in his brain. His eyes bulged out. "There are no hospitals. I think I have internal bleeding. I am a dead as fuck," he announced to me.

I didn't need the stake; he had done this to himself.

"Uh, hey, Rach, could you help me to the bed and put your hot hands on me, I know you can take care of me."

He asked for help. He asked me to heal him. It was the first time I remember I physically healed someone. Like Captain Marvel, I easily lifted him out of the debris and carried him to the sleigh bed. For two hours, I gently laid my hands on his chest and prayed for healing. I did not have any formal training; I did what felt right. I visualized his bones mending and his lungs filling with air, not with blood. I called out for help to random angels. His journey was not over yet, and in this moment, we made sure his life would continue.

That evening, he wrapped himself up with large bandages and began to haul infested refrigerators to the sidewalk. I believe the guilt over being a dumbass and jumping into an unknown pile gave him the superhero strength to move three refrigerators out of our neighbors' homes. Or maybe I over energized him.

Two Minutes Tuesdays

Mardi Gras literally means Fat Tuesday. Living on Bourbon Street for over ten years has changed Tuesdays for me. Tuesdays are the forgotten early weekdays of work in every city in the world, except New Orleans, the state of Louisiana, and of course Brazil. Tuesdays become special once a year. It is a day we celebrate with gluttony on all levels—a great time of partying and revelry.

On August 29, 2005, my life, as well as those living in three states surrounding Louisiana, would be forever changed. A storm called Katrina hit land. The storm caused mass destruction of the city I loved, with 75 percent of it underwater. Such heavy damage made the area unrecognizable. It was the kind of natural disaster that truly brings people together. One gets to see the real fear in people.

During the first part of the recovery from Hurricane Katrina, I was working in Hammond, a small town fifty minutes away from New Orleans. My heart ached since I wasn't in the city physically building it back up. I wanted to help with the rebuild. I remembered an article I had read on a study done in the Middle East. Researchers took the square root number of 1 percent of the population. After figuring out the number, they asked that number of people to meditate or pray for peace at the same time. The study showed that, while this specific number of people prayed or meditated, no one got arrested, and no one went to the emergency room. Basically, all crime stopped in the city during this period. I thought we should put this into action. With such a small population in New Orleans, it wouldn't take very many people to do this.[1]

According to the news, only 270,000 residents were back in New Orleans in January 2006. One percent of 270,00 is 2,700, The square root is 52. I had to find 52 people to pray on the same day for the same thing. This was how Two Minute Tuesday began. I texted and called people from everywhere to help pray for the city of New Orleans' recovery every Tuesday. It would be a year or two before I would start promoting it on social media, but the idea of people praying for one cause—their community—stuck with me. Other research explains this same concept with transcendental meditation.[2]

I asked everyone to pray or meditate for two minutes on Tuesday for their community and for world peace. It totally made a difference in New Orleans. For three years, I constantly reminded people to pray or meditate on the city to help its recovery. We all watched with love and amazement as our great city rose again. In three years, New Orleans was back on the map as a tourist destination and the home of Super Bowl champions. The power of prayer is unstoppable!

We all have time to do this. Whether you are waiting in line to check out, sitting on the toilet in the morning, or driving a commute to work. Take the time to send divine love and visualize your community in the most peaceful, beautiful light. This practice is amplified when we do it in the community. It is also felt when we send love individually.

---

[1] http://www.worldpeacealliance.com/index_htm_files/greggbraden.html.

[2] Rob Roth, "Maharishi on 'The 1% Effect': How Just a Small Percentage of People Can Change the World," *TM Blog*, May 11, 2012, http://www.tm.org/blog/maharishi/maharishi-on-the-1-effect/; World Peace Group, "World Peace Through Meditation," World Peace Group website, http://www.worldpeacegroup.org/super_radiance.html.

Poem Channeled by Rachel Otto's Inner Child

I want a lover.
I want to be touched again.
I want to be held and wanted.
That is not love!
That is desire of the moment.
Lusting in the here and now.
That is a feeling or as they say expression - but it is not true love.
I miss being held.
But when was I held?
Briefly from a working mother.
Not while a child in grandparents' arms,
Not in high school as they lied about me,
Not in college too much distraction,
Not in marriage- it was suffocating.
Why do I miss being held when I never was?
When you want love,
You can't feel it.
You spiral out of yourself,
When you want ALL
You want yourself to be happy.
Neither can it be outside of you.
Both are already in you.
I just forgot.
Took a breath and found one space inside deep.
Found its love,
And let it grow inside.
Love is not on the outside.
It's on the inside.
That how it grows from you.
I was being held inside.

By *ALL* and by myself

CHAPTER 1

First Dimension is pure divine love energy.

One of the cool things I did in Palm Springs was to co-write a book, *The Prophecy Map of Nova Gaia*. It was not my original thought that I wrote about, but instead it was a channeled message. It was a story told long ago in the *Book of Enoch*. When defining dimensions, it is simple to start at the beginning, which is the beginning of everything. The following is a shortened version of the channeled message.

> *The first dimension is a sound of oneness, the OM. A singular oneness with ALL not only a straight line as described in geometry. It is instead, a single perfect note of music or one infinite sound. The first dimension is an untainted vibration of divine love and consciousness.*

The beginning of *ALL* that began with a conscious thought, a oneness. It was a warm, fuzzy, orgasmic feeling. This is what we call timelessness. The thought of divine love came to *ALL*. It had a conscious awareness of Its surroundings. This first conscious thought of *ALL* was divine love.

Divine consciousness had the thought of divine love. **BANG!** OM

A tiny atom created a big bang as *ALL* replicated itself which caused the first pattern of life. This is the sacred geometry of life. This is where everything comes from, the seed of life that forms the egg of life. Within our cells this pattern continues to replicate itself.

In understanding the rest of expansion, we must first understand the different dimensions. In high school I first learned about dimensions through Descartes. Descartes was a mathematician who described dimensions in a linear form in basic geometry. The horizontal line ($\leftrightarrow$) plotted on a graph can be used to represent the first dimension. The first line is called X. Next add a vertical line ($\updownarrow\leftrightarrow$) that is perpendicular to the horizonal line. We call this line Y. The combination of X and Y produces a second dimension. Finally, a third line gets added which forms the third dimension. This line is called Z. When a new line is added it expands into unlimited possibilities.

Get the idea? This model is limited and we must gain a new concept of dimensions past simple geometry. The dimensions are within each other. They can exist in the same place. On Earth we can live in the lower dimensions and higher dimensions, at the same time.

The first dimension is pure divine vibrational sound expansion of one love. Simply, the first dimension is sound. The first dimension exists on Earth inside everything! It is the space in our cells. The first dimension can still be heard in the OM, as well as seen in distant universes. Each of the dimensions exist like a foundation or a connection to *ALL*. The higher in dimensions we climb or ascend, the closer we come back to oneness with *ALL*.

The first dimension is the foundation for the second dimension and all dimensions expand out of the ones before them. Think of it like the history of entertainment. First, we only had songs we would sing. Then we wrote words or dramas with dance and themes. Next was recorded songs on phonographs broadcasted on radios. Photographs expanded into streaming movies. Television gave pathways for 3D movies and Imax experiences. Continual expansion into experiential rides and 4D movies. Entertainment keeps expanding until we realize we are in the lead role in our movie called life or Earth walk.

Divine Love Energy

Love is energy, the energy of everything in the universe.
Love is everything and everything is made of love.

Everything on this planet has a conscious love energy flowing through it and is made from love. Even items made in laboratories contain the conscious love energy from Earth. The spirit or soul of everything has different levels, depending on the vibrational level. The vibration of a disposable plastic cup has conscious love energy. However, its vibrational level is super low on the scale, so it may or may not have an angelic, otherworldly, or other dimensional soul. It still carries the conscious energy of Earth.

We exist in an infinite experience of galaxies, universes in various dimension and parallel universes that range from immensely small to beyond our imagination. In higher dimension we only exist as a collective love energy. You can go into any of these infinite spaces from where you sit. We have total access to *ALL*'s infinite wisdom!

The concept of one God, *ALL*, is still not fully understood by us humans. The idea of *ALL* is beyond our collective understanding. We try to humanize divine love energy by putting human traits on to *ALL*. Unfortunately, that is where confusion begins. Humanizing *ALL* is how many major religions and belief systems are misleading. These groups can portray *ALL* as judgmental. Prizes can be given out to true followers in heaven or prisons like hell for non-believers. Some see *ALL* as a bearded man of infinite knowledge that wants nothing to do with our suffering. This same God encourages war in his name. To see love energy as being vengeful or one-sided is not looking at the full spectrum of God or *ALL*. That's why I was given the term *ALL* for God or Creative Source or Universe or Universal Energy. I am presenting a neutral understanding that we are not separate; everything that exists is of *ALL*. Everything.

Beings of light and otherworldly beings have become confused with fire and violence. They have been turned judgmental and some marked evil. These beings do not burn. Nor are they on fire. They are compassionate beings that burn with divine love. We have been taught in the Bible that when we see God in physical form, it can be in the form of fire. This form of *ALL* is not fire as an element. The earthly concept of divine fire is a burning of compassion or divine love. This is the vibrational energy they illuminate. Divine love *is* energy.

Divine love energy embraces the world in its transition. This will create a change from living in a fear-driven matrix (also called the web of life) to creating a healthy, sustainable, happy life. New ways of thinking and behaving are happening now. The world is coming to recognize and understand that it can no longer exist as it was. We, the human occupants of the planet, need to find pure love and respect for ourselves. We can be in harmony with the world, as we once were. Divine love reminds the individual that we are all divine beings. Divine love is different from human love or romantic love. We have been misinformed about love. We are to be creators on this plane… not workers.

Divine love is being newly defined. Divine love is unconditional, infinite, nonjudgmental, and holds unlimited possibilities. It is unlike the traditional love that we have been taught. This type of love would never put anyone in a compromising position. For example, divine love would never ask you to do something harmful to another person. Divine love would never call for *war* in its name. Divine love would never hurt you either. It has no limits. Divine love is not just for those who pray every day or for highly devoted religious people. You were born from divine love and made of divine love.

New guides have come to our planet with divine love energy. We have access to new assistants to help us like Ascended Masters and angels. The list of guides goes on and on, from fairies to rocks, divine love is the energy of all creation.

Step into your heart and open it up to all the pure love energy. Feel the tickle from the inside, a giggle in your heart, the happiness of the small wins of the day. It is all around you. The more you love yourself, the greater love flows. Find what makes you sing.

It Was a Three-Hour Tour

In 2011 I was rewarded with a free trip to Cancun, Mexico for all the volunteer work with Meeting Professionals International. I'd sat on committees and boards for over ten years putting together programs, budgets, securing donations, and turning in many favors for several hospitality organizations. I was finally president of the Gulf States chapter. For years, I'd been luring people to lunch meetings with cocktails. People showed up for early Tuesday mornings for Bloody Mary meetings. A lesson learned was that there is no such thing as too much alcohol in New Orleans.

Once again, the magic of life got me thinking. It was ironic that the conference was in the one place I truly wanted to be at that exact time.

After all, the end of the world was coming in 2012 as many prophecies said, with some pointing to the Mayans as a reference. Had I truly created this opportunity to be in this exact location? Or was it just a chance that I was brought to this exact place on the Lion's Gate of August 8, 2011?

It was unknown to me at the time, but now I do understand the expansion cycle. The Earth is entering into its greatest transition into a higher dimension of living. This is a cycle that you can follow in history. If you looked deeper into history using astrology, we could figure out the exact cycle.

This trip would mark a place in my conscious journey. This trip to Cancun would be the first major spiritual marker that was my own unconscious doing. I would have never guessed that 2012 was not the end of the world. It would only be a marker of the beginning of the greatest transition in the world. It was just a time of transition and energy, not the end. Spoiler alert! There is no end of the world, no apocalypse coming, just many transitions into new ways of being.

From 2011 to 2023, the trauma the world went through will be written about for ages to come. From the rising of white supremacy to the chaos of the pandemic and climate change. The transition from chaos to divine love will take place over the next twenty to forty years. It is a rebirth of humanity. We were placed here at this time to help with this evolution. This will be the world's greatest transition and greatest joy when we step out of judgment and into love. This will be the greatest time of a rebirth of individual expression. Freedom allows everyone to have happiness.

When I read about the Mayan calendar in a grade school magazine, going to Chichén Itzá had been a goal in my life. That this greatest time in Earth's history was going to happen a month after my fortieth birthday meant it must have major significance to me. I wanted to see and feel these famous temples. I wanted to understand the Mayan calendar and what it meant to those who lived there. I thought maybe I could also learn why the Spanish conquistadors eliminated this culture. I skipped one day of meetings to go to the Mayan ruins. I finally had a chance to understand a history that eluded me firsthand.

I worked so hard to reach this goal. This day seemed to take a lifetime to get to. We finally recovered from Hurricane Katrina, and all seemed to be moving at a new fast-forward pace. 2012 was coming, for years a group of us had been talking about this date. We would discuss the what-ifs and conspiracies about the end of the world based on the Mayan calendar.

It all started out lovely. A brand-new sparkling van pulled up to the resort with a driver and a Mayan tour guide. There were only three of us on the tour. Bob, myself and another conference attendee.

As soon as the van door shut, it was like we were entering a scene from a David Lynch movie. The lighting changed; the energy became palpable. The Mayan tour guide began to speak. His words brought in the energy of Mayan culture. He explained basic numbers, simple words, and the class system to which the culture still adheres. They were highly intelligent and created large complex buildings. Yet, they were cruel and believed in sacrifice and suffering, which was an honor.

We drove past jungles, Mexican shops, cafés, pharmacies, and gas stations in the Yucatan Peninsula. Soon we were out of the city limits where we could only see green trees. We had been driving for an hour, and it was time for a bathroom break.

"This is the last stop for water and the bathroom" the tour guide said knowingly. "You have to follow me to get the hidden key to use the bathroom." He bobbed and weaved through the aisles filled with piñatas hanging happily in the air.

"Aqui" he said, pointing to an old wooden door as he went on his way to find food.

I opened the wooden plank door to a hole in the ground with no toilet paper in sight. Praying that some snake did not pop out and pull me into the dark smelly goo of a makeshift toilet. After paying a few pesos for breakfast with some kind of meat, we were back in the van.

"We are going into nowhere, no cell phone service" the tour guide announced between Mayan lessons. As I listened to his historical references and made my comments. A strange feeling was brewing inside me—excitement, fear, and something else I just did not understand.

"Are we there yet?" Bob said without moving or blinking an eye. He was almost blue now. I didn't know if it was from the other guy talking nonstop over the tour guide, the drive, the strange meat, or too much free beer last night.

"Just another ten minutes till we see the opening in the jungle," the tour guide said as we quickly maneuvered around the rocks and holes.

For another thirty minutes, we drove down paths made for four-wheelers, not tour vans. The jungle grew around us, as the paved roads became thin jungle paths. Suddenly time stopped. Even the sky froze into an aqua blue with no birds, no clouds. . . just the blazing sun.

We had entered a great clearing, like a huge wasteland of a distraught jungle or an ocean of green. Things felt different. I could feel time leaving me, like a weight being lifted off me. We had no way to track time, we were in a timeless state. The sun was directly overhead. It hung there almost perfectly, as if it was high noon like in a cartoon. It felt like walking under water. The humidity was thick. I could barely think as the sweat rolled down my face. It was hard to breathe.

Bob was physically there but not comprehending what was happening. The driver was trying to have fun with the Americans and took a sharp corner. I think he even said, "Ye- Haw" like a *Dukes of Hazard* episode. He drove us into a deep spiral of buses and cars. The cheap breakfast with mystery meat in it tried to come back up for the first time. We prayed out loud "Lord help us".

The Mayan ruins are not for miracles but a place very heavy with emotions. Where pain and suffering collected for centuries. Bob felt the heaviness too and went on his own path of choice away from the group.

It was 95 degrees with the humidity making it feel more like 130 degrees. I sprayed myself down with sunscreen and bug spray. I was ready to find answers as the blinding light invited me into the ancient structure.

In the distance, I could see flickering lights. Watchers knew we were there. They saw us, and they are the caretakers of this unreal place. The lights were flashing around us in this ruin of a city.

Walking through walls of water and heat was to be expected in this jungle. The fuzzy feeling of uncertainty turned into excitement. The rays of the sharp sun would have melted most fair-skinned humans. I had been preparing for this walk for my whole life. With only months away from the year 2012, I was getting ready for the world to end. It was August 8, 2011. I was standing at the jaguar entrance on the date of the Lion's Gate. I knew deep in my bones something was truly transpiring. I could see Bob slowly moving out of the van, doing his best. He got his second wind.

Little did I know how unprepared I was. I entered the unknown of my true self and my life's purpose. It was the seventies sit com *Gilligan's*

Island. I was like Gilligan. I did not know my "three-hour tour" was going to be a ten-year adventure.

I ran ahead in a daze. I went in looking for physical answers to the end of world. I did not know it was a spiritual awakening. I thought I would get closure. Instead, I started to unravel.

I wish I had cleared myself of my worries before I went. If I had smudged with sage or Palo Santo, the smoke would have cleared my energy. My experience may have been more pleasant. Instead, I ran into an energy I did not understand.

Before I go more into journey, I don't want you to make the same mistake. When visiting any historic location, it is best to go in with pure intentions and fully protected. Protected not from people but from fearful energy. A simple clearing and protection meditation before going into the world will keep the fear at bay.

Meditation: First Dimension Clearing and Connection

Clearing Yourself

Before you go into a ceremony, a sacred place, deep meditation or even going to bed, give yourself a break by doing a clearing. Ideally, this would be done before you do your practice or event. It doesn't have to be on any special day or time. Know your spirit goes past all time and space! Any time is a good time to clear yourself of worries, other's thoughts, other people's worries and the collective consciousness.

In the evenings I wipe down my arms and legs, like dry brushing. I imagine that I am wiping off the day, clearing off the negative creep's energy. It can help you break habits that don't serve you. Or letting go of things you have no control over, like world politics.

Vanessa de Luna, my spiritual bestie, told me about a clearing ceremony to help let go of the past. It really helped take the weight of my shoulders. She said ideally you would do this in a large body of water. You may not be able to access one, so a creek or river would be great. Even if that's not possible a shower or bath works just fine with a little imagination. Start by finding a place where you can meditate in peace. For this special clearing you will need a sweet offering of honey, maple syrup, molasses, or pure

8

cane syrup, white towel and dry clothes. It's not necessary, but if you want to go all the way, have all white clothes to wear after representing rebirth.

The Ceremony

Find your center. Connect to Mother Earth and Father Sky or to your personal beliefs. Feel your heart connect as your soul expands into the water before you. Go to the edge of the water. Get in or stand in the water if possible. Say the following:

> I [your full name] release, renounce, revoke, and return to light all the promises, vows, curses, self-inflicted or fair, hexes, spells, negativity from this lifetime and others. I release all vows of poverty, marriage, celibacy, nunnery, or monkhood. I release all vows of service, vows to protect, vows of slavery, and vows of life and death that my soul has ever made. I release all promises made to Spirit that are not for our highest good.

After saying your prayer, feel the negativity release into the water for a few moments. If possible, dip into the water or cover the top of your head with water. Be with the release, letting go and feeling the water clear and cleanse you. If possible, dip in the water three times or pour water over your head three times.

Next put your sweet offering of molasses or honey into the water. You can also rub it on your arms or body and let the water naturally wash it off you. Honey will do wonders for your skin!

Pray, sing, or chant your favorite songs. Do what you feel is your final release, from saying the Our Father prayer to singing your favorite song. Give out joy and gratitude.

Once you step out of the water, do not look back. Keep walking forward. It's time to move forward into your pure state. When you think too much, you go backwards. When you go backwards, you can re-attach the bad habits that you just let go of.

Once you have cleared yourself, it is much more fun to connect to your guides. You will find meditations go deeper and life feels like less of a burden. Clearing creates a pathway for beings of light to come directly into your life. Being cleared of your own doing gives you space to connect deeper to beings of light or angels to achieve greater healing.

A super easy way to clear yourself other than lighting sage or palo santo is to just simply place your hand on your heart and take three deep breaths. On the fourth breath out, just lightly hum. Whatever sound comes out is right! Hum out nine times and feel yourself connecting back into yourself, clearing your heart to allow it to guide you.

Another great way of clearing yourself without any tools or effort is toning. Even if you are not a singer, try toning to connect deeply into the first dimension. The chakras are specific energy centers in your body. The seven main chakras that make up your physical body are also in every living thing. The chakra system even scales up to be the same for the Earth, and our galaxy.

The sounds are based on the chakra energies of the etheric body. The etheric body is an invisible energy that surrounds everything. Understanding chakras is easiest by feeling them within your body during meditation. By singing each of these tones, you can feel the energy build or expand within that chakra. I will list the classic sounds of the seven chakras, or seven energy points.

Try a simple meditation by just making one of the sounds listed below and then feeling it. Where in your body do you feel it? Take a deep breath and slowly make the sound come out of the center of your body. Feel free to add movement or other sounds. Do not worry how silly you may feel or about the sound coming out. Just try it!

Root, first sound	*Uhh*
Sacral, second sound	*Eeuu*
Solar plexus, third sound	*Ooh*
Heart, fourth sound	*Ahh*
Throat, fifth sound	*Eye*
Third eye, sixth sound	*Aye*
Crown, seventh sound	*Eee*

Be Curious, Keep Learning: Balance,
a Channeled Message

You will express your love more fully by being you. Being yourself means understanding that you are a precious being here on Earth. You are meant to do good things in the world. Being yourself means smiling just because you can. Dancing just because you can. Laughing just because you can. Being yourself means having the courage and the strength to understand that, while we are all one, each of us is a unique expression of that oneness. There is joy in discovering our differences to celebrate and understand them.

When you can celebrate our oneness and our diversity of thought and action, then we can begin to bring balance back into the world and celebrate how our diversity brings balance. The sameness of crops in one area leads to too much of one nutrient and lack of another. The sameness of voices leads to lack of harmony. The sameness of opinion leads to lack of comprehension. We are balanced within ourselves and within our humanity when we are our best selves, our true selves—the self that is balanced and being true. Being yourself is where you shine!

CHAPTER 2

The second dimension is not lower or higher than the first dimension. It's just an expansion of possibilities from the singular oneness in the form of light.

The second dimension is more than a spot where two lines crossed as Descartes would lead you to believe. Rather, the second dimension is light. This is the place where the first Creator Beings and beings of light were created. This is where cosmic dragons or beings of light were born.

I remember the early stages of this existence. I could feel myself as a fuzzy ball of energy. I was pure divine love and consciousness. My personal memories of this time are almost cartoonish. I can feel myself as a singular atom. One ball of vibration of divine love and divine consciousness. I can remember, I was conscious. I was a real ball of joy.

We were in original space, or what I call "They Who Have No Name". I just feel the love when I think of this time. It was a sparkly deep purple, indigo place with specks of sound color energy. We vibrated in joy and wonderment as we kept expanding. This, too, was an exciting time of expansion into the unknown. It was vast and full of divine love and energy!

The beings of light multiplied in the second dimension. They are the founding energy for all the dimensions. They give structure to all universes and galaxies. To understand the second dimension is to understand beings of light or angels. Beings of lights are appendages of *ALL*.

I found an easy understanding of spirituality or the metaphysical world through the framework of the beings of light. Dimensions create space where experiences take place, where everything neatly exists. Beings of light help with the organization of all forms of life and communication for

ALL. They are often confused with aliens or otherworldly beings. Beings of light are the true source of our souls and as well as souls for otherworldly beings.

Beings of Light

Using the term angel is over simplifying beings of light. Beings of light can be described in all the dimensions. Angels are defined similarly in many religions and cultures. The Archangel Raphael is found in the Koran, the Hebrew Bible and all Christian Bibles.

When angelic beings were first written about, we had a limited perspective. The first encounters of beings of light had to be overwhelming. It makes sense that they were described as fire because of a limited vocabulary. Angels were depicted in baroque art as childlike heads on clouds with wings. Wings may have been the only way to describe how they could fly. Early in Mesopotamia pottery, we see winged angels in human and animal form. Some breathe out what appears to be fire. Much has been written about the beings of light. In history we can see that as human understanding expands of angels, so does our mental vocabulary.

You can find information about the nine orders or choirs of angels throughout history. Sometimes, ancient ways of understanding the beings of light organize them into a hierarchy. I would like to present the angelic order or choirs in a new way. Let's look at them for what they truly are, which is pure conscious energy.

Using the electromagnetic spectrum as a guide, we can logically break up the beings of light into three known categories: High Energy, Visible Light and Long Energy. I say known because an energy wave is infinite. Each category has many frequencies of energy they give off. We can break down the three energy categories to three main types of known energy.

For example, the High Energy category consists of Gamma Rays beings, X Ray beings and Ultraviolet beings. Visible Light has Black Light beings, Indigo and Yellow beings as members. Long Energy is made up of White Light beings, Infrared beings and Radio Waves or guardian angels. There are many more frequencies and categories than these. I am keeping it simple, but the types of beings are infinite. The electromagnetic spectrum expands infinitely in either direction, just as the type of beings of light.

Just like an energy wave, each group of beings of light are part of the group before them. Meaning the X-Ray beings came directly from the Gamma Rays beings. Each energy section has a specific area of responsibility. Taking a slightly closer look at each of these groups will help us get a better understanding of who can help us heal or guide us to our highest good.

Beings of light speak light language. We can't hear it, kind of like a dog whistle. It is heard and understood when accessing higher dimensions through mediation or prayer. Beings of light are like a vibration of sound. When together, they sound like a full orchestra or sing like a choir. Their energy helps keep universes, galaxies, all that is seen and unseen moving. The closer we get to these guides, the closer we get to *ALL* or the source of life.

High Energy Waves: Gamma Rays, X Rays and Ultraviolets

The First Energy: Gamma Rays

ALL, in pure joy, expanded out to experience everything that has ever existed and will ever exist. From limited knowledge, *ALL* created gamma ray beings first. *ALL* itself in its pure state is too much for any being. *ALL* is like a super unimaginable God sun burning with divine love. For when you are in the presence of *ALL*, you are immediately brought back into the oneness of everything, of *ALL*. In other words, *ALL* is so powerful we would be like a drop of water in the ocean. Too close and we would immediately be sucked up into a pure blissed-out state, and our individuality would become oneness.

The gamma ray beings are the main communicators for *ALL* and are the closest to *ALL*. We are not able to see or hear the gamma ray beings in their natural state. They have to change form or lower their frequency to be on Earth. In meditation I have smelled their sweet scent of cardamom and have felt the colors spark light within my being. Being around them instantly removes blocks from both your physical and spiritual being. You can find other ways of communication beyond words or visions. In time you will find your personal way to connect.

The gamma ray beings are the first in order or in the choirs as described in many religious texts as the seraphim. Mīkhā'ēl is one of the first gamma ray beings in the form of a cosmic dragon. I do think it's ironic how the Catholic Church changed the story. Their version Michael was fighting a dragon, eventually killing it. This represent "killing evil," when in fact, it was the first gamma ray being that was a cosmic dragon.

Gamma ray beings are cosmic or angelic dragon-looking creatures. They appear like Chinese dragons, a dragon with no legs. Serpentine, they float throughout all time and space. We can feel and experience them with all our senses in meditation. We cannot speak to them with our human voice like other beings of light.

Another common gamma ray being is Raphael. Raphael is awesome, of course. Raphael is known to be the greatest healer, the healer of healers. It's been said Raphael carries an ultra-emerald-green light for healing on all levels. Raphael was one of the first gamma ray beings after Mīkhā'ēl came out as the first cosmic dragon angel. Raphael is also an Infrared being, white light angel, as well as a guardian angel. Mīkhā'ēl is a gamma ray, an Xray being, an ultraviolet, archangel Michael, and guardian angel Michael. They are the same wave of energy just in different forms that do different jobs. I would work with lower energy forms of Michael when I needed protection and clearing and Raphael for healing. And yes, it was Raphael who lovingly kicked me out of the heaven of bliss. By the way, he has since let me back in.

The Second Energy: X Ray

The gamma rays expanded out into the X rays' section of the beings of light. They all worked with *ALL* to help create life structures. This is how galaxies began taking shape. The High Energy Wave beings of light made a foundation as *ALL* guided them to within the Divine Temples. The Divine Temples is what I use to describe the heart of *ALL*. The Divine Temples translates or communicates all the information that is gathered and stored in the Akashic records. The Xray beings oversee and guard the Akashic records. Think of Akashic records like *ALL's* personal infinite iCloud storage. It is here where all the experiences and memories of oversouls are held. A giant library in the consciousness that holds history from the beginning of time across all universes. Yeah, *ALL* has a tab on everything everywhere! This is the place where people can learn about past lives, karma, and their individual soul stories.

The X ray beings have been made famous by a painting done by Rafael, <u>The Two Cherubs</u>. It is true they have no gender, but they also have no bodies. The painting is a humanization of these beings. Our human eyes could not handle the flaming energy they carry, just like when using an X ray machine, we have lead aprons protecting us. Beings of light have zero human qualities. They do not fully understand money or our financial systems. They cannot figure out our judgment system either.

Meditate and call in the X ray beings. Feel their conscious wisdom. They hold universal knowledge. This is a great group to contact when you are ready. They have guides to help you clear out your past and begin healing yourself.

The Third Energy: Ultraviolet

The ultraviolets are beings of light whose main job is to aid in getting information to all the beings that were created. Thrones was also a name used for them. Often represented as the wheel of life or the great hoop in ancient history, ultraviolets are the foundation of divine love and communication center. They are part of the flow in life as it moves forward and constantly expands.

Looking at a traditional medicine wheel, we see it teaches us the constant movement of life. Starting in the east, spring; moving to the south, summer; going to the west, fall; and then finally moving to the north, winter. The cycle is repeated not just in a year cycle, but in daily life. The ultraviolets are beings of light who create the energy to keep this forward motion going. Think of them as fuel for Mother Earth.

They are expansionists. The world as well as the universe is always expanding. The ultraviolets keep life moving forward. Sometimes we get stuck and out of the flow. I find the teachings of the medicine wheel to be the best way to really understand ultraviolet beings and how they work on Earth. We are to flow forward, not backwards.

Zadkiel is a famous ultraviolet being of light. It is often called upon to cleanse and purify situations. In some healing modalities teach about the violet flame or the Saint Germain light. It is used for protection, healing, and initiation.

Visible Light Waves: Black Light, Indigo, Yellow Beings

The Fourth Energy: Black Light

ALL created the visible light waves beings of light to help control what was going on in the physical plane. Traditionally they were known as Dominions, Virtues, and Powers. Since the high energy waves group gave us a framework on how to exist, the visible light waves group keep it organized.

To me, the black lights are the hardest-working group of the beings of light. I would call them "back of the house" in restaurant terms. They do the unseen work to keep structure. They are constantly reworking the web of life to keep those who choose God's will to keep on their individual contract with *ALL*. Since Earth has free will, this group works to keep everything in order for billions and billions of souls on their personal will or contract. They are like computer programmers who never get a break, keeping the system on track as *ALL* desires. Whatever condition the world is in, it still is on *ALL*'s path, or following God's will and the black lights make sure of that.

ALL created the black light beings to work directly with Divine Temples. The Black Lights help keep everything in order. They are the structures of time as seen in astrology. The Divine Temples create "space" by supporting all parts of the universes and galaxies.

The Black Lights also work with the Indigos to create *divine time.* Divine time is when the universe is in alignment with *ALL*'s will. Things just happen perfectly.

The Fifth Section: Indigos

The beings of light each have their own responsibility. The Indigo beings make sure the souls of the stars are going into all of the beings and that life is flowing. They're also the carriers of compassion and bring love and joy. The Indigo beings were created to continue to work with compassion and to do the work of love from the Great Goddess. Sometimes referred to as the Nine Muses, the Indigos or the virtues guide life.

In astrology, they have names like Venus and Mars. Indigos are not about physical beauty but, rather, internal beauty. This group can be called upon to heal physical issues, but they also help us let go of negative thoughts that might keep us depressed. They show all beings how our individuality is the key to our Earth walk . . . that we are created exactly the way ALL or God wanted us to be.

Indigos also bring arts and music to all beings. It's the movement, the sound of divine love, a beautiful painting, an ideal meal, a dance, or a feeling of inspired elegance of life. They can be seen in everything and can help you be your best self.

Indigos are a great group of guides to ask for help with creativity, like removing writer's block. These are the beings who can inspire you. They can help you on a superficial level. Literally, they are the beings to call on when healing skin issues or even ask them to come in before a photoshoot to brighten your skin tones.

The Sixth Section: Yellow Beings

Formerly known as Powers, the yellow beings are stars or suns. Yellow beings keep life moving forward with the ultraviolets. They work within the web of life. These beings of light are the worker bees of *ALL*. The yellow beings' purpose was clearly defined within God's will. The yellow beings help keep people on track with their will, or God's will. When people choose free will, the yellow beings change the web of life to keep you aligned with God's will. The saying "nothing is a coincidence" could be attributed to the yellow beings. These beings help keep your life on track.

The yellow beings can help you if you are depressed or lost in conspiracy, the world of "everybody hates me." They give you back your power, your connection to the world, and your confidence! Let the yellow beings help you find your own confidence and your own power of who you are.

Long Energy Waves: Infrared, White Light Angels, Radio Waves

The next three sections are a great group to get help for daily needs. The Long Energy Wave group can do *everything* you need in the here and now. They also build our future dreams. This is a group of angels that most religions talk about. Historically known as archangels and guardian angels, they are whom we communicate with the most. They are the most present on Earth and can help in the quickest ways.

I have found this group is good to help with electronics. We often forget that everything is of God or *ALL*. That means even the car you drive comes from organic materials that were once pieces of the Earth. Think about it from the iron engine parts, the leather seats, to the plastic cup holder. All of it comes from the Earth, the plastic was once oil, which is just decayed plant matter. When you are in need to extend your battery life or a power boost, ask anyone from the long energy waves for help.

The Seventh Energy: Infrared Waves

Infrared beings or principalities are our great assistants on our Earth walk. They are to assist us by bringing spirituality into our daily lives. They are like building blocks creating a foundation of divine love and divine consciousness. These angelic beings help with our communication, both with others and with ourselves. When you are aligned, you can communicate with them in a more efficient manner.

The Eighth Energy: White Light Archangels

Hands down the most popular of all the beings of lights are the archangels. In major religions, these beings are consistently described as the messengers or the way to communicate your prayers to *ALL*. If you are meditating or connecting with each of the choirs, you will notice that some angels appear in several different sections. Like humans, each of the beings of light can do different jobs or "wear different hats." Just like a person could be a mother, a sister, an executive, a hiker, or a lover. Light beings can take on different roles.

I feel compelled to tell my interaction with Metatron as a story of the white light angels. Metatron is also a gamma ray known for sacred geometry. In the Bible, it's known as the "scribe" for God. Its divine love energy is the foundation of sacred geometry. Different versions of Metatron have been on this planet as great leaders like Toth, Euclid, the father of geometry and Pythagoras. And it too has been vilified by religions.

On full moon nights I would host an Earth healing circle in Audubon Park in New Orleans. I was guided to bring in the energy of Metatron. I felt our small group was ready to be initiated into this higher knowledge. The consciousness of Metatron is ancient knowledge. This knowledge cannot be gained from books or art. It is instead gained directly from the energy itself.

Vanessa de Luna, found a fantastic prayer for Metatron. A prayer to help us understand the energy of sacred geometry within each of us. I had just purchased a large crystal sound bowl, now our healing circle was ready to connect to the great energy.

I led the group in an opening prayer at a golden sunset listening to birds on the twin trees in front of us. To the left side was a green bench with egrets. I began saying the long prayer. Soon we created a deep connection to this being of light and its energy.

At the end of the prayer, I began to play the crystal singing bowl. It was a wonderful sound. The uplifting vibrations filled the space as we began to feel the energy. Gently, I played it by swiping around the rim. The sound carried across the small pond in front of us. I could see the vibration like rings or small waves in the water. When I struck it again, there was no sound! I struck it a little harder. Nothing. I opened my eyes to see what I was doing wrong as I rubbed the suede handle across the top of the bowl, still nothing.

Silence. The people in the circle were deep in meditation. The birds had stopped singing. It was as though time itself had stopped. No wind, no people walking, no one within sight. A bright light came as I looked at the green bench where the egrets were perched. An older man with beautiful, long silver hair, curled perfectly at his back now sat on the bench. I could not see his face. Only his back in a neatly pressed seersucker suit that was white with golden silver lines. He sat looking straight forward at the pond.

A glowing light surrounded him. The sun had completely set. There were no streetlamps in that part of the park. He was glowing.

I knew immediately it was Metatron! They came because of our love, our gratitude. It was a moment of truly being with divinity. I knew this was as close as we could get to *ALL* on Earth. I held my gaze directly upon it. My voice could not even come out of my throat. I tried to OM or say thank you, but nothing but air came out of my mouth.

We all just sat together in oneness, in balance, in love for all of Earth. Even now when I think about this time, I can still recall that complex feeling of just knowing. At some point, he faded right in front of my eyes. He didn't float away or walk away, but just faded. The sounds of the bowl instantly came back without one hit or swipe from me. A beautiful white egret flew to the spot on the bench where he'd sat as the meditation ended and the group came back. All the beings of light want to help us on our Earth walk we just have to ask them.

The Nineth Section: Radio Waves

Every sentient being has its own guardian angel or radio wave being! They are not just humans and dogs like in the movies. Everything, from plants to rocks has an angelic spirit or being of light to help it. The radio wave beings were specifically created as guidance for each person. Some people have several guardian angels, from past loved ones to gamma ray beings. You just tune into your radio wave being in your heart.

By opening your mind in a simple meditation, you can connect to your guardian angel or radio wave being. Ideally, make your back straight. Open your heart to allow the divine consciousness (also called Christ consciousness, Krishna's consciousness, or Noah's consciousness) to flow. Choose an opening prayer that is right for you. Many people like the Our Father prayer. The Hail Mary also has a common prayer you can use. Choose a simple prayer that you connect with. Use what you identify with from your background or culture. Find your own words that express your humbleness and desire to connect.

At the end of your prayer, say, "Thank you for all your healing and guidance. I send my gratitude and love to you. I ask for communication with you. I understand that I can't speak your angelic name. Please tell me what to call you. If there is more than one who works with me, tell me all your names. I ask this request to be carried out with joy. Thank you. Thank you. Thank you."

Be silent and just enjoy the peace. Keep your mind free of thoughts and just listen. This is your time to connect directly with your personal guardian angels. You will receive their names within forty-eight hours if they do not tell you immediately. Listen in your dreams, songs that pop into your mind and other messages that come to you.

What they give you is only a name, not what they are capable of. What do I mean by that? Well, the first time I did this exercise, I got the name Jeremiah. I was with a small group of spiritual people. No one had heard of this angel. They thought for sure I had done something wrong or made it up. I was embarrassed and kept praying and asking for names. I was very disappointed I kept getting the same name that no one had heard of.

While doing this meditation in a group, I felt a thump on the back of my head, again. I received a very clear message from my radio wave being. "You can't say our names. You do not have the capability to speak our language. Our names are what we like from your plane or feel you can say. I have many names—Jeremiah, Ezekiel, and Shouphin. Call me what you want. I am here for you."

I did feel a little silly that my guardian angel called me out. Its point was made. If you want your guardian angel to have your grandmother's name, fine. Understand it's just a name for you to use.

Years later, I read a book that named your guardian angel by your birthday. Funny enough, for my birthdate, Jeremiah or Jeremiel was named the angel in this book. I guess I was not wrong. Again, listening to others did not have my highest good in mind; instead, they were speaking to what they were comfortable with.

Call on them if you need advice or just want to thank them for the help. Send them gratitude. Sending healing energy to an angel just builds up what they give out. Once someone said, "Isn't sending energy to an angel like bringing sand to the beach?" No, it's not. Guardian angels use the energy you send them to help with your requests. If you are praying for your own healing, they amplify what you send to them. They can also send your love energy to people you are praying for. It's a great way to give back. Send all beings of light healing energy. Giving this offering of love only expands the healing they send.

Channeled message from Jeremiah:

> *Beloved, you are not supposed to*
> *work. You are here to create.*

The Message

This message was received in summer 2016 at Lily Dale Assembly, New York. I invite you to read it and sit with it in meditation. Think with your heart, not your mind.

> *There is nothing more and nothing less than love. Love is all. Love is God, and love is the void. Through this great fire of life, one gets an opportunity to choose it or just accept it. Those who choose it take the longer route. They look for proof and evidence of good. Good does not equal love. Bad is not good; therefore, it is not love either. Love just is. If you are one with ALL, you make no choice. You are you. You are one with God. All you can ask for is to be one; oneness is what we want you to achieve.*

> *We are the helpers, the gatekeepers of the passage to the new consciousness of the new world. You have many names for this new life and love; yet it is the old way and already resides within you.*

> *Give up hope for this world! For it has already happened. Just know. Hope is no longer needed when love is there. Feel the truths in your heart and know the love of God / spirit / energy. Love is the kick-starter—the source of All. It will set you free to know love, energy, or God. Holding on to hope is holding on to fear. You must know we don't hope you will grow; we know you have grown.*

Time doesn't exist, so stop trying to set dates for changes or shifts. It has already happened. Just love it. Be it. Know it. Stop trying to make it happen or not. It is—just like God is and you are. Be one with love, with energy; be one with the source. Let go of doubt and worry and see it already here. So much help is here. So much is already done. Don't look back and don't look forward. Be in the here and now, for it will never be this way or this moment again.

All universes will become one. All possibilities become one as you return to the source of all. See love. See change. But don't stop taking actions of love. It's not a time to allow people to come crying out of pain and suffering of their own doing. But instead, shout for joy and the understanding that you don't have to try for anything, if one accepts love.

Children of the light, all of you, come to the understanding of empty minds and of open thought and of free-flowing love. I (the being of light) can only see what I want to know, and you can only see what you want. Choose to see more. Your time for choice is coming to an end. Soon, all things will just be. Be excited for the Lord of Lords chooses you!

CHAPTER 3

The third dimension is where physical
universes and worlds were created. It is the
dimension the physical world exists in.

A quick recap, the first dimension is pure divine love energy. The second dimension is conscious vibration of light and sound. The third dimension is the result of the two colliding! Physics helps us understand this transformation of energy to physical life. Atoms, gases, elements, all part of the foundation of the universe.

The third dimension is host to the divine temples. The *divine temples* have many channels, many layers of dimensions. The *divine temples* are part of They Who Have No Name (Space, the Great Void), have many deities or understudies. The understanding of gravity helps explain their physical presents on Earth. You can see into the soul of the *divine temples* through black holes. Space is the backdrop of the *divine temples*. Space is just there to support the planets and stars. Space allows light and sound to travel. Space is not void; rather, space is *the* support system. Space is macro that holds up the Earth. It is also micro as it is inside every cell.

Space is part of the void. We cannot comprehend the void yet. Often called dark matter, void feels like it is void of sound, light, and vibration, yet it is not. Void is not negative. Void is part of *ALL*. I think of void as a purifier. Clearing out old ways to make room for new love. The void is also a womb space, where all things are created.

Once in meditation, Raphael gave me a pair of dimensional goggles. For the next week, I saw the craziest things in my daily life. The sky was constantly prismatic, or rainbow colored. I could see everything's aura. Aura is a color of energy that surrounds all things. I could see guardian angels for every individual. The golden, silvery sparkly thread of life that connected us all. It was too much after a few days. My brain could not process all the information. I got the message. We humans don't yet have the capacity to really see what the void is.

The divine temples are where stars are born and where stars transition back to *ALL*. Every star in the universe represents every soul on Earth. The star is the physical form of your soul. Every star bears a soul and connection with *ALL*. It is called "God spark." The conscious love connection to everything that exists. When a star dies, an oversoul has completed its journey and returns to *ALL*. There are trillions of suns or stars throughout all universes' dimensions. They all have a God spark to carry a connection to *ALL*.

In the third dimension, *ALL* became physical. *ALL* is everything. The elements were created. Universes, stars, suns, and moons, everything that is tactile was created in this dimension. Most universes exist in the third dimension.

The third dimension is the physical reality of Earth. It is real and can be experienced by all the senses. All planets, the stars, galaxies and universes are founded in this dimension. We are all made of the same love energy substance in the physical realm of the third dimension.

A Life of Clichés

You get what you pay for in life.

No good deed goes unpunished.

It's always the darkest before the dawn.

Out of the Woods.

You've got to wet the well before the water flows.

Take it with a grain of salt.

A penny saved is a penny earned.

Stop in the Name of Love.

Has our understanding of life become a cliché? Betcha a dollar I can tell you where you got your shoes at! I am such a good psychic I can tell you something. If you are wearing shoes right now, I can tell you where you got your shoes at. No matter where you live, I know where you got them. I can tell you, without knowing you.

"You got your shoes on your feet." (Sigh.)

That is a Bourbon Street scam. Daily, I would have to say out loud, "Yeah, I got them on my feet." It does describe living in a third-dimensional world, both Bourbon Street and all the clichés. One would think after ten years of living on Bourbon Street they would leave me alone. Seeing me walk or ride my bike on the same path every day did not stop them. The hustlers would call out to me. Just like any spiritual lesson, it happens over and over until we understand. Life in the third dimension is about surviving. It is very physical. It is real, often harsh, and it feels unforgiving. You can keep your dollar.

On our Earth walk, we are here to experience Earth. Each of us has already set up our itinerary for our Earth walk. If you would like to see your itinerary for yourself, check out your astrology! Each person was born under a star or part of a star—and yours marks you. I do believe we all come from stars, but specifically, every soul on Earth has a star lineage.

Your astrology chart is a map of your life, or what may come in your life. It is a peek at God's will. Your will or God's will is the contract you and *ALL* made before you got to Earth. *ALL* is part of every sentient being. Since *ALL* is within us, we are the creators. It is our choice what we want to experience. Using astrology as a guide can help you on your Earth walk.

If you choose to look deeper into your personal astrology, I do recommend going to a professional astrologer, like CeCe Stevens or Susie Cox. Check your area for a local guild. They will have information to help you with your life planning.

I like to use astrology for guidance. From the little I understand of astrology, I do know you are more than your sun sign, which is what you can typically find written about in the back of magazines. Look at your moon sign as well as your sun sign for a better understanding. I am a Scorpio, proudly, with a type A personality. I am driven, highly sexual, intelligent, and very confident; these are a few of the qualities of the sign.

Wait, did I just judge myself? Am I a stereotype? Maybe. In the third dimension, astrology is an easy way for people to understand their personalities outside of their community or family.

I have found that understanding astrology can help you in daily life. A famous astrological event is when Mercury goes into retrograde. This is not an ideal time to buy a car, computer, or large appliance. Signing new contracts during Mercury in retrograde may be a bit tricky too. Learning what planet is in retrograde can help a lot in life. Tip: don't get a new haircut while Venus is retrograde.

Astrology can help in other ways than telling you your future. Astrology is a tool for timing. It can tell you the best days to sell an item, when to start a new project, or even the best time to ask for money. Astrology is a wonderful tool if you know how to use it and do so with a professional who can guide you. Astrology guides you towards your highest good for the best possible outcome. Astrology is a gift from the cosmos.

If you really want to know your future, you just need to look inside your heart. Astrology is a wonderful tool, one of my favorite tools to use. I use the information not to plan my life but to guide me to my greatest joy.

Back to the Three Hour Tour: Spiritually Lost in the Mighty Jungle of Life

The indigenous tour guide left after Bob had wandered off. The guide said, "Bus is leaving in an hour." as he walked away. The tour guide had left us at the main temple in Chichén Itzá. This was our time to seek out our truths in these ancient ruins. I brought offerings to leave in the temple for blessings. I made intentions of saving my marriage and New Orleans. I also wanted the New Orleans Saints to win another Super Bowl. I wanted to stop the destruction of the world that was predicted for 2012. I wandered the grounds.

The other guy on the tour found something and wanted to show us. We backtracked passing hundreds of people. An unworldly maze suddenly appeared in a clearing that was one kilometer wide. The freshly renovated stone fence looked like a labyrinth from the hilltop. I had read about a maze with unusual white stone walls were not painted or made by man. Could we have walked into this ancient labyrinth, the Man of the Maze?

We had entered a secret section of Chichén Itzá. With great curiosity we went into the unknown section. I took small intentional steps. A feeling of numbness came over me. We had entered a vortex. The green grass started glowing at my feet. With a few more steps everything around me turned to dust.

Little did I understand the depths that I stepped into that day. I had already been doing the best preparations for doomsday. I had been hiding food and supplies. I had closets full of lotions and man-made products I feared I would never see again. I stood inside the Aztec looking maze that very few Americans had ever seen.

I was taken to another time. I could feel the fear of all the men who entered this space. I could feel anger, fear, and confusion. The lush green grass had left. Only a small red tan patch of Earth could be seen. I was stepping on a path that had been walked for thousands of years. This path was a heavy walk full of anger, fear, and panic.

The experience changed my life in ways I would have never expected. I had done my research, but it still could not prepare me for this walk. With my eyes fixed on the ground, my soul was soaring. I had just pledged my undying love to Bob. We had just made it through so much. I had always felt the calling to be a healer. At this moment, I wanted so badly to gain new universal knowledge, but instead, waves of anxiety covered me.

I felt a fiery breath across me as I stopped touching the ground and stood up. Bob became silent, a strange look came across his face. He looked angry. He went in deeper, stomping and punching the walls. He felt anger and fear as I did. Instead of watching it as I did, he stepped into it.

We each had lessons. Our perception is everything and nothing. Different thoughts or religions are right in their own truths. The various beliefs look at a topic from *one* person's perspective at *one* time in space. A singular perspective from Earth. There are billions of perspectives, each one right because it is someone's. Who am I to say one is right or better than another? Voices were crying out to me—suffering for the state, sacrificing for the good of all. These were harsh lessons the jungle held. It became completely overwhelming as the heat rose. I could see suffering for centuries appearing.

It was teaching me lessons on the sorrows of Earth and the understanding that suffering is only part of fear, hatred, and anger. I could see the manipulation of people. They would give up their spiritual gifts in trade for power or money. Thousands of years of an old matrix or paradigm of a world of money, fear, power, and greed.

This was how I learned fears are from Earth and are earthbound. Suffering and evil do not exist outside of planet Earth. These myths we know are manipulated into good versus bad. Many stories to teach love have been corrupted to teach guilt, enabling, and control. Universal truths and love are a life of no judgment that awaits at the end of this ruin, not just at the end of one's life. More information buzzed in my ears; my heart raced as my steps were not left behind me.

Time felt like an eternity, lost in this labyrinth. Just as in life, wandering around clueless. I felt the vibration of the vortex as I stepped inside. It was like an invisible wall.

This was different. It was a deep contemplation of the self, what it was to be human in a third-dimensional world. Slow down. Look at each step. Slow down. You move too fast to make the morning last. Just tripping down the cobblestone, feeling groovy. I had Simon and Garfunkel singing in my head. My "clair" senses felt like something had turned them to 11 on a scale from 1 to 10.

Maybe I shouldn't have walked in. Maybe it would have been best if I'd stayed out. Were the things I truly desired petty and worthless? Was I a worthless human being? Was walking in nothing but beating up myself? Self-doubt, fear, and sadness over the reality of this world struck me. It started getting heavy, the swirling pain of suffering. Humans suck. We are mean to each other. We make fun of each other. We are kept divided by greed and power-hungry sickness. Was *Seinfeld* right to end the television series with the characters all going to jail?

This walk was stepping past the collective consciousness. In the maze we jumped around in dimensions. Walked into other realities, past all time and space. The stench of rotting corpses and fresh blood carried me through as I walked down timeless hallways. Lost in pain and suffering, the realities of how the world was being manipulated and controlled for money and power. I walked in pools of my own tears. Streaming down, my tears carried thousands of years of pain, suffering, wrongdoing, and anxiety over what would come next.

Later that evening, we had our first real-life understanding of what we had experienced. In literal terms, it was foreshadowing what was to come. The trip ended in a horrible fight in public, yelling and crying and with so much drama and pain I felt I was back inside the labyrinth. There, Bob had an epiphany and knew I was going to leave him. It was clear as day. A few months later, he ensured it would happen, just the way he had seen it.

The trip was my "not-ready-for-this-but-it's-happening" spiritual wake-up call. All the years of my wanting to come here and research into cultures and religions meant nothing inside this maze of ruins. This first labyrinth had me walking in and out of portals and places randomly. I did feel like this labyrinth jinxed me at first.

We never fully understood what we saw or felt; it changed us forever. Lessons were learned. You cannot help other people unless they ask for help and there is a fair energy exchange. The experiences of this event became a marker in my Earth walk. This time my spiritual awakening was loud, and I had to answer it. I had entered a cosmic labyrinth, not knowing how long I would be trapped.

Meditation: Mother Earth, Father Sky

In 2017 after completing a forty-day Christ consciousness meditation, I had hoped for divine information to be given to me. I basked in a clear conscious and pure divine love feeling I had hoped to get. Yet, no immediate information came to me. I continued to do my daily tasks with greater confidence. Still awaiting more information, I worked.

I may have even had a stink about me. To "stink of enlightenment" is when people carry an air about them that they know more than others in a spiritual sense. A few days later, the information I requested was granted. Not in the most ideal place, a bathroom. As I stepped out of the shower, I stepped into the seventh dimension of heavens. Then she appeared!

The Holy Mother Mary appeared to me! She was true divine love with all her faces of the goddesses. Mother Mary gave me many gifts and information. Two of the most important gifts were the healing energy of Mother Earth, Father Sky. The other gift was discernment. She literally opened my eyes to ensure I couldn't help but see truths and love in a new way.

She made me see how much we all are covered in shadow. How many wonderful healers, psychics, and other gurus are covered in old paradigms and shadow. I began to see examples in my own life. One event was a famous yogi guru who wanted me to collaborate with him. I could feel how he was "sucking" the energy right out of me with every awkward hug. I was appalled and felt drained whenever I was near him.

In my bathroom Mother Mary taught me this meditation. She said we are to be both Divine Love and Divine Consciousness. She continued, a healing meditation for all to connect to Mother and Father daily. A prayer to connect all beings on Earth to higher vibration of consciousness.

It is a simple connection that can be made anywhere at any time. Once you do it, share it. Remember when doing any guided meditation or prayer starts with your imagination. Then you can be free to expand. Other beings or guides may show up as well. Know that energy work is for the highest good for all of Earth. Find your own personal way to connect. Life changes and healing begins.

1. *Ground yourself.*
   If it is possible for you, please stand up. Spring grass with bare feet is ideal but not necessary. Daily I go outside early in the morning to connect. Again, in the evening I will do this. Stand with your feet flat on the ground. (Shoes can be on) Breathe in through your nose and out your mouth. With each exhale, feel like you are letting go of worries. Imagine you have roots coming out of your feet. Spread out the roots in a wide area. Feel secure in expanding outwardly into the ground with your energetic roots.

2. *Go to Mother Earth's core.*
   Send your energetic roots down into the Earth. Feel as though you travel down the roots into the center of Mother Earth. Imagine that you are surrounded by a ruby and orange energy of brilliant light. Begin to pull up this energy from Earth's center. Pull up the hot magma love through your roots. Begin to feel the bottom of your feet tingling, maybe even a warm sensation. This is Mother Earth's energy. Visualize it as a ruby red-hot magma or hot lava pouring into your being.

I have come to understand that many beliefs connect to the spirit or universe first. For this lesson, or this meditation, it is not the case. For this I was shown to connect with Earth first, as that is where we stand. Earth is where we presently exist. Mary taught me it is important to anchor in the first thing every day, then we can reach up higher. Later we will go deeper in this area is also called soul seed.

3. *Bring up divine love.*
   Feel this ruby red-hot love energy at the bottom of your feet. Pull it up into your ankles. Feel the divine love rise up into your knees. Faster up your thighs. Feel it go into the pelvis. The energy will rise into your heart area. As it rises, you may feel a block, or it feels stuck. A block is something you have created for yourself. It could be an old promise you made to yourself, or a belief that no longer serves you. It doesn't matter what the block may be forgive it. Forgive yourself, forgive the situation. Let it "compassionately burn." Do not go into the past memory of what may have created it. This is clearing out old ways- and we are always clearing our past. This is one process that we are constantly doing. Unfortunately, there is no "one clearing" one process, one plant medicine, one experience that totally clears out your blocks. Society, school, social media, other's negative creeps can keep coming at you, challenging you. This is why it is important to find a way to clear daily or let go of the past, your worries and what no longer serves you.

   Allow divine love to unblock the chakras. Removing cravings or possessions. Feel the divine love energy lock into the first chakra as it expands upward. Allow it to clear the second and third chakras.

4. *Pull* up *Divine Love into heart.*

   Allow the ruby red-hot love energy to flow into the heart space. Feel how the energy connects you directly to the core of Earth. When the energy reaches your heart, you may feel like an oak tree rooted strongly in the ground. It will make you stand tall, with strength and confidence. You are now connected heart-to-heart with Mother Earth.

5. *Invite Father Sky in.*

   Enable the opening of the top of your head. Feel now how your crown opens wide up. Invite Father Sky to come in through your crown. Father Sky has many names, depending on your culture. It is called Holy Spirit, the St. Germain light, the Archangel Metatron, or Lord Zadkiel. They all have similar definitions as the connecting spirit to *ALL*. Visualize a white, ultraviolet, sparkling light coming down from the infinite universe into your head.

6. *Expand your third eye.*

   Feel how Father Sky's ultraviolet light energy expands out your third eye. You may see sacred geometry patterns, pyramids, diamond shapes. A brilliant crown of light expands across your head. Feel it opening wider than ever before. Allow the ultraviolet light energy to go past the horizon, past all time and space.

7. *Clear with divine conscious light.*

   Allow Father Sky to deliver divine conscious light into your being. Feel the energy clear out your throat and ears. Feel the ultraviolet, sparkly light travel down your spine. The energy frees your voice and opens your ears to hear other's truths. The conscious light energy clears your throat allowing you to speak your truths. It clears out your blocks with communication.

8. *Bring down divine conscious light.*

   Feel the conscious light pour through your spine down into the ground through your roots to Mother Earth. Down your spine the light energy of *divine consciousness* flows. The energy coming up your feet is *divine love*. The two energies of Mother Earth and Father Sky pass through your entire being. You have become a conduit between Mother Earth and Father Sky. You are connected to both energies. Celebrating the love for each other. Think of a thunderbolt as the consciousness of Father Sky striking Mother Earth.

9. *Create new energy.*

   Allow the two energies to join in your heart. A blast of new light comes out of your heart. The new energy of both *divine consciousness* and *divine love* surrounds you. It cocoons you in the balanced energy. Feel how this new energy goes out past the horizon and travels through all time and space. Bask in this new energy of one. Feel how the mother energy connects to above, the father energy connects below. This is the moment that we are healing ourselves and the planet. This connects you to everything.

10. *Pull it all together!*

    Now take your hands to your second chakra or your pelvic area. Hold your hands with two to three inches of space between them. Imagine creating a ball of this new energy in between your hands. Feel the new balanced energy come from your hands. Feel it gather strength from your second chakra. Create the energy ball or sphere of light in your hands. Pull up this energy ball from your pelvis area to your heart, the fourth chakra.

11. *Imagine yourself being healed.*

    Visualize yourself in the ball of energy between your hands. See a full-body version of yourself standing.

35

Sending *divine love* from your heart into your ball of energy to yourself. Say out loud, if possible, "I love [your name]," three times. Just for a moment feel the love. If you need any physical healing, see a golden-white light going to that area of your body. Imagine the light there and hold it. Love yourself. Keep sending love out of your heart until you feel it has done it is complete.

12. *Heal others.*

You can heal others with this new balanced energy. Send healing love anywhere in the world. Only after you heal yourself can you heal others. Begin to imagine other people between your hands. You can imagine a person, an animal, a group of people, a community, a city— anything that needs to be healed or helped. No permission is necessary, as this is a direct connection with *ALL*. This meditation is for the highest good of the planet as well as the individual.

13. *Expand out the ball of healing love.*

Lift the ball of energy above your head. Imagine the ball grows as you open your arms bringing them down to your side. Fill yourself with this prismatic ball of energy, divine love, and divine consciousness. Next expand out to the universe. Depending on what your individual needs is what color of light you send out. For example, a silver bubble is used to reflect what others give to you. Only love is allowed in. When going into large group events you will need protection. This may be visualized as bright white layered with fuchsia light to protect yourself from others' free will. An emerald, green light can bring Raphael's healing energy. Later we will explore more colors related to chakras, and other guides as other options for specific healing needs.

14. *End with gratitude.*

> Say thank you as you reach down and touch the ground.
> Touch your heart next with a thank you. Reach up saying
> thank you to father sky. Repeat this motion three times.
> End by hugging yourself.

I really encourage you to try this. Of all the meditation and exercises I list in this book; this is the one that everyone instantly feels. Even when my friends and family who do not always understand my work or beliefs do this with me, they feel a divine connection. It's a real heart opener.

What I found is the more I do this, the more that initial feeling of *wow* goes away. It's not because I have already done this meditation a hundred times but, rather, because I live in that heart space as my norm. I have become accustomed to living in divine love, to feeling all of the oneness and consciousness as I do my daily tasks. I totally understand why people say that, after years of doing spiritual practices or meditation every day, it no longer appeals to them, or they no longer get that fuzzy feeling. It's not that they are over the spiritual journey. Rather, it's that they've integrated the practice into who they are. They live in divine love and divine consciousness. They are guided by their hearts and guides. They are living in balance.

Channeled Message from www.Marigoldslove.com

Printed with permission.

Oh, beautiful source, I ask from my heart how can I learn to be a more loving human? Learning is the first step. Loving is a noun. Love is just being. Just be love. Emanate love. Be love. Embrace love. Sit in love. Soften into love. Be the noun love first, then the verb love. Be the noun love. First know that your mind, body, and soul is love. Then you can act on that knowingness from your heart and do love. Doing love looks like extending a hand to someone who needs love. Giving a heartfelt hug to one who needs love. Giving love to someone or even a place that doesn't know that they are in love too. That they are the noun love. When we step into our Knowingness, we can do love by simply being in love. This is a transition that comes from the heart. When the loving act comes from the heart instinctively, then the transition has been made. When the loving act comes from the mind, the transition is still happening. There is always a beautiful exchange of energy between the heart and the brain, but to become love, the acts come from the heart and the brain follows. When one is doing love or giving love from the mind, the energy exchange between the mind and the heart could be stronger. Strengthening this infinite energy exchange while letting the heart lead takes practice and fortitude, fortitude of the heart not the body or the mind. Fortitude of the heart means having strong boundaries, strong loving boundaries that let your heart know what it is capable of without overextending oneself or overriding the capacity of the heart at that moment. One when being Love, the capacity of the heart is infinite. But, like most humans in physical form, there is a transition, a liminal space between doing love and being love in which the capacity of the heart is still growing to its mature form. In this transition, this arc of becoming, there are capacities to be learned, boundaries to explore. Going beyond one's boundaries leads to resentment. This is a good sign to have experienced resentment as this shows one where a boundary is. When one is feeling filled up with their own love from Source and from their own heart, the boundaries are expansive. One is feeling low and not filled up, the boundaries contract (while in this transition phase). This is OK. It is all learning. It is all becoming Knowingness. It is becoming Love instead of doing Love. Give yourself a break and check in with your boundaries today. Where are they? What is your capacity? Where can you give less to be more? To be more loving instead of trying to do more loving? It is a subtle shift that can have profound energetic resonances. Tune into what you can do today that allows you to be more loving, for yourself, for your connections, for your brothers and sisters of humanity. This could very well mean going back inside and staying put until you feel filled up with your own love again, with love from Source. Or this could mean going outside and helping a friend. The decision is yours. There is no right or wrong answer. The task is to tune in, find your boundaries, ask your heart where the boundaries are for that particular moment, and see where it leads to.

CHAPTER 4

*The fourth dimension is the home of
fairies and mystical beings.*

The fourth dimension permanently opened its gates in 2012, or so. Natural magic or the mystical can now be felt by all sentient beings. For example, fairies can now be seen everywhere, instead of being limited to small pockets of forest, hidden lands, or dreams. Magic, which has limited knowledge, is free for all beings. Before 2012, the fourth dimension was limited to your dream state or a place where the third dimension was explored without limitations but traditionally ruled by fear and anxiety. Dreams are part of the collective consciousness, which also include night terrors or nightmares. Here divine love can prevent them from expanding into physical reality.

What was once hidden in the shadows and in dreams is now open and available. With the opening of the fourth dimension, the secrets in mystery schools are available to anyone. Now everyone can choose to see all perspectives, all energies, and all knowledge. It is open for anyone to connect to the land, to plants, or to animals. There is a new understanding that shadow work is light work. There is no good versus evil. Magic is available to every being. The truest of magic energy is divine love.

Many creatures from the fourth dimension are well known. This is where the fairies live, the trolls thrive, and the imps and the mermaids and mermen live openly. This is the dimension where we can interact with and not just feel the elementals. It is where fire is not just a red flame but an energy. From the horizontal plane, the east, or the wind can clear off what is no longer necessary. The south is of light and energy of all kinds. The west is of water, teaching the changing of life. The north is Sophia Gaia, grounding, the foundation of all life. On the vertical plane, we become closer to Father Sky above us and Mother Earth below us. Here in the fourth dimension, unicorns are not just horned goats. Stallions and winged horses fly with dragons in the sky. It is the rainbow-colored land of joy and happiness right at our doorstep!

Many truths were compromised by humanity in the name of war, greed, and power. The Jungian shadow side of the human ego has been ruling the planet with the help of otherworldly beings. Many of these magical beings who once freely roamed this planet have been condemned to myths, stories, or the underworld. These beings who were once a part of our daily lives, had to be hidden away or forgotten about or stories had to be created to make us fear them.

Even sexual pleasure was vilified to keep all individual happiness away. In the Western world during the Victorian age, Puritans, and other religious groups worldwide damned the naked body. These groups made individuals feel guilt, pain, and even sorrow for their natural bodies. This is no longer needed to control our daily lives. We can self-govern with grace and ease, instead of a restraint demanded of us.

There is no evil, no divine abundance, no zombies, and no monetary system outside of Earth (no other dimensions or worlds go without anything). There is no lack of anything. To be abundant may be considered wasteful on other planets. It is a human need to have more than necessary. Earth was created to be one physical place where everything could live as equals with free will. All forms of beings, from light to otherworldly beings, exist on this planet right now. The fourth dimension has opened our physical eyes now to see this.

Every planet of every existence has a presence here on Earth. Most likely, they are in the exact opposite form of what they are on Earth. For example, the first dimension is only sound. A first dimensional being may come to Earth to be a crystal. Other universes may be giants to us yet come to Earth as ants. Again, they too come to walk, to experience physical joy, to feel touch, to learn how to giggle, to enjoy food, or to be entertained. They come to physically use their five senses to experience joy. The smell of a rose, the taste of a fresh peach, the feeling of comedy, the view of the Grand Canyon, or the sound of a favorite band are all different ways of experiencing an Earth walk.

My buddy, Ernie Fruge, the mayor of Bourbon Street knew everyone in New Orleans. From bartenders to doormen to concierges of every French Quarter hotel, Ernie knew all the players on Bourbon Street and most of the French Quarter. He was known for his money-making schemes during Mardi Gras. He always took care of me. When he found out I was moving out of state, he got depressed I would not be around. We had fun together. He had a joke for everyone. I was the one who made him business cards proclaiming him Mayor of Bourbon Street.

When he died, they called it suicide. His close friends knew it was a prescription sleeping drug that pushed him. I was heartbroken. I was deep in my spiritual journey in the desert when he transitioned over. I wanted to hear Ernie call out to me, "Lucy, I'm home," one more time. It was our little joke. I called for him in the heavens but could not feel his energy or presents anywhere. His soul, or life force was caught in misunderstandings and conflict. His soul did not choose suicide. It was the sleeping pills that forced his hand. He had sleepwalked his way into his own death.

Once called purgatory, Ernie's soul went into hospital heaven. This is the transitional area of becoming a being of light again, clearing the human ego and fear away. When people hold tightly to beliefs that are not true or go against universal law, they need to detox in hospital heaven. It's not a waiting area. It's a place for decompression or for lessons you did not learn. Here is where the healing happens that did not happen on Earth.

Ernie was a good man. He lived a good life but did not have all the correct information. It was hidden from him as it had been hidden from most of the world. Understanding the magic of the fourth dimensions takes away lies told to us. Which allows us to feel and experience all the wonders of life. Ernie had to not only detox from alcohol and prescription drugs, but he also had to find his connection to his higher self. It was time to unite with his soul family. Time to learn that the love I have for him is not limited but, rather, part of the divine love the universe has for all of us. Ernie is no longer in hospital heaven. He is with his family and does come to visit me regularly. He comforts me still to this day.

The fourth dimension has always existed around us. It's just that now we can feel and see it regularly! It's right there for everyone. Living in the fourth dimension opens the third eye of everyone who wants to see or know more. In the past, to gain sacred knowledge, you would have to pledge your life to secrecy or pay thousands of dollars to gurus and teachers to get information on ancient symbols and mantras. People spent their entire lives searching through jungles, deserts, and even Antarctica to find symbols, tools, and ancient knowledge from indigenous people or signs of otherworldly beings. Currently, men and women are still being prosecuted for trying to uncover old history and legends of the past. Just as I will be called a heretic for what is written in this book. This is not a time of judgement, instead it is a time of curiosity.

This is the dimension to manifest your dreams into reality. Remember you are part of the Creator; *ALL* is inside of you. I was once told, "Fake it till you make it." Now, I understand that, here in the fourth dimension, it is not faking it; it is creating it. You can create your own dreams and bring them into reality, not by a spell or by paying someone to make it happen for you but, rather, by speaking your own truths, being who you truly are.

In pop culture all we hear about is manifestation- make a vision board, manifestation spells, light your manifestation candles. You don't have to manifest anything in your life. You only need to create your own future. Dream boards or vision boards are tools to help you open to your dreams and the creator you are. As with most of life, it is simple. Do not try to define the way you will achieve your goals. Instead, stay focused on the feeling you want to have. How does it feel to have the dream job? How does it feel to have your ideal partner? This is the focus rather than how to get what you desire.

There are hundreds of books written about dreams, dream analysis, and symbolism in dreams. From my personal experience, dreams are your personal tool of processing. Sometimes, dreams create the future. Sometimes, they're programs running from TV or internet shows repeating the last thing you watched or an issue you still need to resolve. Keeping a journal is a great way to see the flow of your dreams. Try not to get stuck in the over analysis of your dreams and visions. We are to be present in real life, not lost in trying to figure out if a dream means we will have children someday. Dreaming is a tool we can use to create and process and to communicate with other parts of ourselves and our guides. In a journal, go back every few weeks and see what you wrote to see what your personal pattern with dreaming.

Dream big while staying in the present!

Little Red Riding hood

One of the greatest gifts Bob gave to me was trips to Frauenau, Germany. He would work or teach at the art school, and I could be a student at play. This summer school was tucked away in the Bavarian Forest. Frauneau means the belly of the frau or women. We were just a hike away from the Grosser Rachel Mountain. The great Rachel is Germany's third highest mountain peak. The summer of 2005 we visited Bild-Werk Visual Arts School, escaping the reality that we might not have a home in New Orleans. It was also the summer of the hundred-year flood. Bild-Werk school was still open even with flooded streets.

I would explore the area on my own. This year I was going to hike to a kinder pool at the foot of Grosser Rachel. I was up for the adventure in my new bright red raincoat, hiking boots and a paper map. This was before cell phones were glued to our hands. A freedom for which I still pine for.

I filled my little Octoberfest bag with my favorite sausages and cheese from the butcher. I made a quick stop at the bakery for a pretzel and sweet treat. Then a final stop to fill up my water bottle before I was off. It was a day to commune with nature herself!

The clouds kept threatening to rain on my walk as the sun shined down on me. I marched through a back alley, past the galleries and houses, down to a farmer's path. One side was a creek flowing heavily with water and on the other side was grain fields. When I got up on my tippy toes, I could see the town over the top of the golden grains.

Walking through the farmer's field, the sun warmed my face. I had just come upon the old wooden bridge as the sun sent down glorious rays of light. I could feel the heat instantly as I skipped across the wooden planks. The water below was rushing. We had been cold and wet for weeks, so this was a rare sunshining day.

Immediately everything around me changed. The bridge took me to another place. I was at the edge of the Baden-Würtemburg Forest. The ground was golden brown from all the pine needles. Pops of bright green ferns reaching for light. There were pinecones of every size and shape. I couldn't believe all the different varieties of fir trees. From wide and tall, short, round, skinny and frail. Different varieties of mushrooms poped out of the bottom of old stumps and decaying wood. This was a true forest bathing experience before social media named it that.

My *Snow White* dream was coming true in this magical forest. I saw the most elegant and graceful buck. An adult with his eight points in velvet. I saw his family on the other side of the trail, two fawns following behind the mom. I was just full of giggles and joy on this hike. I had already walked four miles to get to this point. I was just gliding up a hill on divine love for the rest of the hike up.

I was singing out loud and laughing in my head. I was on the trail to the kinder pool; .5 kilometers till I reached my destination the red sign noted. I was excited. Suddenly, the sounds of the forest changed. It went from birds and winds to sounds like an angelic choir. At this point in my life, I was more into conspiracy than spirituality. I wondered if I ate the wrong wild mushrooms. We were warned about the mushrooms, not for the psilocybin, these wild ones were full of radiation from Chernobyl. I thought I was losing my mind because I could hear angels singing to me.

The voices got louder the closer I got to the kinder pool. The kinder pool was a place where locals went to exercise. This was not a tourist destination. As I reached the wooden deck of the open area, I saw that I was not crazy. The Vienna Boys' Choir, the actual choir was practicing. They were going to perform that evening. This was where they'd stopped to practice with no one around except me and the birds.

It was *unglaublich* (unbelievable). I spent an hour listening to this choir as joyful tears ran down my face. I sat on one of the wooden reclining chairs cheering after each song. I was dizzy in the daydream of sound in the most perfect forest setting. It was a surreal moment. The choir members all got a treat and drink before they filed back into the bus. I thanked and cheered them on, as a crazy American girl would do.

I was ready for my walk and refreshing dip in mineral water. I prepared myself for my kinder pool walk in the ice-cold water. Here I marched around in circles in two feet of water. There was a place where you could stand under the ice-cold spring water. I did my rounds proudly with the angel sounds still echoing in my head.

I laid on the wooden plank recliners to dry off after my splashy march and cold shower. I felt blessed by the mountain. I got into my delicious German snacks. Still singing in my head. I watched other people coming to get their daily walk. My two hours of private forest spa time was unmatched by any paid spa service I'd ever have had. With the boys' choir and the spring water, it was an unworldly experience. It was one of my first vortex experiences.

I packed up, leaving nothing behind. I was all dried off and readied myself for my walk back to the hostel. As I walked down, I went over and talked to the trees. I smelled their different barks and noticed the variety of colors and patterns. I soaked in every second of this magical forest. I floated down the trail, noticing everything.

I even acknowledged the troll that protects the stream. He pointed the way to the bridge; it was around the bend. As I neared the pedestrian bridge, the sun moved lower in the sky. The mountain gave a dark shadow over my path. It was getting close to dusk. I knew animals came out to drink from the creek. I decided to pick up my pace. I could feel the clouds begin to creep in.

As I started across the bridge, I noticed a large figure coming toward me. At first, I thought it was a farmer with a cart in front of him. He might be pushing something. We were both moving directly toward the bridge. It was the only crossing possibly for miles.

I got a full visual of what was approaching me. It was a *huge wolf!* Not the skinny wolf you see at the zoo or the hungry wolf in *National Geographic* but a true gray wolf. It was big, almost make-believe! It was the ancient wolf from the stories of the Brothers Grimm. The Brothers Grimm were from this area in Germany, this could be what they wrote about. It was taller than me and wider than a Softail motorcycle. Its eyes glowed yellow. In the shadow, it appeared to be black with shiny silver highlights. It scared the bejesus out of me! I stood frozen at the end of the bridge. I felt trapped. The wolf wanted to cross, and I wanted out of his way.

A frozen moment in my memory, like the time I saw a snow owl, it was all in slow motion. I could hear the heavy breath of this monster. It would have no problem taking me down in one chomp. My heavenly experience from earlier in the day suddenly became terrifying. The reality of this great beast crashed down on me instantly. My dream day was now my worst nightmare.

I acted instinctively. I bowed to him. A full-on *Alice in Wonderland* curtsy. I pulled my red hood over my head. The rain appeared as the sun disappeared. I felt like all the light left me alone in the dark with the big bad wolf. Yet the joy from my day filled me with love and shined out.

The wolf acknowledged my bow and nodded to me. We were only ten meters apart from each other, a single lunge for him. I quietly said, looking down in all humility, "Thank you, great wolf, for appearing on my path today. I do apologize for being in your path. It is not my desire to be in your way or to detain you from your journey. May I pass to the right of you?" I said thank you once again, peeking up slightly to see if my request was heard.

The great beast stood taller. I nearly had a bowel movement. Its gaze met mine. I was terrified to be face-to-face with this monster of a wolf. I looked at it with all the love I had inside of me, praying it was the correct response. The creature's yellow eyes glowed as if it was a Disney film. He was huge, as big as a cow; even his heavy fur could not cover his muscular stature.

The giant wolf stepped forward and then to the side as if to make room for me. It was not frightened by me, since I had nothing but love for it. With grace and ease, I stepped as close to the bridge railing as I could. We both walked forward at a medium pace.

I could smell its nappy fur as I passed by the huge creature, looking down, so as not to provoke it. Soon, we were less than a meter away from each other. I could have reached my hand out to pet it as it passed me. Its energy, just its presence gave a different meaning to my whole day. I truly experienced the magic of life. Like the doe in the medicine animal stories when she was trying to reach *ALL*, I knew only love could conquer all.

There is nothing to fear in life when we approach any situation with respect and love. The great wolf taught me this, like the medicine of the deer. When we are on our path, God's will, we can live in grace and ease with the guidance of love. Nothing can stop you, not even the big bad wolf.

Guides

In meditation, I have been seeking my guides' advice and knowledge. I never asked, "Who are these guides?" My guides came in all types, from common angels (beings of light) to past loved ones. Since guides come in all shapes and forms, the more expansive question is: "What are we seeking?" I ask the guides in meditation or through my heart, and the appropriate guide shows up. I just ask for help or an explanation.

Guides can also be ascended masters who have come to help or teach us our lesson. Ascended masters range from Jesus Christ to Bob Marley. These beings give guidance to us on our Earth walk. Nature and otherworldly beings are other guides who are out to help us, like a personal human resources department on our Earth walk. We have unlimited, unconditional help always surrounding us.

When communicating with guides, know they do not respond to yes-or-no questions. A pendulum answers yes and no, guides give you guidance toward your choice (free will), toward your higher good. I often ask a question in my mind only to have the answer download overnight, finding myself with full knowledge and understanding the next day. We all need to create a connection with our assorted guides to get help. That connection is not just to divine love but also to divine wisdom from the conscious light. The guides bring us that connection with grace and ease.

It's been amazing to watch the transition from third dimension to fourth dimension over the past years. I was part of the transitions by holding space. I started my spiritual learning in a very third-dimensional world. I understood spirituality by attending mystery schools, studying three lineages of reiki, engaging in experiences with shamans, and attending angelic healing training and conferences—the very old-school way of spirituality. I have put in years of meditation, mantras, private healing sessions, moon circles, and living in *ALL*'s will. And yet, it's only the beginning of a lifetime of service to divine love. It was my guides who led me to the place I am now.

In my early studies, it was all about secret words, ancient symbols, ritual, and ceremony, with emphasis on the date and time of events. I loved studying Wicca and participating in the seasonal rituals. This involved the burning of candles and incense for specific events. It was important to "feed" the deities or show them gratitude on their altar with offerings of fresh flowers and fruits.

I noticed at the very end of the transition from third into fourth dimension, the prayers went from huge pomp and circumstance to simply ask and receive. No longer do we have to wait until the blood moon, or the full moon is in our first house. Instead, we just need to connect within our

God spark and ask a guide for help. At the now moment, I live in gratitude and walk in a present meditative state. I am consciously walking in my natural surroundings with my guides surrounding me.

Candle magic, blood magic and other spell casting was never part of my studies of Wicca. For me, it was about respecting nature, learning the cycle of life, the moon cycle, flowing with the medicine wheel, and listening to your body and nature around you. I haven't practice Wicca for over twenty years. As a girlfriend pointed out, it seems capitalism has expanded into the mystical arts, as Wicca isn't what she used to be.

I receive help with my dreams from other guides as well. When I feel like I made a mistake, I ask the guides what lesson I need to learn for my highest good. With my unlimited teachers, I do not make mistakes anymore. I am learning lessons.

It could be said that, over the years, it became easier for me to see and hear the guides because this was what I put my attention to. However, with the current downloads and a consciousness opening, I have taught people how to connect, and within minutes, they are communicating with greater detail than one would expect.

Communication with your guide is very personal. Some may leave your answer in an email or push a book in front of you. Other guides may come in visions or during meditation to give you messages or direct help. Some may hand you symbols or objects, give you feelings, and show you visions. Guides may put you in the exact situation you need to understand. All communication is done with gratitude and humility.

Guides are angelic beings of a higher frequency. In the fourth dimension they exist in all forms from Ascended Masters to otherworldly beings to fairies. We can receive their guidance and healing much easier. Learning about the different guides will open doors to universal knowledge and give you a great sense of self. They are here to heal, guide, and find what it is you need to stay on *ALL*'s will or your will.

Take time to explore your guides, how they work and connect with you. Consider starting with your past relatives. Are there any that you feel may be an easy guide to start with? Talk to them. Converse in your mind or heart or out loud to a photograph. Find a way to say what you want or ask your questions to them. Then just wait and listen.

Negative Creeps

Here in the fourth dimension, the negative creeps can also guide us. Again, this is not limited to earthly fears. Negative guides—or in Kurt Cobain's lexicon, negative creeps can sneak into our feelings and thoughts, showing their faces in physical pain. These low frequency guides are often manipulated by our collective cultural experiences and guide us in ways not for our highest good. Like nightmares in the fourth-dimension dream world, they can get into our subconscious, giving us a feeling of being unworthy. They can even be sent to you by loved ones wanting you to feel their pain or suffering. This is why clearing yourself on a regular basis is needed. The negative guides can put you in a conspiracy mind, a state of mistrust, self-loathing, and other forms of depression without your knowing it or being aware of it.

Negative creeps are part of the old matrix, the old thought patterns that *ALL* is outside of us and not part of us. It's a way of control. It is also part of black magic or blood magic. Negative creeps are low frequency energy that are in the second and third dimension used to control our actions and thoughts. They do not exist in dimensions above the fourth. Here, where the fear of the human ego gathers, I call this the egew. We have an opportunity to listen to the negative creeps both knowingly and unknowingly. Negative creep energy can be found in everything from video games, songs, movies, social media, and people can carry negative creep energy into our life.

When you feel out of sorts or have negative ideas or thoughts you normally don't have, go clear yourself! Water is a lovely way to release what is no longer needed. A traditional smudging or smoke bath or essential oil sprays can also help. Even a shower can help clear off negative energy. Call out in prayer to what you connect with or believe in to clear you; whether you're petitioning Archangel Michael or Green Tara or Lakshmi and Lord Ganesh, ask for help removing what is no longer needed.

Going to healers or shamans can really help release the negative creeps. In my meditations for private sessions, the first thing we do is clear off what is no longer necessary. When I get overrun with negative creeps, I call up my favorite healers and friends for help. I am grateful for Cindy Hamilton Bowels for being able to clear off negative creeps instantly off me anywhere

I am. When a voice inside your head tells you not to get help, that's when you know you have a negative creep. The negative thoughts are trying to keep you in a downward spiral.

Negative creeps can also be called entity attachment. These are programs or spells sent by one person to another. Some are highly detailed, like a ritual. More often, it is a simple negative thought sent while unknowingly doing magic. Words can hurt others and incite others to do harm. It's true. Speaking hate out loud creates more negative creeps.

Negative creeps can come in all forms. Their influence can happen over and over, one event right after the next. Others may come in the form of feeling loneliness or sadness. Processed foods can enhance negative creeps, just like exercise and meditation can clear it away.

In our current time we now have more negative creeps than ever before with marketing. Cults have a long history of using negative creeps to gain not just money but control people's whole lives. Negative creeps are real people too, not just low energy thoughts. That is why discernment is so very important. Love does not hurt you or others in any way, divine love does not hurt in ANY WAY. A "love/hate" relationship is a sign of negative creeps.

Know that you are more powerful than any form of negative creeps. With divine love you can create a path of happiness without low frequency thoughts.

How To Know Faires are Real

As earthlings, we are gifted with sight, hearing, tasting, smelling and touching senses. Every sense we have is able to acknowledge reality. The different waves of energy angels emulate define how we perceive them. This personalized view of beings of light is why we have so many different religions. Each person understands all of spirituality from their surroundings. In the age of media and global unification, more information is available.

As a side note, this is where the clair senses come from. It is a metaphysical way or psychic way of using our senses. With our inner child and higher-self we can open ourselves to this way of communication to all our guides. It is with the "clair senses" we find our personal connection to fairies, nature, and beings of light. Let's look at some quick definitions of these senses:

❖ Smell. Clairalience, I was told, is the oldest of our senses. Having clairalience means being able to smell what is not physically around you. For example, working with Mother Mary or Quan Yin, you may smell roses.

❖ Hear. Clairaudience is hearing messages clearly. This is direct communication with guides like beings of light. An example for me is hearing a song before I do a session with an individual. What I have found is that lyrics of a song can give advice to me or to who I am helping. It's as though the guides gave me insight through songs. It makes session much easier when hearing the answer.

❖ See. Clairvoyance is to see or have clear visions of the past or future. The most commonly known and the most desired clairvoyance may come in the form of readings or psychic sessions. Some clairvoyant practitioners use deviations like tarot cards or runes. Rituals can be used to put them into a psychic state so they can see into the past. Those who tell you your lifetime achievements are either over exaggerating or reading the contract of your will. You have to follow your own discernment. You will know whether someone who says they are clairvoyant is real or is really "full of it." Free will does not allow for our future to be set in stone.

❖ Feel. Clairsentience is being able to feel emotions. Like getting goose bumps when something is said that strikes a chord deep in you. Clairsentience may show up as a feeling that you should just leave a place because something is wrong. You can feel what is for your highest good. It is our personal experience in the fourth dimension.

❖ Taste. Clairgustance is being able to taste something that is not physically present. Once, in meditation, I was in the heaven of Source. Well, a place where we humans are allowed to feel that divine love. It was in the form of water; the living water religious practices often talk about. I remember cupping my hand and drinking this high-energy water. I remember thinking, this does not taste like any water I've ever had. I drank more. It was like my taste buds were exploding. It was exactly like an "everlasting gobstopper" from my favorite childhood movie Charlie and Chocolate Factory. It was every perfect flavor that sparkled on my tongue.

❖ Know. Claircognizance is knowing. It is the key to the fifth dimension, Claircognizance is when you just know the answer. You just know the whole situation with grace and ease. You can ask a question of the beings of light, and—poof—you just know or understand it all. This is where I often get in trouble. I have been called a know-it-all. I used to say it was because I read and listened to others in my youth. Now, I understand that I am connected to higher energy. I have a higher guidance. Yet, no one likes it when you know more than they do. No one wants to feel "less than." I have learned to keep what I know to myself unless I am asked or paid.

Meditation: How to Communicate with Beings of Light

We are always surrounded by beings of light, and they want to help us. The beings of light don't speak English, nor do they even have mouths. The sound of energy of their vibration is light language. Not all of us can understand light language. We ask them for help through prayers, listening for the answer in our heart.

While in prayer, it's best to go to them with humility. I was taught by Walter to go humbly. "I am an ignorant being." Ask for their help by acknowledging that you need their help. Let them know you understand they are here for us. Be grateful and humble when asking. I know of situations where it may be necessary to demand help. These are circumstances of very high-level energy work, and such a style is not applied in a normal situation. Please don't just demand your guides' help. Instead, send love and appreciative gratitude.

Honoring them in daily gratitude by simply acknowledging them through prayer is better than waiting until the last second in an emergency. Trying to make a deal to get out of a situation usually doesn't work. Create a working relationship, talk to them.

When help is needed, ask a being of light. Remember when asking your questions, they do not give out lottery numbers (unless that is your purpose) or respond to questions of *yes or no* or *good or bad*. To receive the complete answer, you must be open to the response and hear the message completely. Realize that the answers may be given anytime from immediately to months later, you just must pay attention. Typically, answers come within the first twenty-four hours to forty-eight hours. Answers may be in a song, an email, a movie even. You will know in your heart when the answer is given.

Opening communication with your guardian angel is simple. By following your heart and listening with your heart, you can find your personal way of communication.

Offerings of lighting a candle, singing a song, saying a prayer, or other signs of gratitude are felt with love. I have created altars for my angelic guides and leave them gifts of fresh flowers, fruits, and nuts. These are just ways of acknowledging them, not treating them like the "golden calf" or creating a spell. Gifts of gratitude show we love our guides! Using your favorite prayer is perfect too. Or creating one just for the occasion works as well.

A sample prayer:

> I humbly call upon [whoever you are praying to for help, Mary, Jesus Christ, Raphael, Ganesh]. I am in appreciative gratitude for all of your love and protection. I [state your name] come to you today as a respectful human being asking for help and guidance.
>
> Would you please help me with …
>
> Allow me to let go of my worries about …
>
> Would you please send your healing love and light to …
>
> Please open income pathways …

To end, I am thankful for all you do. Thank you. Thank you. Thank you.

Guides: Nature

During one meditation, a guide told me to look to nature for answers to our questions. The spirit guide went on to explain we no longer need old thoughts, old rules, and old ways of living. He said to look at what exists in the *now* around you. What is the world around you saying?

Guides are not always human beings or beings of light. They come in all shapes and sizes and can communicate with you in different ways. It's not only quartz that has a vibration. All things have a consciousness to them. Some may openly communicate with you. The natural world holds the greatest guidance.

The guide told me to talk it out with standing people (trees). They would listen to all my stories. I began to connect with all the trees and wondered if others could hear them. I had friends tell me of exciting experiences on DMT or ayahuasca that allowed them to speak to trees or plants. This was the inspiration for me to make my own way to learn how to communicate with nature; I knew that I could do it without any substances.

I was hooked on nature guides. Still am. Once you can connect and hear them, it is a lot to take in. The first real acknowledgement that I was talking to trees and birds came from grandfather crow. In Palm Springs, California, we lived at the base of the San Jacinto Mountains. I got very overprotective of the birds in my yard, including the nests of doves, mockingbirds, and hummingbirds. One summer, the mockingbird pushed one of its baby birds out of the nest and called for grandfather crow to come eat it.

I was confused by what I had seen and heard. What was wrong with mockingbird? Here was the little helpless bird not able to fly, chirping for its life. Mockingbird got grandfather crow's attention and brought him to my backyard for an afternoon snack. I freaked out. This *huge* black crow shot down to snatch up the baby bird. Not on my watch, I thought, as I started throwing rocks at the crow, telling it to leave the baby bird alone.

Before I knew it, a mockingbird started diving at me! *What the heck?* I thought, *I am trying to save your baby!* It started screaming at me even more. Before I knew it, the little baby bird found its way out of my yard, I could no longer protect it. Grandfather crow was upset at me. He began to follow me to work and on my walks with Sophie, my poodle. He would sit on the electrical pole with his son eyeing me. The next day while we were on a walk, he stood at the end of a block, right in the middle of the street. He stood at least two and half feet tall. He started yelling at us and flew directly at me. I mean directly to me only four feet from the ground as though he was going for my throat. Both Sophie and I froze in fear.

Like some computer translator had just clicked on, I could hear what grandfather crow was bawling about. First, he yelled to me about the circle of life, that he too had a family to feed and take care of. He was doing what mockingbird had asked of him. I had no right to interfere with nature. He explained to me that the young bird was not of his making and that I was getting into bird drama that was not about me or my feelings. He yelled at me to go read about cowbirds. Finally, I would understand the whole situation, not just my perspective.

All this happened as grandfather crow did a flyby, I could feel the tickle of his feathers as he passed my face and went straight up into the air. I was confused by the whole thing and raced home to see what a cowbird was. Why did I feel like Simba? And why, suddenly, was the Disney production of "The Circle of Life " playing in my head?

This made me think of what my papa had told me when, after watching *Bambi*. I'd tried to get him to swear he wouldn't hunt anymore. He explained to me in his kind, compassionate way, "You see, Peanut, the people came and took over the land to build houses and farms. They pushed out the animals to a small area. They no longer could use all the land. There are many deer now living in a small space. We need to hunt them to keep their population down and help control diseases. If they got sick, well, it would kill off too many of them. The deer might disappear. We have taken away their natural way." Was papa watching me as *grandfather crow?*

Grandfather crow was right. A cowbird does not build its own nest or even raise its own chicks. It pushes its eggs into other birds' nests. Sometimes, cowbirds push out the other birds' eggs, and in this case, that's what happened. The cowbird had pushed its egg into the mockingbird's nest. The male knew it wasn't his chick. He tossed it out and gave it to grandfather crow to seal its fate. It was a hard lesson for me to understand. The cycle of life is not as pretty as we pretend it to be. It also showed me I can connect to nature; it was real, not my imagination.

It led me to create When Nature Speaks to You, a deck of eighty of my original photographs. These magical images of nature were printed to help teach anyone how to connect to trees, plants, and rocks. When Nature Speaks to You is a simple way of connecting to guides through daily meditation.

I took photographs from my heart in various places across North America. Literally I would hold a camera or my cell phone at the level of my heart to take the picture. From Lily Dale Assembly in New York to the Stupa in Sedona, Florida's sunrise, vortices in Joshua Tree, the giant Sequoias in Kings Canyon, New Orleans city park to caves in Mexico. The cards are pictures of nature's guides. These guides speak to you directly. The standing people (trees) are our antennas to the universe. The stone people are some of the oldest beings on this planet. The plant people teach us sacred geometry. The sky people show us a bigger perspective. And the water people remind us to flow and to be reflective.

Learn to connect with standing people or trees. They have much to tell us. They help by transmuting energy, literally. Trees breathe in carbon dioxide, and with the help of the sun and water, they turn it into oxygen by photosynthesis. Standing people are here to help us process the past and release current fears or anger. They are also the antennas of the planet, listening and absorbing our pain. To me, trees represent myself, my community, or friends. These guides show themselves; you can see their faces like trolls or fig trees with warlock faces. They are nonjudgmental, like all of nature, allowing whatever form they come in to speak to you. They show strength and confidence, as well as support.

Plant people are a magical link to everyday life, from the food we eat to the clothes we wear. They hold great healing properties! They are the real-life fairies and mythical creatures that surround us today. They work with all kingdoms on Earth, bringing balance. In nature, as one plant can be toxic, its relief is always nearby. In the modern day, we use medicine, essential oils, and other plant medicine. We eat the fruits plants bear and have trained the plants to provide unlimited substance for living. Connect to the plant people to feel the magic that lies within you, allowing them to open you up to higher dimensions of healing and understanding.

As we step further into understanding nature and knowing that we are all connected, we see how our actions have consequences. We are just now understanding the massive underground communication systems of plant people; they communicate not through fiberoptics as humans do but, instead, through a beautiful lattice system created by mycelium, a small fungus with gigantic, worldwide reach.

Mycelium is the underground communication for all plants people. It is how trees talk to each other and share nutrients. The network sends messages like fiber optics. As the raindrop delivers a message to a plant, it relays the message to the mycelium. This message is shared with all the plant people. It is the unseen biomatrix that Mother Earth uses to communicate.

Plant people have been misunderstood throughout history. Mycelium is a fungus among us that has been theorized to be the forbidden fruit in the garden of Eden. Ancient artwork depicts a red mushroom shape with white dots. Others have written that mushrooms, specifically the psilocybin or psychedelics, gave humans their first conscious expression. NASA is doing all kinds of research on mushrooms. It may be the key to space travel. Not to mention, it begins the discussion that maybe this magic mushroom is the blueprint for all life consciousness on Earth and beyond.

As a side note, about plant people, we have a misunderstanding of genetics. Humans have also manipulated the plant people's DNA for centuries. In our modern age, we have awarded the highest scientific award to Norman Borlaug, who was able to modify plant genetics to increase their strength. What was called the Green Revolution may not end up being for our highest good. Yes, it does help certain plants survive drought and increase the amount of fruit they produce, but it may lead to other factors that are not good for human consumption. I am saying acknowledge plant people. They are more than the nuts, fruits, and vegetables you eat. Thank them for the nutrition they will give you. And if possible, buy local, organic, or non-GMO products. Sending your love to them always helps raise the vibration.

Stone people have much to say. Crystals are known for their vibration; their communication or energy is what powers our watches. Crystals and minerals have been collected and held in high places, but every rock or stone has a story, too. They represent family to me, a foundation where your paths can be laid or where you can talk to ancestors, connecting to your personal history. The stone people want to share with you, their knowledge. They may have a face or form of animals, humans, or otherworldly beings. The stone people come in all sizes and shapes, with different textures and colors. Feel into the story of the stone people. I have a knack for finding heart-shaped stone people on my walks.

I also have a confession; I had a five-year affair with a mountain. Yes, a mountain loved and protected me unconditionally. I fell in love with this giant. In Palm Springs, my backyard was the San Jacinto Mountains. There is a tram that goes to the peak or highest point. In the evening, I would watch the little light of the tram go up and down. This was my first time falling in love with a mountain. Being born on the great plains, I did not have such strength, such power in my view in my childhood.

This mountain was awesome to me. He would send me gifts of flowers to my doorstep and color the grounds around him in various greens and yellows. He would wish me well on my journey and be the first one to greet me when I came home. He made me feel safe and protected. He would stop fires from raging too close to my home and send coyotes away. He spoke to me every day and greeted me in the morning, whispering goodnight. He watched over me, fed me, and entertained me. He was everything I had ever wanted in a companion. We danced under the blood moon. We chuckled as he rumbled under my feet. He cooled me off with streams of water.

Stone people are not just crystals you find in shops. They are the ground you stand on. Listen to them. They, too, have much to teach. The foundation of what we are is beneath your feet.

Indigenous people have many names for water people, just as we do today. Waters like ocean, river, creek, stream all flow with a different deity. My connection with water people is strongest with the orisha Oshun, of the Yoruba people. She teaches me about the divine feminine through fresh water; Yémaya is an orisha for the ocean is another water person. Flowing with divine love and unlimited potential, water is the Wi-Fi of Earth. It connects all beings and teaches us how to allow transition. Water people come in all forms, from solid to liquid to gas. Water people are guided by the moon as well, giving them a constant rhythm of life.

Water is the life source itself. It is the ultimate cleanser—whether we're drinking it or bathing in it. Every doctor will tell you to drink water. It is what our bodies are made of. Water is constantly being recycled. It has enormous history within each drop. In meditation, you can breathe underwater. *ALL* or God has been called "the living water".

Flow with water people.

Rainbows and orbs often represent fourth dimensional beings. When seeing a rainbow, clearly ask a question or for healing. You can find rainbows more than just in the sky. See rainbows around plants and animals. Rainbows may have portals and vortices. Orbs may want to guide you. You can understand more about them by their color, number of them and size.

With the help of our Earthly guides, we open up parts of ourselves to higher universal knowledge. Soon, you will be just looking out your window for answers, instead of turning to tarot cards. With our nature guides, we can learn how to heal and get our own personal message from the universe instantly. They will tell you if the weather is changing or if you should leave a situation and can help you with discernment. Unlike humans, who may get caught up in money, these guides are only for your highest good. They will never mislead you. You may misunderstand and have to ask again, but they will never send you the wrong way.

Meditation: Nature Guides Connecting

To connect to your nature guides you must be connected to yourself. It is also important to ground yourself. Make sure you are present in the current moment. The deeper you are connected to the Earth, the easier it is to communicate. Choose one being or guide that you are going to connect with. It can be in person or a photograph will do.

Next, introduce yourself through your third eye or sixth chakra. Your mind's eye introduces you to various guides. Talk through your heart. With gratitude and humility, tell them your full name and your nickname if you have one. Get personal with them. Let them begin to connect with you. Feel as though your conscious love reaches out to them, connecting into their energy.

I recommend that you meditate with nature for at least five minutes, allowing as much time needed to create a stronger connection. Listen to the guide with all your senses. Sometimes, a guide will jump right out with the answer, and other times, you will have to listen and look deeper into yourself. Colors are one way a guide can communicate with you. Smells, sounds and even feelings are ways of understanding messages.

If it's a tree or bush, you can touch it or hug it if it has no thorns. If it's a plant, gently feel it, careful not to break or damage it. Smell it. Feel into its aura or the energy that surrounds it. Take your time. Just be with nature. Do not rush the moment. Savor it. Be present. Really allow the being inside of it to show itself to you. If you want, ask it what its name is or what it would like to be called.

I will never forget connecting to the world's largest tree at Sequoia National Park. The tree was named General Sherman to honor an American war hero. Before I could even introduce myself, the tree said, "Please, please, please tell them my name is Shirley." I started laughing hard, I forgot my question and instead learned the history of the standing people that surrounded her. I think Shirley was the most talkative tree I have ever met.

Ask your question out loud for the best response or in your heart. Yes-or-no questions will not be answered. Guides do not understand finances or debt. The question could be simply, "What is my lesson for the day?" If you talked to the same tree every day, it would have a new message for you each day. You could release your deepest secret or ask a personal question. They don't tell anyone your secrets. And they don't give out lottery numbers or do anything related to gambling, as they have a hard time understanding money to begin with. They want to guide you to happiness, to joy, and to a deeper connection to yourself.

Some guides do not speak at all. They will give you messages or feelings or even colors. You have to listen first; digest and then listen with your heart to find the truths for you. Do not quarrel with the response. Really, do not tell them that's not that answer you want to hear; they will quickly close and may not respond to you in the future if they feel you are not listening. Like this conversation I had with the bird people:

"Where is my happiness?" I inquired. "What am I supposed to be doing?"

The same message was repeated. "God has always taken care of you. Why would they stop now?"

The message from the bird people went on to explain there would be nothing I would ever go without, unless it was not for my highest good. You may not have realized something you desired was a block or holding you back from other happiness, the bird people explained to me.

Perhaps it was a situation, a job, a person you no longer needed in your life. It might even be painful to let it go of. You may lose friends or have a difficult time with the transition. Every action you are guided to take is intended to bring you joy. Even if you do not see or feel that immediately. The bird people taught me, when we stay with what we are guided to do, we can grow and find joy.

With the help of guides, you can heal, understand, and expand at a much faster rate than you could without them. You can ask anything for help. Talk to your car if it sounds bad. Ask it to hold on till you can get to a proper place to fix it. Seriously, if you can talk to trees, then you can talk to your car. Feel its energy and talk to its guide spirit.

Always end your request in appreciative gratitude. We must thank our guides for our ability to ask them to help us. If possible, give them thanks by way of gifts. Most love fresh water, but seeds, food, or acknowledgement. Polishing your crystals or your car would give them love in return. Even singing or dancing in their honor shows your respect and is a way of giving your love back to them.

Father Sky

I don't know the sky.
I'm sitting here looking up, and I don't know the sky.
I know my sky; I know the sky in Palm Springs.
I know the sky in New Orleans.
I know the sky in Omaha Nebraska.
I look up at the Big Bear sky,
And I don't recognize the sky.

Father Sky said, *I have stayed the same. I am always constant. It is you who keeps moving.*
There's another guide saying it's consistent like Father Sky,
Using the sun's light conscious light.
It's Father Sky's daughter, the moon,
Who dances with me at night.
The moon teaches me of space, dark at night.
The Void, she says, *is space, not of dark matter but a place where everything is bright,*
A womb of our creation, where our dreams can manifest in light.
I see the sky now. I see my eyes are Father Sky

Channeled message from www.Marigoldslove.com

Stopping to smell the flowers and notice the trees is more than just noticing the beauty surrounding you. Stopping to smell the flowers and notice the trees is about giving thanks to the fellow energetic beings that live around you and honoring the connectedness of all life. What do the flowers have to say about the global events of late? What do the trees think of humanity's current crises? The shared knowledge between the Earth, the plants, and the animals is not a secret born out of exclusion by the Earth, the plants, and the animals but a secret created once humanity forgot the language of the Earth, the plants and the animals. Just as human dialects and languages have gone missing because there has been no one left to teach the words or listen to the songs of their Elders, so too has humanity let the languages of the stones, the birds, the waters, and all the other living languages of our mother tongue to be forgotten.

Do not despair! Within each of us is the capacity to *remember* the languages of our natural landscape. Observe a small child and you will see that they know how to listen to the ground or speak to an animal. The small child has not been taught to forget their gifts of communication with the natural world. Slowly, the small child is taught to forget and by adulthood, most in our modern world do not remember.

But within each of us is the capacity to *relearn*. Within each of us is the capacity to remember how to communicate, how to listen, and how to speak. It is more challenging, of course, as an adult.

But it is not impossible! Within our DNA we have all the tools we need to remember. Just as science has proved that ancestral trauma may be stored within our genetic codes and passed down from generation to generation. Similar are the neural pathways that will allow us to relearn, remember, and rejoice in our ancient ways of communication.

The first step is to remember how to communicate with yourself. However, practicing this is perfect for you. And then, it's a matter of shedding all of the layers of human history in your outer shell that is blinding you from your gifts. However, you choose to do this is also perfect just for you.

And once you begin on your path of remembering, it's like you become a child again, fresh, and curious about what all life has to offer, about how all life forms have meaning, and asking the deep questions and listening deeply to what all life around you have to say. Just wait, there is a story within every ancient tree, rock and landscape.

You have the capacity to listen. You have the capacity to learn.

CHAPTER 5

The fifth dimension is divine consciousness.

The fifth dimension is not just a sixties band name. It is the place where our higher consciousness begins to open up unlimited possibilities. This is where we begin to align with our higher self. A popular term to describe the fifth dimension is *Christ consciousness*. When I first heard this term, I did not understand it. At first, I was afraid of it. I thought it was another way the Roman Catholic Church was co-opting spirituality. Later, it was explained that it is also known as Krishna' consciousness, Buddha's consciousness, Archangel Michael's consciousness, and Abraham's consciousness.

Understanding the science and spiritual meaning of consciousness can get complicated. Science has researched consciousness that goes beyond my comprehension. It's not that I failed biology in college, it's not my strongest subject. I have read much on the claustrum which is considered to be the "seat of consciousness." Different articles have different theories on how, but it is the communication in the brain that is most linked to consciousness. Some say it produces an oil that travels up and down the spine. If it does have an oily substance that gives a conscious experience traveling down and up the spine, would that explain why the only commonality of all meditation is to have a straight spine?

I was told by my guides that 72 percent of the planet Earth has moved into the fifth dimension as of 2020. The more people become conscious; the more planet inhabitants will grow towards peace. I got really excited thinking we were headed in the right direction, until I remembered that 71 percent of the planet is covered in water. Which means only 1 percent of where humans live is conscious. Yeah, we have a long way to go. It does make me think that if most of the oceans are becoming conscious, would this explain why orcas are attacking boats? Have the orcas "woke" up? That's a bad joke, as the term woke is being used to stop consciousness by those who still want power. Yeah, that's a little fishy.

To me, divine consciousness is allowing divine love to rule our actions in divine time, to acknowledge the consciousness of everything, seeing the golden thread that connects us all to *ALL*, at the perfect "now" moment. It also opens the doors to all our guides and is the highest good of all. It is a powerful understanding of the connection each of us has. It is universal knowledge and the peace that comes with understanding life is not defined by good and bad. This is the true state of just being, being who you are in divine love, knowing tolerance is for the highest good and compassion is the only answer.

It is through divine consciousness that we can understand the Second Coming of Christ is not about a single person. It is about every being finding the same consciousness that Jesus did when he walked as a man on Earth. He came to show us how to exist in complete divine love and divine consciousness. He taught others this way of living.

Since I have already turned off many people by my beliefs, I have to say Jesus doesn't love just one religion; nor does he love guns. Jesus was a true pacifist, and my heart aches for the way his name is used. He is a true ascended master who lived on Earth and tried to show we silly humans that we can be better.

I asked Jesus once in a meditation, "How do you deal with all these religions making money off you, not helping others, making millions to build bigger churches, and using your name to conquer lands and murder people? How, Jesus, do you deal with humans using your name in such a horrible way?"

Jesus said to me, "I love all. I cannot control the actions of man. I can only show them the way. It is their free will. I only have divine love for all of creation. I do not judge others' actions." *Wow*, I thought, *to be that compassionate, to be that judgment free. Wow. It is something to work toward.*

Jesus, my brother, does not have any human ego issues and is truly something to try to emulate on Earth. I get it now.

In a recent meditation going to Jesus for help, I found that he was not the same as he'd been during all my prior encounters. He was the *Christ*.

He was everyone. The second coming of Christ has happened! He has been reborn in all of us! We are the physical Christ consciousness, Krishna's consciousness, Michael consciousness. Whatever you feel comfortable with, divine consciousness is available for everyone. We can all carry the Christed light!

Now

Now is the time to become conscious and understand it is our individual dreams that can create our new future. I know for a fact that we can dream bigger than those apocalyptic fears. I know that divine love is the strongest of all loves, as it is not judgmental, and that it is unlimited, infinite power. Divine love is the true energy that everything is made up of. The entire universe runs on divine love.

If you are conscious, if you are part of the love, not of the fear, you are already doing things to take care of yourself and self-governance. Live a healthy lifestyle. The responsibility of being a healer is to heal yourself first to help heal the world. This is all happening now. Add gratitude for your daily life and then just live in joy!

> *Now is the only time that exists. You can*
> *change any thought in this now moment.*

I can guarantee that this present moment is real. This is the only thing that truly exists at this time right now. Whenever you are reading this in two months after I typed these words or ten years from the first publishing of this book, the present moment is the only thing that exists. I say we take this present moment, and we blow it out with more divine love and divine conscious light than we have ever felt! Be present. Be in love.

Divine time happens in the *now*. Divine timing has no way for us to access it; it's one of the great gifts of the divine. When you allow the universe to take care of you, everything happens in divine time—exactly when you need something. When you are fully aligned with the universe, if others are as well, an event that happens in divine time becomes even more magical.

Now is the time to dream of our free future, which is free of debt, free of fear, free of hate, free of war, free of stereotypes, free of pain and suffering. Divine love healing knows us as sentient beings and knows that we are capable of living on Earth without money or trade. Money is not the answer, for anything in divine love and divine consciousness. Money is a tool that man created for control. In the world of 2020's you do need money to live. It's your perspective of money that can control you or not. Do you worry about bills or work towards goals? Do you want brand names, bigger and better because others have it and you don't? Or do you want more money for clean water, food, and basic needs? Unfortunately, we need money in the present moment of Earth's history. That could all change in the future now moments.

> *The now is focused on healing everyone to heal the world. It is time for us to work together for the common good, for the highest good.*

That's me being a dreamer, a seeker of a future of oneness, a person with faith that clear living is possible. I do not believe this will happen because of a natural disaster or war or the destruction of current systems. I believe free society will happen in small communities, slowly. Free stores are beginning to pop up. People wanting to live off the grid is more common. And many are working with technology to help us in ways we can't even imagine yet.

Right now, choose your dream for the future. Right now, take your action steps or inspired action of divine love and divine consciousness to create a future for everyone.

In the Now,
Love thyself,
Heal thyself,
Self-governance
Live judgment free
In appreciative gratitude.

I was given a simple suggestion on how to live every day. Use these principles of divine consciousness and it will lead to oneness.

In the *Now*,
Love thyself,
Heal thyself,
Self-governance
Live judgment free
In appreciative gratitude.

Let's look deeper into these simple statements of how to be.

In the *Now*

To live in the present moment is to understand both that you cannot change the past, and the future is yet to be. The only thing that exists is the *now* present moment. This also means not living in past experiences. Our past lessons push us forward. If we get caught in old paradigms or actions, we stay stuck or become at dis-ease with ourselves. Being stuck in the past will hold you back from all your dreams and keep you from expanding into your higher self.

If you go toward the opposite rabbit hole to a never-ending fear of the future, you can't move forward in your life for your highest good, either. Our future dreams inspire our now actions of love. Now is the only thing that exists. Be present in this gift Source gave to us! The balance space between the two extremes is the present, our *now* moment.

Stay in balance. Stay in the present moment, which is the true gift from *ALL*. *Now* is the time to dream about your future of joy. In this moment, are you without anything? Just stop and feel what is happening to you as you read this. This is being here and "now".

There are many books like *Be Here Now* by Ram Das that go into this at a far greater level, explaining this present moment. I recommend *The Power of Now* by Eckhart Tolle or any of his books or recordings. My friend on Bourbon Street recommended I read this book. *The Power of Now* gave me a great, integrated understanding of living in the present.

Love Thyself

To love thyself is divine love! It is to engage in unconditional energies of unlimited possibilities. Let love rule your mind, body, and soul. Connect to higher realms for healing. Source, *ALL*, the Creator lives within our physical bodies, not outside of us. I'm talking about when we truly love ourselves—not an egoistic, narcissistic love some have for themselves. Instead, the unlimited judgment-free love of *ALL*. As we love who we are, it means we love the Creator. We acknowledge we are the same, a oneness within. It gives us back our control, the power of our being. We are cocreators of this world! Create what you desire out of love for yourself! You must love yourself first. To love yourself is to respect yourself. We must respect ourselves to respect what is around us.

How do we love ourselves? Self-love is the answer to all our problems. One way I was taught was to say I loved every part of my body out loud. My teacher Walter Lübeck suggested I do this by looking in a mirror naked. I was to start at my toes and say, "I love my toes. I love my feet. I love my ankles." He learned this technique of self-love. Thank you to the original author who suggested this method. It is a lovely way to announce love for all body parts.

I thought this would be pretty simple. Yet the first day, I could not get past loving my stomach. I cried for hours with the pain of my own self-loathing of my body. I tried it again the next day. This time, I reached my arms and could not keep going. On the fifth day, I was able to look at and profess my love for my entire body. It was not until the seventh day that I started to believe what I was saying. Finally, after three weeks of every morning looking at my body and saying aloud, "I love you," I finally got over my own fear of myself. It was eye-opening to me. I'd thought I did love myself, and I hadn't realized the negative thoughts I really did have for myself.

There was another technique I was taught by an amazing sound healer, Sharon Carne. She explained to me once that we need to hear our own voice to connect our heart to our thoughts. She went deep into explaining that our own voice carries spiritual information. When we hum, it connects us to our heart. It allows us to think from our heart, instead of our brain. She referred to in-depth report entitled "Assessment of Nasal and Sinus Nitric Oxide Output Using Single-Breath Humming Exhalations" published in the *European Respiratory Journal*.[3] You can read about the science behind this simple technique. I recommend learning more with Sharon with her meditation of the heart. Check out references in the back of the book.

Start by putting your hand over your heart, either your physical heart or your heart chakra. Breathe in through your nose. Then exhale a sigh out to release worries, fear, and anxiety. On the next breath in, imagine

---

[3] M. Maniscalo, et al, "Assessment of Nasal and Sinus Nitric Oxide Output Using Single-Breath Humming Exhalations," *European Respiratory Journal* 22 (2003), https://erj.ersjournals.com/content/22/2/323

your nose is in front of your heart. Breath through your heart and exhale out a sigh, a moan, or whatever sound you make to release the tension. Do this three times.

On the next exhale out, instead of sighing, hum. Hum however you can, whatever sound it makes, however long you want to hold it. There is no right or wrong way to hum. Humm nine times. After that, feel the connections, your self-love, and the control of you through divine love.

Heal Thyself to Heal Others

Eat healthy, take care of your body, and keep your chakras aligned. When you are healthy, you can help others. You feel it in your community. When we are at peace with ourselves, we can heal our physical body and our past! We need to be healthy to help others. That means taking supplements or eating your healthiest diet.

The silly example that comes to mind is the speech you are given on an airplane before it takes off. The captain clearly states that, if the oxygen masks drop in an emergency, you need to put on your masks first before helping others to put on their masks. You are no good to help anyone if you are weak, sick, or out of breath.

Healing yourself also means forgiving yourself. Forgive thyself and forgive others. We need to forgive ourselves for whatever we think we have done. This is not just about physical healing. It's also about releasing old karma, giving away the dharma we have been holding onto. There is no original sin! Find forgiveness for the self and heal your wounds, your trauma. I understand we want to share our experiences and get help from others, but there is a point when you must release your pain and heal and not stay in suffering or victimhood. It is your choice to step out and heal.

If you are not ready to forgive others, then forgive the situation that caused the hurt. The Ho'oponopono prayer is wonderful for this deep forgiveness. This ancient Hawaiian pray is simply, "I am sorry. Please forgive me. Thank you. I love you."

I recommend reciting this nine times daily. For a deeper meditation, do a full mala or recite it 108 times. I find it is such a release in many situations that we feel we have lost control. Do read more about it, as it deeply allows you to forgive.

Self-Governance with Divine Consciousness

Using divine consciousness allows us to connect into Mother Earth and Father Sky daily to receive divine wisdom. Divine wisdom teaches us to be responsible for ourselves, and to respect ourselves. Respecting and loving yourself means you will respect and love others. You are responsible for yourself first. When we respect ourselves, it flows into all aspects of our life. In return, we respect all parts of nature and this world.

This is not saying to go against the government to find your own rules and laws. It means to pledge to yourself: a pledge that you will keep your body physically healthy. Pledging allegiance to yourself that you will not talk badly about yourself or put yourself down. Say it out loud when you are ready "I pledge to myself that I, (state your full name) will (insert your personal goal) such as keep as healthy as possible". You are the priority in this lifetime- your own life. Taking care of your physical body is self-love.

Divine consciousness is a connection to all the ascended masters, to all the guides, and to every being that has ever existed. You can connect into the divine collective consciousness and seek knowledge, not just from your great-great-grandfather but also from otherworldly beings. You can connect to the compassion of the world's greatest teachers and even the understanding of contracts from a modern-day lawyer. Consciousness is not limited to spiritual experiences. Again, spirituality is just living. When you have a conscious connection, you allow yourself to open up to Universal knowledge and to more guides than grains of sand on Earth. Divine consciousness allows for self-governance.

Self-governance also respects *universal laws* as well as the laws of your community. Stop lights, speed limits, helmet laws are not created to limit you, they are created to allow all beings to live together with ease and grace. Find the balance of what your truths are and the community that reflects your beliefs.

Discernment is part of self-governance. It is an action of love for yourself by understanding if someone is tricking you. One example of me not using my discernment was during my divorce. A very cool spiritual man was attracted to me. To impress me he took me to an amazing secret temple in the middle of nowhere. He had me recite a long passage in another language. Being new to this religion, I was not familiar with the practices or the belief system, but I thought had a new friend teaching me.

I found out later this person admitted he'd used "natural magic" to put a love spell on me. His personal astrologer told me that the prayer we had done was a form of a marriage commitment. We had made a vow to each other in ancient script. For months, I had become completely obsessed with him. I didn't want to work, only wanting to be with him or talk to him on the phone. I would drive for fourteen hours straight just to see him, only to turn around and drive back fourteen hours. I tried to understand these three months, but they are like fragments of faded images.

It is an example of people intending to control another person. Typically for your money, sometimes, it's your energy. Other times, it's for their pleasure, not for your highest good. When you are conscious, you are part of love, not of fear. You are already doing things to take care of yourself. This is what self-governance is about, to live a healthy lifestyle. The responsibility of being human is to love yourself first and to live as an example of love. Discernment is the ability to know what is for your highest good and what is not.

Live Judgment Free

I believe the hardest part of the principles of living on Earth is being judgment free. To be judgement free we need to start with ourselves. When we stop judging ourselves, we also stop judging God or *ALL*. We have to acknowledge our divinity and accept that *ALL* is part of us.

We are not here to judge ourselves, *ALL*, or others. In fact, nothing judges us outside of Earth. Judgment is a human quality of control. It's about creating power by creating hierarchies, which lead to stereotypes and miscommunication.

To be judgment free is to understand that things just are. Through divine consciousness, we see we are all made of energy. Energy is neither positive nor negative. When we judge, we create good and bad. We separate ourselves from our God spark, our Creator, and say we are better than all creation. It is as though we are swimming in human egew, allowing fear to rule by judging others. Not even the beings of light judge us. Why do we? Please don't confuse being judgement free and discernment.

I remember seeing billboards saying, "What would Jesus do?" In the eighties I did not understand the message. Rather, I would question it. The thought behind this phrase was shortened to WWJD. This phrase is truly to be judgment free. What hurts today is that the same religious group who have used Jesus to claim land, destroy entire cultures, and judge others are no longer saying WWJD. Alternatively, these groups are fashioning crosses from bullet casings and are against anyone different from them. We do not need to step backward in old judgments but rather move forward in divine love. I think now, WWJD? He would be tolerant. He would be accepting. He would be compassionate. He would turn his cheek.

In Appreciative Gratitude

We are requested by the gamma ray beings to give gratitude every morning and release the day in the evening with gratitude. To live in a state of appreciative gratitude is to find the perfect balance of your life.

It is an automatic response to say, "God bless you," when someone sneezes or to say, "I love you," when you end a conversation. I have an instant, "I'm sorry," when a situation arises, and I don't know what to say. These automatic responses may be polite, but do they hold any meaning for us? Instead, when we say something, we need to have our authentic self behind it and really mean it. In other words, say what you mean.

We truly need to appreciate the world around us and be grateful for all that is. Living in this state is not just about meditation and prayers. Living in full appreciative gratitude expands divine love and divine consciousness to everyone around you. It really helps when you are on the low end of the wheel of life. You can learn how to be okay with your own feelings. It's easier to find balance when we are grateful for what we do have and for what will come.

When you live a conscious life, you are putting yourself first. You take care of your physical, mental and spiritual needs so that you may better serve the community. It means when you look in the mirror that you love who you are.

It means finding your daily practice or your daily ritual or whatever it is that makes you feel comfortable. You need daily contact to find your personal connection to divine energies and the Great Spirit, *ALL*.

Whatever it is, you call it Jesus and Mary, Shakti and Shiva, Mohammed, or Moses. Whatever it is that you feel comfortable with is right. Take the time to connect to your beliefs daily.

Los Angeles: The City of Lost Angels

One reason for leaving New Orleans was that many of my French Quarter friends are no longer on this plane. Hurricanes, overdoses, suicides, cancer, and gun violence have taken several friends and family members of my Louisiana relations. One friend was Herbert. Herbert was the kindest man. Every day, we would talk about the world and how to make people happy. He never understood why people were so angry all the time, even in New Orleans. One evening after work, he was shot in his car for no reason. The city I loved so much was now taking away all the things I loved about it. This joyful feeling was getting harder to maintain in New Orleans. Anxiety, money, alcohol, drugs, and violence ruled New Orleans.

One day the anxiety got too much for me, I just walked away. Literally. A brown paper bag with my pj's and jewelry, I left my fabulous life and marriage to find a consistent, healthy, happy way of being. It was a hard decision to leave New Orleans after twenty-two years of planting roots. I could no longer take the fear, drama, and violence in the city I deeply loved. I left many friendships and still miss all the wonderful artisans, businesspeople, and committees. I love New Orleans and am very grateful to have experienced the whole cycle of life with it. The city taught me to understand cycles of fear, suppression, and power, making me want a new way of living.

In 2016, my wish to be in Southern California finally came true. With a new partner, Shane, came new dreams and new explorations of what could be possible for us. A job offer from a dear friend came to give me the final push to move to Los Angeles. I had a calling to go, and I answered it.

After months of looking for a new home, we found a place in Sherman Oaks. It was in a boring apartment complex that I experienced higher dimensions. Here I truly understood there are no coincidences. Although everything happens for a reason, sometimes we are not supposed to know the reason. And sometimes, it is not a lesson for us; we are just the participants.

I have very little memory of the four months I spent by myself in the apartment in Sherman Oaks, and it was not due to any drugs. I would dream for days about being in intergalactic meetings. In a daze, I would get up to drink or eat, only to be pulled back into the high council meeting. I would not go out of the apartment. I did not have a television, just a small laptop and my phone. My only furniture was an air mattress and a couch the previous owner had left.

It was in this apartment in Sherman Oaks that I first understood the consciousness of all things, not just living, breathing beings. The apartment may have come with a couch, but it did not come with a refrigerator.

My friend took me to a used refrigerator store since I had a very limited budget. I went to the very back sale area. Not picky about color or size, I just wanted a simple appliance to cover my basic needs. There, I found a lovely cream-colored fridge with heavy dents in it. It had been overlooked, and it fit perfectly in my budget.

A few days after my new appliance was installed, it started fizzing and making weird sounds. I noticed my laptop was doing the same. At first, I thought this must be a result of power surges, but no one else had the same problem. I knew the fridge was beaten up on the outside, but the mechanics were still good; there were no leaks in the air compressor. I noticed it wasn't just the fridge acting strange. In fact, anything plugged into the wall was freaking out.

Something made me go into meditation to see what was happening. I had cleared the place before I moved in. I had set up the angels for protection and felt very safe. As I went into meditation, I asked Ultraviolet Michael to help me find what was causing the strange actions of appliances. I was also feeling a pain in the back of my neck at night. At the time 5G was being set up in the area. I thought, *Are the rumors true? Is this new technology going to harm us?* The little conspiracy girl inside of me began weaving fear of technology and controlling AI.

In meditation, I began to astral travel, not to other places but, rather, to other dimensions of the apartment. I was able to get to the seventh dimension, where I spoke to the consciousness of the refrigerator I'd just purchased. I asked why it was having problems. Was it the 5G or Hollywood witchcraft that made it not want to work?

This was where I found an astral portal that had been created by a former tenant in the apartment which I was residing in. It was started on their computer, from a game they were obsessed with, possibly some type of gambling game. It was linked to an artificial web of life that looked like it was created in Silicon Valley. This could have been an early form of AI.

I had seen this type of matrix before, not in the movies but, instead, at the witchcraft shops I had recently visited in LA. It was weak. This matrix was held together by candle waxed computer codes and controlled by lost souls. It was my first encounter with human egew (the dark oily residue of all human egos). The collection of centuries of fears, anger, hate, greed, power are all of the worst parts of being human. Egew is an oily substance being powered by nightmares.

This was energy that was attacking me at night, trying to tap into my brainstem. It was not an alien abduction. It was the greed of man. This greed was trying to confuse me into fear, into a downward spiral of victimhood, lies, and a conspiracy theory that Russians were invading. This was when I understood the thought that created QAnon. I saw where the split in healers started, where black magicians pretended to be kings, a false underworld, a hell of our own making.

In the movies, this was where a montage would happen. I would gather special crystals, get holy water, and pull out ancient Lemurian (a spiritual community who lived at the same time of Atlantis) texts to slay the energy. It was a battle, but not like that. I called out to Michael, to devour the petty attempt at control. Michael said it would free the souls that were controlling it and free the apartment from its grip. In flashes of light and sound, I was released from pain and the controlling grip of human egew. Divine love carried me out. The source was released. Michael to explained to me that it was of God, or part of *ALL* and that it could not be destroyed. As artificial as it felt to me, it was still a creation that existed within *ALL*'s realms. It would no longer harm me or come after me. Selenite would protect my computers & cellphones from getting caught in this mess again.

It could only be destroyed when the whole world no longer lived in fear, which was inconceivable to me. This "thing" was now a part of our technology; as long as we acknowledge it, it cannot harm us. The selenite is a clearing stone that will keep it at bay. Selenite will keep the consciousness of the technology clear of the human egew or the collective fear. True protection is pure divine love. This was not a battle of the soul or good versus bad. It was the collective consciousness trying to spread fear with technology. I asked if selenite would help my refrigerator as well, since it, too, was acting up.

The refrigerator told me another story, not the one I expected. It showed me what it was like when it was new. It was a real treasure brought into an apartment like mine. It showed how, at first, it was full of fresh vegetables, milk, and cheeses, and its owner cherished it. Then the food was slowly replaced by beer as a new man came into her life. Soon, beer replaced even milk. The children would hold open the door as if something different would magically appear.

The next scene it showed me was the man being angry. So angry he punched the refrigerator, not once but multiple times. His anger went from the empty fridge to the lovely woman who had once filled it with wholesome food. I could not watch the rest of what it showed me; it was enough for me to understand.

I went to the conscious energy of the fridge and told them they were safe. I showed them it was a different apartment and that I had filled it not with beer but with farmer's market eggs and vegetables. I showed them I loved the refrigerator and how important it was to me. I needed it to keep my food cold, so it doesn't spoil. I kindly put my hands on it, the same way I would do reiki on a human on the outside and loved it just as I would any being. I gave a full healing session to my new acquaintance, as I knew how important it was for me. I did not have the funds to replace it.

It worked! No strange sounds or smells ever came out of it again. The dents popped out, and the light inside got brighter. Every day from then on, I acknowledged it for its pain and its life as being a part of my own. Even to this day, when I have problems with a machine, whether it's a credit card machine not working or my car, I acknowledge the energy it carries. I tell it how much I do need it to do its function or even pat it and say, "I love you." We are truly all connected. We all carry divine energy from *ALL*. When we can live in that understanding, we create stronger connections and find respect in all of Earth's creations.

When I meditate into higher dimensions, I can hear the consciousness of all things. Sometimes, it's more than I can handle. Like when the wood screws in the kitchen cabinet start complaining they can't hold up any longer. Or when the stones I collected start asking for attention like puppy dogs. I know it's time to step out of the fifth dimension or the fourth to keep my sanity. It is enough to acknowledge the energy within everything. You do not have to do their bidding.

More and more machines are being made by humans. AI or artificial intelligence is at its infant stage learning from the collective consciousness. Cell phones, computers, machines are now becoming part of the collective consciousness. No, I am not going down the Terminator path, but I am acknowledging that more intelligent beings may want to control human nature. It is with discernment that we should use AI technology.

AI technology can help humanity if we don't worship it or allow it to control us. Advice or help in screening medical issues will help us live longer. AI can enhance our lives, yet we need to make boundaries before we enslave a machine with consciousness. Since we use super computers, we must also respect them. We do not need to fear AI, instead learn how to work with it for the highest good of the planet.

I do believe that taking time to connect with an object to feel its information is important. When acknowledging all things from the mundane to the newest AI robot technology, you are acknowledging that everything is made of energy. Energy is the divine love of *ALL*. Therefore, nothing on Earth, *nothing* in the universe is not of *ALL*.

Channeled Message by www.Marigoldslove.com

Raise your consciousness and feel the heaviness in your mind disappear. Raise your consciousness and feel your heart expand. Raise your consciousness and feel any stickiness feel less sticky.

As humans we feel the weight of the world from the ground up. Consider noticing the weight of the world without making it a personal issue that is yours alone to solve. Consider noticing your personal issues not as problems that you have to solve but as human experiences that are gifts for you to explore. It is often repeated in spiritual circles that we choose each and every experience that we have. This may be true, but it doesn't mean we have to love it or even like it. The best we can do is to really tune into what is happening for us at a cellular level and see if any one cell in our body can be shifted, to consider a different perspective on our own situation or another's. As humans we are like ants in that we often only see what is right in front of us, without zooming out to notice the big picture or all the other creatures around us. There is nothing wrong with this and there are also other ways for us to move about our world, for we are not ants. We have a consciousness that is shared amongst our own kind. We have a consciousness that is shared amongst every living thing on this Earth. We have a consciousness that is shared amongst even the plants and minerals and animals. Some allow themselves to consider a consciousness that is shared between us and the stars, us and the Universe, us and more than just our Universe.

Do not be overwhelmed by these ideas. Just consider expanding your viewpoint to beyond what is right in front of you or what is bothering you. There could be a gift in there for you to discover. There could be wisdom for you to find. There could be a tension point you reach that not only invites you to shift your perspective but demands that you shift your perspective in order for you to grow.

For today, put on your expansive lenses and see what gifts are waiting for you!

CHAPTER 6

The sixth dimension is the dimension of bridges
and portals to other dimensions and passages
to all past knowledge and higher selves.

This is where we create the paths to our future. Its where cosmic grids show the golden thread of *ALL* as a massive, infinite collective of divine beings. This is the great web of life. In this dimension, we step into our galactic selves, where we feel our divine connection to things outside Earth.

As I understand dimensions more, I see the glorious plans of *ALL* are right on track. Becoming more conscious of the sixth dimension opens us to divine love and divine consciousness and to unlimited possibilities, unlimited wisdom, and new levels of *free will* we are yet to fully understand. This dimension is in harmony with all dimensions, connecting the great web of life. It is here within the sixth dimension that the energy of our individual chakras exists. This is where our auras exist with each other. We get to see and feel the colors and energies of the chakras in the fourth and fifth dimensions; it is in the space of the sixth dimension they get blocked or one-sided.

Another way to think of this dimension is like a massive highway system with tunnels that pop you instantly to the area you want to be. This is where the understanding of *nadi*, a Sanskrit word meaning tube or channels, comes into play. Think of it as similar to the blood vessels in your body, allowing divine love to flow through your chakra system. When looking at Earth, we would talk about the meridian system, not just longitude and latitude but also the hidden maps of the world's energy system. Meridians can also be found in the body, but I like to use nadi to describe humans' electrical system and meridians for Mother Earth.

Right now, the space race is all about how to sustain life on journeys that require light-years of travel to other planets and solar systems. What if, instead, it was just a matter of spiritual technologies that opened the sixth-dimensional highways? Yes, it does sound a little like *Stargate*, the TV show, but what if that is the way to explore space?

There are many ways to travel through this dimension. Portals are bridges that look like a matrix. They are within your spiritual world and accessed in meditation or sleep. Portals happen within. For example, if you wanted to go to heaven or within your own chakra energy, you would use a portal. Portals are the rainbow bridges, the cave you go into when you ascend down the tree of life or into Mother Earth. These gateways are within our consciousness and can be guided by our inner child or higher self.

Vortices are physical locations that carry energy to other dimensions or directly to otherworldly beings. A vortex is what we call the sixth dimension on Earth. Vortices occur naturally and are found everywhere in nature. Vortices can be conjured or opened by sentient beings, as well as by some people carrying the vortex energy. I really understood this energy in Sedona at the now-torn-down stone cross at the airport parking lot. The most obvious vortex I had felt was at the St. Louis Cathedral in New Orleans. Step inside the church, and you can feel the vortex. Many would think it was the energy of church, but instead the church was built on the vortex of energy. As are many of the great temples and religious buildings.

Vortices are felt through our five senses but have specific feelings for the individual. The first experience of a vortex I felt was in church. I could not explain why I would tingle all over when I entered the narthex of the church. I would get that same feeling when I visited other temples, synagogues, and Gothic cathedrals. In my youth, I had a fear of the outdoors and nature. I did not feel the natural vortices until college. It was not until my parents moved to Sedona, Arizona that I heard about the vortices and finally understood what that feeling was. Fuzziness is the simplest feeling. Others include a spiral feeling in your heart or stomach, tingling in your hands or feet, buzzing in your ears, the smell of something that's not there, and water tasting differently. We're using all our senses—visual, auditory, tactile, olfactory, and gustatory.

Do you see colors or flashing lights? What do you hear, feel, smell, or taste? These are the different ways to calibrate or experience vortices. They create bridges for our guides and otherworldly beings. This is how you feel and understand what different vortices do.

I am grateful that, as a child, I capped myself from this higher knowledge. Meaning my higher self, and my oversoul, did not allow me to have all my spiritual gifts at once. I admit, when I first felt this block or cap of my own spiritual gifts, I blamed others for limiting my spiritual growth. After much meditation and self-reflection, the answer was me. I had done it to protect myself. I gave myself a naive childhood, instead of one of worry and regret. In America, for some reason, maybe on talk shows, we have an underlying belief that our parents caused our misery. For some parents, unfortunately did create trauma and make their children's lives a living hell. At one time I thought my own mother cursed me. I know differently now. In my case it is not my mother who loves me to blame, it was too many movies getting into my psyche. I learned that I can't allow fear and guilt from outside sources to control my life. I had a lovely childhood, and I am so grateful for every moment of it.

We are to be our own guide. Each one of us has a "soul lineage" that is recorded in the Akashic records. The beginning point of our soul is called the oversoul. The oversoul is not who you are in this lifetime. The oversoul is the conscious love energy that chooses to come to Earth and experience joy. The oversoul is the soul star as well, the conscious energy source. Literally your soul is connected to one of the billions of stars in the sky!

As many stars as there are in the skies, there are souls on the planet; cliché or not, it's true. Our oversoul waits in a queue or a line for its desired life to be lived. When the right situation arrives, it pops into a life form as the umbilical cord is cut. The first cry of life, that first breath, is when the soul enters the physical form.

Everyone's soul has an oversoul or a soul seed star, a higher self which is an individual's perfect state in present life. A middle self is also called the ego and an inner child, which is created in present life.

It is necessary to be connected to your inner child, also called the subconscious. This is you between the ages of 3 to 12. When you are the most connected to magic, to nature, to your own imagination. The inner child is formed before the influence of schools, religion, or family. The inner child is your intuition and your joy. Being connected to your inner child is more than just acting like a child. It is about being imaginative, creative, connected, and curious in a childlike mode.

About age ten, depending on your cultural background maybe sooner, the reality of life in a third dimensional fear driven world may cut off your connection. After this the middle self begins to form. It can be your voice in your head telling you what to do. The middle self pays bills, works jobs to make money and deals with everyday reality. Still, you must be connected to yourself or the ego as some call it. The middle self constantly changes with you. It can be open to both positive and negative influences easily.

Your superconscious or higher self is you, in your most perfect, ageless state of being. This part of you guides you for your highest good. It helps keeps you on ALL's Will instead of the chaos of free will. We can achieve our highest self on Earth, I believe that is what Jesus and Muhammad tried to teach us. Psychologists, scientists, and healers have spent lifetimes exploring all these parts of the soul.

Once in guided meditation, I went to my soul home to check in on little Rachel, or my inner child. For me, my soul home on the outside is the house of the Seven Dwarfs from the Disney classic *Snow White*. Everyone has their own unique soul home, it's whatever you can imagine. As I pushed open the door to get my normal greeting of a hug from little Rachel, she was gone! It freaked me out so much that I stopped meditating. I felt my body lunge forward. I closed my eyes, and she jumped out of me and giggled. "I am not there. I am *you*!" That was a huge moment of alignment for me. It was confirmation that I do walk in balance with my inner child. Being aligned means your soul parts, higher self, middle self and inner child, we are connected to ourselves. Life becomes easier.

I realized I had achieved the dreams of my inner child by the time I was fifty. The dreams of my ego, my middle self, were not for my highest good. I had spent most of my life trying to achieve goals that weren't in my life contract. When I had my dream job of my inner child instead, the old promises I made to myself were released. I was able to free myself from judgement and forms of self-loathing. It's very freeing to know we are in constant change. With more experiences in life dreams change, new understanding comes as we must be in flow with life changing, as well as ourselves. My ego's dreams were limiting. They were influenced by movies, trends, and objects. Without the limitations of my middle self dream's, I can dream bigger and achieve more.

Dream of the Future

Our dreams from the fourth dimension get funneled through the sixth dimension. This is when all the TV, movies, music, and entertainment come out as our great desires through the collective consciousness. They collect here to become our future.

Fear of an apocalyptic world is currently buzzing through the collective unconscious. We need to take this time to expand out to a high-vibrational love that gives us goose bumps. Create a divine healing love that gets you giddy and dream about the future of your happiness.

We, the individual cocreators on Earth, hold the key. The key to our unlimited future is our collective dreams. It is time to dream it up as magnificently as possible! Our true Earth walk experience is one of complete joy for all beings.

To stay in this vibration of divine love, dance, eat dessert, enjoy your favorite activity, and be around people who are fun. That is all that *ALL* or Source has ever wanted for you. As humans, we have selective forgetfulness. We have forgotten our past. We have forgotten who we are. The time of the *now* is to be present in your divine love and connect with divine consciousness to become a cocreator of the future.

In the sixth dimension, we get to see what happens not only in our community but also in other cultures, concepts, and worlds. As an individual, it is up to you to experience spirituality, which is just another name for Earth walk. Here, we have an opportunity to go higher faster. We can love more and make changes happen in the drop of a hat without ritual, without symbols, and without calling in any specific deity, because we are the creators. We carry the God spark; we are the cocreators.

There is great beauty and wonderment in participating in an Earth walk. Amazing things can and do happen in life on Earth. The unlimited future of divine love is going to be utterly unbelievable. It is up to us—to all of us. If you open your heart and truly listen to this message, you'll see that divine love is our greatest guide. Step into your heart at any age, at any time and begin to love. It is up to us to daydream, to dream of a divine future, and to visualize our new future for our individual needs. Create what it is that you desire the world to be like, not what has been told to you for lifetimes.

The collective consciousness is changing from a direction of fear to allowing love to rule. Since 2018, a small shift in the movies has taken a positive turn. We've started to see a response of love instead of fear. *Wonder Woman 1984* is a good example of a story in which love, not fighting is an answer. In 2022, with the new Marvel multiverse series, from Spiderman to Doctor Strange, unlimited possibilities with love as the answer have opened. Even the new Captain America has shown that fighting is not the answer. This will help the collective consciousness move toward love. It's a start, but it's not enough.

Finding a way to unplug from the collective consciousness allows the individual free will to expand into infinite possibilities. When we "go along" with the status quo, we give up our freedom. That's what is so magical about *ALL*. This great energy wants you to be the individual you are, to just be you. As a collective, we will all grow as one in love, not one with hair color and size. We get to be who we are, and the universe wants us to be just that. The oneness is just understanding and allowing divine love to rule.

To help you with this dream, I did a guided meditation just for you. When you are ready to expand, check out: https://vimeo.com/waychilllife/innerchildfuturehealing.

Chakras

Balance in life is only found when we balance our energies within ourselves. This will be achieved by self-love, self-care, and self-governance. Another way we will expand these energy systems is initiation or upgrades through our main or traditional chakras. Chakras are part of an energy system that exists within everything. They are disc-like in shape, in every color imaginable. They stack on top of one other in a specific order. Each chakra holds a different type of energy, both receiving and giving. Seven of them are commonly used in Hindi, and yogic practices. In early Jewish mysticism the seven heavens of the Merkabah have similarities to seven main chakras. Today many people believe we have thirteen main chakras and an unlimited number of secondary chakras.

Many books and lifetimes of studies have been dedicated to the chakra system. In my understanding, chakras are a gauge of the unseen energy of a being or object. Reading this energy can show everything from physical disease to mental issues. Knowing your own system can help you find balance. I have found that working with the chakras by clearing the blocks directly creates healing channels within the body.

By understanding the basic sets of chakras, we can expand out to other types of chakras. The original or traditional seven-chakra system began in India sometime between 1500 and 500 BCE in the oldest text called the Vedas. From here, it expanded into the secondary chakra system—every joint in the body has an energy to it that holds healing information. For example, when your wrists are in pain or trauma, it usually means a relationship needs to be dealt with. There are wonderful books that go deeper into this information listed at the end of this book.

Chakras are read by intuition and by seeing colors and feeling energy. When I first was taught how to read chakras, it was by asking my inner child, what color is that chakra? Now I can feel the energy over the phone to the point where I can feel it stronger on one side. I have learned that a chakra can be blocked. If a chakra is blocked, you don't receive love energy from others. It could be blocked on the giving side, then you don't give out love energy. It is these blocks which stop the flow of energy. It may stop you from speaking the truth. Any blocks may stop you from your highest good—in other words, stop you from being a cocreator and getting everything, you want!

As we expand into new understanding of the chakras, I want to talk about the layers of each chakra. For this new information instead of going into all of it, we will keep it to 3 layers: the main, front (high) and backside (gemstone) of the main chakra.

For me, we receive information through the back side of the chakras. For example, behind your heart chakra is the emerald chakra. (Side note, it's super dark green, not black, though it feels like it's black.) Here, in this astral place in the sixth dimension, you find the source of the divine consciousness. This again is also known as Christ consciousness or Krishna consciousness; it is the place where we can connect to all the universal knowledge.

The front of the chakra is how we give out our energy. This space of the chakra is where we want to flow "true north" or toward the universal truth. The high layer or front of the chakra allows us to move forward into our dreams. This is how we create our own future with the energy we emulate from our individual chakras.

Your aura or the energy that surrounds you is directly related to the chakra system. You can even download an app on a smartphone that can take a picture of your aura. The colors that surround you are in direct correlation to what chakra energy is guiding you or what may be blocked. Aura photography can be even more insightful when you have a trained person explaining the colors and the orbs that are around you. For me, this is great fun and an easy way to see if I am in balance with my energy.

Plants, animals, mountains, the Earth, everything has a chakra system; everything can be broken down to love energy. Plants, trees, and animals follow the same rainbow colors of the human chakra system.

In the glossary in the back of the book, I'll provide simple definitions or descriptions for you to explore on your own. Again, this is an area that is constantly expanding, and much research has been done. Like the rest of this book, it's just an overview of the chakras taken from my own experiences and basic knowledge.

You can read more about chakras, but truly experience each of them for yourself. The greatest understanding is already inside you. As you experience each chakra, write, draw, or express what it means to you for your future guide. The colors and sounds are consistent for all chakra systems. Getting to know them is up to you. A great meditation is to feel each chakra. You can go through all of them yourself. Begin in your soul seed and travel up your silver-golden thread of life to each of the chakras. You can imagine them as spaces you have to clean up—you know, unblock your chakras. How ever you wish to clean the chakra works! You can imagine that you are sweeping, dusting, or pushing the garbage into the center portal where your golden thread of life comes out. Mother Earth will recycle all the energy! Take as long as you need to "clean" or clear out each chakra.

Another way to enhance a chakra meditation is to make the sound of each of the colors of a rainbow to enhance the portals. Listening to a prerecorded meditation with sound bowls, tuning forks, gongs or computer-generated hertz frequencies. You may be guided to do toning or making your own sounds. Toning sounds listed in the second chapter match up with the chakras.

There is a meditation you can do at the end of this chapter. But to help you out, I created, "Way Chill Living—Full Chakra Meditation." You can find it on YouTube at https://www.youtube.com/watch?v=TAtkE9xcnoE&ab_channel=WayChillLiving.

The Traditional Seven Chakras

First Chakra, Red

The root or first chakra keeps us grounded and centered. The traditional thought of the first chakra is "are you going to run away or are you going to fight?" Let's reword this for a nonviolent question. How about instead ask "are you connected to Mother Earth?"

The first chakra holds the energy of grounding, or the connecting to the rhythm of Mother Earth. Without this connection, you cannot travel to higher dimensions and may have problems just functioning in daily life.

Easy ways to connect to this chakra is to put your hands in the dirt; put them down into the ground. Hold a rock, not a crystal, a rock, granite, iron. Put your feet deep into the sand. If you live in the city and this may not be possible, another trick is called a sole water. Using Himalayan pink salt in a glass of water—ideally one teaspoon of pink salt to one full glass of purified water. Some recipes call for lemon, I think that's just for taste. The tradition of drinking salt water does ground you. A good time to drink sole water to help bring you back to reality is after a sound bath, yoga, or any type of meditation when you do not feel fully grounded.

Another way to feel the root chakra is the pendulum swing. This is an exercise where you let your arms hang loosely as you put your back into tabletop position. Bend at your waist and make your back flat. If that hurts just naturally hang over your toes in a loose way. In this position, you will gently connect to the Earth and feel its movement. You will find yourself gently swaying with the natural rhythm of the world. At first it may be just your arms, but you may find your whole body feeling the natural movement.

After teaching Rainbow Reiki and angelic healing five days a week for six weeks continuously, I became lightheaded. It was a super fantastic feeling like I was on the best designer drugs. I was so wrapped up in a higher spiritual consciousness. An old friend told me the truth about the way I was acting. I was abusing friendships. I was "living in the clouds" and not in the real world.

While I thought I was on the high road to a higher understanding, she said that I "stunk of enlightenment". I was flying without any direction, spaced out and not grounded. I was not connected to nature. She taught me a hard lesson by ending our friendship. Grounding is not just reaching down to touch the ground or holding a stone. Being grounded is living in the now consciousness of Earth. It's about feeling secure with nature, with your surroundings. It's about feeling the rhythm of the world beneath your feet all the time.

The first chakra, your root chakra is the foundation for you to move forward. Make the connection here and the other chakras will follow. The stronger you are connected into yourself, into the Earth, the further you can explore in meditation.

Second Chakra, Orange

The second chakra, also called the sacral chakra, is bright orange. This is the womb area for women and the prostate area for men. It is so important for your physical well-being to have all the chakras in balance, but I find much "dis-ease" builds up here from sexual trauma and shadow side guilt. Sexuality has been confused with divine love and gender issues. Neither is part of universal law. When people want to fight with me about the new movement to binary or gender-free, well, I get it. Angels do not have gender. Could gender possibly be a way of stereotyping people? When we live judgment free, I believe this chakra is going to be much healthier overall.

This area helps with your financial well-being as well. This is where creativity and abundance are grown. Even though I understand abundance is considered unnecessary outside of Earth, it is a part of what we need here. Orange is the color of money, not green. It is what we create in our life, our relationships, both in our attitude and physically around us.

The cave of creation is not just limited to the womb; it is where all creativity comes from. This chakra holds creation energy for everyone regardless of gender. Scientists, bakers, and artists are all creators, not only a mother creating a child. We all have a sacred womb or cave in our energy to create our future, our dreams, and our own personal way of living.

Third Chakra, Yellow

The third chakra, your solar plexus, seems to be the most lacking chakra. Sometimes I call this the "Ra" chakra because Ra was the Egyptian sun god. It is your self-confidence, your personal sunshine area. It also makes me think of sunflowers, fields of blooming big bright sunflowers.

I have experienced the most blocks in this area. Which makes sense since it is the area of how you feel about yourself, your personal power. It even carries the energy of how you feel others think of you. I have noticed that many among the group called millennials have blocked third chakras. Their sell-confidence has been beaten down by bullies. Social media became popular with them, conveying mixed messages of self-love, yet having to match up with high standards of beauty that came out of the Western world in the nineties. We went from pop colors to all black and from the grunge trend to elite, high-end fashion.

This is the area where stomach problems build up over self-doubt and self-blame. I know for twenty years I had massive issues and blocks in my third chakra, causing me to puke when I was super nervous, like when I vomited on Bob's new boss, on Bob's college professors, and on Bob. Come to think of it, my issues went away because of the work I did to forgive myself and because I realized my body was trying to tell me to stop doing things for Bob and start doing things for me.

Social media and the collective consciousness tend to affect this chakra. When you are connected to self-love, the negative comments do not affect you. This area needs to be strengthened and not just with sit-ups and exercise—though a strong core will support your physical body as well. This specific area can be affected by the food you eat, as well as any toxins like alcohol. Self-care is important in all of the chakras. Here, you can really feel it.

Fourth Chakra, Green

The heart chakra is the most accessed and easily blocked chakra. This is where we connect not only to unlimited love but also to unlimited knowledge through *divine consciousness*. Here is your balance of divine love. Green is love of nature; the farmer is often thought of as the archetype for this chakra. It is nurturing, loving, compassionate, the green valley of the goddesses.

This is where I often find swords embedded in people's backs, put there by scorned lovers or even inserted by the individual, believing they are not deserving of love. People also block their own hearts in fear that love itself may hurt them or because they were hurt when loving another. This is where we can understand *divine love* versus human love. Human love puts limits in place. Human love says, "If you loved me, you would do this." Human love is full of guilt, false promises, and trends. Whatever your culture is, that will tend to define what you "love." Divine love, on the other hand, is unlimited, unconditional, and judgment free. Divine love is turning the other cheek and using compassion and forgiveness to deal with situations.

When you feel the divine consciousness with divine love in your heart chakra, it opens you up to higher understanding. The heart chakra has the link to the God spark that allows unlimited divine love flow. It is being in the joy of the moment and self-love.

Fifth Chakra, Blue

The fifth chakra is about communication. How do you talk to others? How do you listen to others? How do you communicate to the world who you are? Here the cotton balls are removed from your ears, your throat is cleared, and your thyroid is balanced. Sometimes we tend to think automatically we know what people are saying or are about to say. Other issues are not speaking your truth, keeping your great ideas to yourself, or not sticking up for yourself. There are several ways we block our fifth chakra. These blocks build up physically in your body. Just as I had stomach issues or colitis because of my own negative thoughts, here, too, you can cause issues, in this case, with your thyroid.

This is also the chakra to forgive anyone who told you that you cannot sing or are horrible public speaker. You are your unique self. There is no perfect note or perfect voice. Yours is perfect for you. Maybe you won't be the next Whitney Houston, but you still need to be able to hum or hear your own voice—to speak up when necessary. Let go of what others have put on you. Remove this block from your fifth chakra so you can have your own voice, your own opinion, and your own perfect way of being you. This is a great spot for a pretty turquoise necklace or earrings to help you strengthen this chakra.

Sixth Chakra, Indigo

Our third eye is the personal portal we all carry to our "clair senses," our spiritual gifts we each carry. As a child, I dreamed of being like Samantha in *Bewitched* and learned how to crinkle my nose. It is not the nose that carries this magic but, rather, the third eye that puts our dreams into motion by saying what we desire.

I remember meeting with a reiki group for the first time. I had just gotten my attunement and was ready to expand. When it was my turn to lay on the table and have everyone put their hands on me, I asked everyone to help me open my third eye. After they completed my eight minutes, one person said, "The window has always been wide open inside you. You just never went to ask your questions or look for the answer."

I believe we all have intuition, a connection in our third eye, the sixth chakra. This is the eye that sees in meditation, past the collective consciousness. This is the eye of consciousness of what is going on in various dimensions and what will happen in the next moment. Once it is opens, you can find out what your gifts are. Maybe you can smell things not there or feel the age of an object or talk to animals. Maybe you know when someone is hurt, or you can feel the pain of those around you. With so many gifts, it's just a matter of looking out your window, asking, and stepping into the answers in this energy space.

Seventh Chakra, Violet

This is typically a chakra not "read" but, instead, connected with or not. Similar to the first chakra, we need this connection to be conscious, to be one in the full rainbow of life. This is our connection to Father Sky, infinite possibilities, and unconditional love. Other names used to describe this is Holy Spirit, St. Germain's Light, Metatron, Living Water of God, and the Breath of God. This is the communication space between our physical selves and the universe.

You do not want to get lost in this area. This is where people become "space cadets" because they get lost in the seventh chakra. If you do not ground yourself after being in this area, you do feel disconnected from your body. Typically, when we meditate, it is here we go up through. That's why it's so important to always come fully and completely back into your body.

Also called the crown chakra, the seventh chakra does have higher chakras above it that help with deep connections to ourselves and the world around us. It's not the end or top of the chakra list. You can keep going up! Check out the end of this book to find where you can read more about the new information on other parts of the chakras.

The Arizona Sky

The Arizona sky taught me great medicine.
Each morning is a new day, a new opportunity.
Every day, I was greeted by the pink canyons—
The stone people, which represent family to me.
The sky is filled with blue first—
Clear communication ahead and then pink streaks of love.
The yellow and orange that the conscious sunlight gives is full.
Of self-confidence, self-love, and self-respect,
Sprinkled with more abundance and creativity than we could imagine.
I was reminded how important family is—
Not just our parents and siblings
But also, our universal family, our extended family
Friends, the animals, the trees, and the plants.

Respect *you*, and the family will love and respect you back.
Father Sky also reminded me to shine who you are every day.
No matter what covers you—clouds, pollution, or smoke.
The sun always shines. Even when you may not see it, it is always there.
Keep your conscious light on, and love flows every day.
Keeping life simple, we expand our beings.
When you want love, you can't feel it.
When you want *ALL*, you want yourself to be Happy.
Neither can you. Either is already in you. You just forgot.
Take a breath and find one space inside you,
Any space and find its love and let it grow inside you.
Love is not on the outside.
It's on the inside, and that's how it grows from you.

CHAPTER 7

*The seventh dimension is filled with
infinite heavens and locations.*

The seventh dimension is the training grounds for bringing divine love and divine consciousness to third dimensional Earth. In meditation and dream time, we travel to the astral realms. Some places are dream spaces filled with possibilities. Others are heavens or homes of every being of light to deities. Locations include everything from going into the center of Earth to the deepest part of the ocean, geysers, to mountain peaks of any planet. Different heavens offer different types of help depending on what your needs are.

Some belief systems have a heaven where *ALL* exists only as the final destination. All major religions and indigenous culture have locations outside of Earth. Several describe underworlds and overworlds like Shangri-la and Satori. In the seventh dimension, we can visit otherworldly spaces of all kinds. We can gain understanding from our perspective or from the perspectives of otherworldly beings or aliens. Our guides are not limited. We can reach out across the cosmos for help.

I have often contemplated what does the seventh dimension do? What guides are reaching out across the universe to us? What if inside our physical body, deep in every cell, individual atoms have access to all the universes? What if the quarks inside each atom, which disappear and reappear, go to other realms, other parallel universes? What if we simultaneously exist on Earth and on another planet? Sounds like crazy questions but they are actual theories in quantum physics.

Modern science has ushered in quantum physics. Since I am not a physicist, I highly recommend the book *Quantum Physics (Idiot's Guides)* by Marc Humphrey, Paul V. Pancella, and Nora Berrah. This is a great place to start. The authors explore all the theories and paradoxes of quantum physics in a palatable way. There are several other books, like one the Dalai Lama wrote that connects science into a spiritual journey. There are other resources with scientific explanations of my experiences. Understanding that only the now moment exists opens the doorway to unlimited possibilities for the future. The perspective quantum physics gives many people a better understanding of the "woo-woo". I admit that going deep into many of these theories hurts my brain. Just acknowledging there exists an explanation is enough for me. The seventh dimension opens new scientific theories that have yet to be uncovered.

Guides: Otherworldly Beings

Other guides, sometimes called sky people by indigenous groups, are not just clouds but are other life forms. We forget we are not alone on this planet or in the universe. The sky people have many forms from clouds to comets and constellations. They bring in a higher knowledge of the future and otherworldly help. They are guides that allow universal knowledge to flow. The otherworldly guides or extraterrestrial guides can lend a helping hand when asked. They can also show us our personal challenges.

For example, comet Neowise in 2020 referenced our past fears. It suggested that we clear out what is no longer needed. The sky people bring great healing and understanding on a cosmic level. This energy or information translates into our everyday lives.

Otherworldly beings come from different locations and universes. These beings are inhabitants from other places, like Dog Star from Sirius, and Martians from Mars. There is a huge population of otherworldly beings like: Lyrians, Anakunki, Mantis, Draconian that played part in human history. Other commonly known otherworldly beings are Reptilians, Pleiadeans, Arcturians, and Venusians. More common names are aliens, little green men, and blue people. TV shows like Star Trek got us to imagine what different beings would look like or act like. Television shows keep the story going like *Ancient Aliens* on Discovery Channels and other documentaries open us up to their possible history on Earth.

Sidenote: Watching random episodes of Star Trek is remarkable that the characters of their journeys do match up with beings I understand. I think the character "Q" is just like the Anakunki beings.

Otherworldly beings are all part of Earth's history, but they did get caught meddling with Earth's purpose. *ALL* was shown how the otherworldly beings had begun mating with beings on Earth. Beings from various galaxies were mating, eating, and experimenting on humans and animals for thousands of years. They pushed human evolution forward rapidly. Someday science will show our connection to aliens or otherworldly beings in our genetic codes. Our physical body contains the story of not just this planet's history but also the original gene therapy and AI. AI may be a new area for humans, but it is not a new concept for the rest of the universe. Since otherworldly beings follow *ALL*'s will, for them, Earth is an intergalactic amusement park of free will.

Otherworldly beings come in all shapes and sizes. They are also a great help in clearing your body and removing implants or negative thoughts. Just as Archangel Michael can cut cords of attachment, extraterrestrials are able to remove strange technology and our own fear from the human egew.

Connect to all your guides. Unlike in the movies you've seen, or books, they are not here to harm us. Maybe there was a time when they may have eaten us like cattle. That has not been allowed for thousands and thousands of years. They have walked or floated on the planet with us for a time unknown. Shows like *Ancient Aliens* show historical proof of time when many gods ruled over humans. Very possibly the gods were otherworldly beings. Looking at Mayan codices and Native American painted symbols feel as though they tell a story we might not be fully open to. Looking differently at history can take away the fear of these otherworldly beings.

What I have found with my experiences with otherworldly beings, both in meditation and in real time, is they do not want "to rock the boat." They understand the fear humans have of them. They will continue to stay in the shadows, guiding us from afar. They too believe in one God, one Source. *ALL* as the only creator of everything. A specific type of meditation, called astral traveling, eliminates the need for a spaceship. Astral traveling, or astral projection is a deep meditative state where your conscious middle self goes to a heavenly space or to another planet. I find it's easier to understand the messages or receive help from otherworldly beings in astral traveling. In real time it has been harder to communicate, sometimes impossible.

If a guide ever tells you what to do without you asking for help, **IT IS NOT A GUIDE.** Go find professional help, either a psychologist or a healer. If you have too many guides talking to you or giving you advice, pick one to be the head guide. Ask your guardian angel to help you pick the best captain of your team of guides. It's your tribe, so you decide who will help keep everyone in order. You give the directions and ask the questions. Use them for the highest good and everyone will benefit.

You have nothing to fear if you choose to go this direction. I do often find it very curious that we look up in the sky to see these beings. We searched with telescopes and huge audio devices. Yet hardly anyone stops to look within. Like much of spirituality, it is not outside of you—it is you. It is within your DNA. This is a great example of the separation myth or dream. We feel separated from *ALL*, from nature, from ourselves because we allow the group thought or the collective consciousness of those who want to control our flow, instead of our own experience.

I have friends who have physically met their otherworldly guides. The truth revealed to them was to believe in themselves. I know of people who have traveled all over the world, calling for these ancient relatives. They would spend large amounts of money and time with no luck connecting with otherworldly beings. If you want to connect, ask from within. If this is what you desire and what is for your highest good, they will appear. It might be in meditation, or it might be when you are out on a walk, or it might be when you are at a public conference. If you want to talk to your guides, create a safe place for both of you. It is a great way to step out of fear and into what could be the greatest information for your highest good. We must stop looking outside ourselves for answers. We must look within. When requesting assistance, always end your request in appreciative gratitude.

Contact in Joshua Tree

In 2017 my second husband, Shane and I moved to Palm Springs, California. It was a huge transformation from living in a small lead painted apartment to a 3-bedroom house with a pool and fruit trees. I went back to what I knew best when in a new area, volunteering. Volunteering can help you make friends. I took the advice of CeCe Stevens by signing up to be a volunteer for the conference Contact in the Desert, the world's largest UFO symposium.

The first evening while waiting to get job duties assigned, I started to introduce myself to others. I met a beautiful, tall woman with long hair and a perfect nose. It was the most perfect nose I had ever seen. She had a simple appearance yet an elegance about her. Her arms seemed longer than normal. She was a guest at the conference. She was a regular, she was someone who religiously attended all the conferences. She had come early to see if the organizers needed extra help that evening. As we waited in line, I was awestruck by her. I could not explain why I was so drawn to her.

Then I just said it. I could see it clear as day. I asked her bluntly, "Do they know you are here? I mean, do they know who you are?"

She was shocked I'd said this out loud. She slightly blushed and said, "I am no one, just a conference goer."

I looked her straight in her eyes without missing a beat and said, "Yes, I know you are attending the conference, but do they know you are an otherworldly being? Do they know you are right here in front of me? That you are a paying guest to this conference that is all about how to communicate with you?" I could feel a Mantis energy from her.

Her eyes lit up. They went from bright blue to greenish yellow. I knew her secret and was not afraid to find out what she had to say. She was delighted I saw her, not afraid but tickled. I called her out in public when no one was paying any attention to us. She began speaking light language to me. I knew what she was saying. I understood completely without any fear or anxiety, I got her jokes. She was precious! She was one of the few of her kind left on this planet. Most of her people no longer came to Earth because they were tired of all the fear and hate.

I could not speak back to her, as my tongue twisted in my mouth. I did not want to fake a response. Instead, squealed with giggles because I understood her. I asked why she stayed silent. She said, in all her years, all her travels, I was the first to call her out so instantly. She knew who she was but did not have the courage or strength to try to explain her presence on Earth. She was born here. She was human. She was here to experience Earth just as I was. She just did not drink the memory-clearing potion. It was her hope she could help us elevate. She rocked my whole world. Then my name was called to get my T-shirt and volunteer job duties.

I would see her every now and then during the conference. We did not create a connection over social media. It was not necessary, for she granted me access to light language. Now, I could hear and see everything from a new perspective. I truly understood aliens are not outside of Earth or even trying to take our gold or brains. They are in the same positions we are in. They are souls here to experience free will and joy. They too are just beings of light with a different history. Or is it our same history that we have forgotten?

Toward the end of the conference, the final panel discussion was held in the outdoor amphitheater. The panel included all the biggest names from the History Channel's shows. *Ancient Aliens*, UFO documentarians, and historians who have uncovered Area 51. Also present were the filmmakers of Skinwalker Ranch. They debated why aliens are on Earth, how long they have been here, and what they look like. Meanwhile I downloaded the creation story as told by Enoch from the ancient Hebrew Bible. As they debated on stage over personal theories, I was shown all the answers. I was given simple understanding as if it was common knowledge and no longer needed to be hidden.

It was an unworldly feeling standing in the heat of the conscious sunlight. While questions were being asked by the audience, more knowledgeable authorities gave me answers. As stood in on the side, I was guided to all the answers. This became the starting point for my writing in *The Prophecy Map of Nova Gaia*. It was an old story that needed to be told again.

This conference changed my perspective. It enabled me to make new connections on higher levels. I gained understandings that I never thought possible. It was my first experience that really opened me up to communication with otherworldly beings.

A few months later, Vanessa de Luna came to visit me in my new home in Southern California. We had a connection to intergalactic beings in New Orleans. It made sense when she came to visit that we would go to Giant Rock in Landers, California. The building called the Integratron was built close to the site. It was built to be a communication hub, like a cosmic airport. This new technology was confiscated by our government, but the building still stands. The Integratron is open for private sound baths and a few public events. I had been lucky enough to go to a workshop during Contact in the Desert.

We could not get into the building that day. It did not matter as the land that surrounded it was where the spaceships landed. When we arrived, it was so bright and sunny, we were blinded by the light. From the sunlight reflecting off all the surfaces, you could still see dark figures on the hills above us looking down. They would follow us until we drove off the property.

In the shade of Giant Rock, we created a space to connect into the higher beings. Vanessa and I gave our offerings and a request to the otherworldly beings. She began to channel a great story. As she spoke the words, I could see it like virtual reality playing out right in front of us. We watched as a golden sphere came down from the heavens. A portal opened in the great rock. It was not an alien or extraterrestrial that came out of the ball of light. It looked like an Earth woman. I recognized this figure; it was Mother Mary. She was carrying a child, a new peace to be delivered to Earth.

She was surrounded by other prismatic blue humanoid beings with much joy. She softly walked forward. An army of men prepared for war surrounded this enlightened being. You could see the terror in their eyes. I am guessing around the 1940s, given the men's crew cut hairstyles, uniforms, and thick black glasses. More blue men came out of the swirling ball of light. The blue men weren't carrying weapons. Instead, their presence felt more like ones of monks or priests with the holy woman.

Like a black cloud covering the sun, we saw fear. The human fear took over the men. One of the soldiers began shooting at the blue beings. All the soldiers joined in. The big-eyed priests turned to stone with the gunshots. It was a massacre, a typical response from Americans—shoot first and ask later. The monks gave their lives to protect the holy woman with the child. She hurried back to the ball of light. The portal she had come through pulled her in quickly. In a flash, it was all over. No blood or bodies lying on the ground. Only orange and blue quartz like statues lay on the ground. The bright light closed the portal never to return to this spot.

Vanessa came out of her trance of telling this story. She pointed to where I had seen the portal. "There," she said. "See where they left their mark." In a daze, she stood up and walked over to a smaller boulder right next to Giant Rock. It was a perfect engraving of an image of a mother and child. I had explored this site many times and had never once seen this perfect cutout of a female form with child.

I gathered a few rocks that held the energy of the blue beings, including the large orange rock that inspired the message. Vanessa left three days later. We did not speak again of our experience. It would take her more than seven months to speak to me after our download session at Giant Rock. It would take over a year for the constant fuzzy feeling, buzzing, and downloading every evening until the crack of sunrise to stop. We'd had a true contact experience.

Meditation: Astral Traveling

I was taught in my youth how to leave my body (for situations like going to the dentist). I did not know this was called "astral travel" or "astral projection". Shirley MacLaine's book, *Out on a Limb,* gave a description of projecting yourself outside of your body. The projection of a soul was linked to Earth by a silver cord. The silver cord represented the cord of life. At age twelve I began to astral travel with no real direction.

Nearly twenty-five years later, I went back to these basic techniques. By this time in life, I had been taught by several gurus, teachers, and shamans. Each of them had their own ways of getting to the same places that were out of reality and into heaven. Their different methods all had an influence on me. Astral traveling as in life, can have different modes of transportation, an airplane, a car, motorcycle, or roller skates.

Music, vibration: The language of all universes and dimensions

When I first stepped into meditation, the chants of the Tibetan monks brought back memories. I found listening to Tibetan monks the easiest way to get lost in meditation. Then I went through a stage of anything by Tom Kenyon. Next, it was Dr. Todd's Lemurian Choir as my preferred way to meditate. All these sounds or music took me to other places, introduced me to guides and sharpened my experiences. I did notice a stronger sensation when I sang along. These feelings lead me to toning.

Toning is another great method of using vibration in a meditative state. Practicing with others or even following a YouTube video is a great start to make these sounds. To connect with others on the same note, pitch, and tone is magical.

It is all about the sound vibrations. Find something that speaks to you. At one point, I was singing heavily ancient mantras in group guided meditation. I noticed a few people stopped going to meditations. I asked why. My voice was out of tune. The sounds were too shocking, and my tempo was off. Going back and listening to meditations, it was true; I was off. I was new to practice. It did make me aware that maybe I should have practiced more. There are thousands of sounds to put yourself in a meditative state. It's whatever you prefer—whatever is your vibe.

Mantras, prayers, and songs are all ways to find your balanced state. Maybe you need to start with nothing at all! Only you and *ALL* and silence. For some, silent meditation is only achievable in groups (not necessarily in person). Silence is needed for transcendentalism. Ideal for many people. I was once told that I should be able to meditate in Jackson Square in the French Quarter during a festival. I was taught that having silence around you is not necessary. Just try different methods out and see what fits best for you.

Now, I love listening to my own gongs, sound bowls, drums, rattles, and chimes. The more I get into the language of sound, the more unlimited I feel. Sound can give a physical feeling of divine love. The vibration of sound is an extension of divine love. Greater experiences in astral traveling happen with the right sound.

You will get messages after astral traveling. They may give you homework or recommendations of what to do. I highly recommend journaling or writing down your journey. Record the experience immediately. Write when you are in a conscious state. Do not think about what you are writing. Write it quickly, as much as you can remember. After you write it out, go get a drink of water. You will need it! You can analyze the experience later. Deeper meanings will come as you look up medicine animals, spirit guides, or other symbols in the traveling.

By following these simple directions, in a safe environment, you can go anywhere! Always take care of yourself afterward. Make sure you are completely back in your being.

1. *Ground yourself and clear the space around you.*
   This is a running theme before you do any kind of healing work. You must be connected to the Earth to properly travel out. In fact, daily grounding to Mother Earth is a good idea. Grounding is also called earthing. There is a lot of research on connecting to the rhythm of the planet. Clear the space around you. No, I don't mean clean up the space, I mean remove other energies. Like turning off computers and cell phones. If possible, use sage or palo santo to "clean" the space. Or call on your favorite angels to remove all unnecessary energies. Feeling a safe connection is important. Clear above yourself as well as below yourself.

2. *Relax. Get comfortable.*
   In a perfect world you should be able to sit in a lotus position for hours in meditation. Most of us can't. Keeping your back straight is the only common element in meditation. Sitting up against a wall or lying flat are great positions for the highest good positions. Just get comfortable.

   Closing your eyes or using an eye covering helps. I have learned how to meditate both with my eyes open and closed. Neither has been a better experience for me. When people saw me with open eyes in meditation it freaked them out. In addition, most clients preferred closing their physical eyes. It would allow them to focus on their third eye. It is fun to experience the colors and space change around you with your eyes open.

It is all an experiment. Find what works or feels right for you. As thoughts pop into your head, let them go. As worry comes in or the "to-do" list for later views for attention, tell yourself, *I can think about that later.* Think, *I want to be present in each breath I take.*

3. *Begin to take deep breaths.*
   There are *so* many breathing techniques, the internet is full of classes, videos, and workshops on how to expand the breath. A simple technique I use is to breathe in the love and healing light and exhale out the worries for the day. Along with any pain in the body. Listen to your breath. There is also the technique of breathing in one nostril at a time. Switch your thumbs back and forth, closing one nostril at a time as you exhale out. Find your preferred way to get into a meditative state.

4. *Set your intention or location.*
   Where do you want to go? Do you have a specific heaven or dimension? A time in the past you want to forgive. A place in the now you want to visit. Maybe you want to go to a chakra space, the waters of Fatima, or up into Buddha's heavens, maybe visit Aphrodite's heaven. You must pick a location.

5. *Use your imagination.*
   To begin with guided meditation, use your imagination. Don't get caught up in detail. Instead, use your imagination to get started. Listen to only one voice—*yours*—that is guiding you. You can prerecord yourself leading a guided meditation and then listen to it if guiding yourself is too difficult and you get lost. Do not try to analyze what's happening or not. Go with the flow. Start with imagining the environment, and soon it will just flow into colors and other feelings. Again, there is no defined way to use your imagination. Just try!

6. *Walk in.*

   Step outside of your body—literally. Using your imagination, see yourself in a spirit form by looking through your third eye or sixth chakra. Imagine yourself walking down a bright, prismatic crystalline cave.

7. *See your golden-silver thread of life.*

   Your golden-silver thread of life is located beneath your feet, and it goes deep into the heart of Mother Earth. Step into the portal. Always start all traveling here at your soul seed. When you start grounded at this point, you are secure to go as far out as you want! This allows you to travel to all dimensions. It is the key to set intentions about where you want to go.

8. *Integrate and expand.*

   Now go anywhere you want to! Let the angels or other guides take you on your journey. Find healing. Maybe you have past relatives wanting to share or ultra-terrestrial beings who want to heal you! Listen for messages and feel into it.

9. *Thank them.*

   Be humble and grateful to all beings you encounter. Do not ask them yes-or-no questions. Receive all gifts given to you. Don't deny any gifts or tasks given to you. Thank them all before exiting. No arguing either, respect all the way! A traditional way of thanking is using prayer hands and bowing to the right.

10. *Call when you are ready to come back.*

    Call for an archangel like Uriel or Zadkiel to bring you back quickly. They will come behind you and bring ultraviolet light to integrate wisdom and love. Allow the angelic being to open the energy of your chakras and expand them. This energy is a part of the integration that will always be with you. As the chakras expand, the angels become protective of your new energy. *(The actual integration of what just happened may take from twenty-four hours to forty days.)*

11. *Go back to your reality, your life.*
Go back through the ultraviolet light. Step into it through the vibrational, ultraviolet, deep indigo, ocean blue, valley green, sunshine yellow, vibrant orange, and red Earth. Step back into your body. Be present here and now on planet Earth. Make sure you are present. Cough. Stretch. Drink salt water if you feel woozy. Always completely come back to the present *now*.

CHAPTER 8

Eighth dimension is the Great Void and of Universal Law

Guidance toward God's Will allows creativity and manifestation for the highest good. Here in the eighth dimension, we begin to experience infinity and how hard the beings of light work to keep *ALL*'s will moving forward in divine love, no matter how low the human vibration is. We also find the great void in the eighth dimension, what we might see or understand as space.

This is where we get the explanation about there being no coincidences and the understanding that chance only happens in gambling, and even that can be controlled. Here, we must take our medicine—learn our lessons on our Earth walk so we can expand into our next archetype or find the perfect state of oneness. Here, we step into self-realization and see the great void more like a womb, where all possibilities exist.

The old saying what goes around comes around works here too. Universal laws are upheld here. If you participate in black magic, whatever spell you cast comes to you as well. Whatever karmic mistakes or lessons are not learned will keep showing up in your life until you finally understand that you are in control of your life.

Here the beings of light, like great web designers, constantly reroute individuals to stay on their paths, while others use free will to go off their paths. I think of them as always busy working to keep *ALL*'s will moving forward in divine perfection. This is where we understand "universal laws"—what holds true outside Earth, not just on Earth. Since we are learning about all dimensions, it's important to know they are part of Earth's structure and give us understanding of the greater whole—the cosmos. Universal laws exist in all dimensions. Here in the eighth, all the laws come together to help push us closer to oneness.

Universal Laws

Let's look at twelve universal laws:

1. *Law of divine oneness,* first dimension. Everything that exists and has existed comes from one source, *ALL.*
2. *Law of vibration,* second dimension. The first sound of the om, the atom is the energy of *ALL.*
3. *Law of correspondence,* third dimension. What is happening internally also happens externally.
4. *Law of attraction,* fourth dimension of dreams and nightmares. Where your thoughts flow, the energy will go. This is probably the most well-known of the laws due to the book and movie *The Secret,* and Esther and Jerry Hicks with Abraham.
5. *Law of inspired action,* fifth dimension of using both divine love and divine consciousness to create our highest good. Nothing can happen until you put the actions out into the world.
6. *Law of perpetual transmutation of energy,* sixth dimension of understanding that we are in a constant state of change. The golden web of life is constantly reweaving itself. Think of the old saying, the only constant in life is change.
7. *Law of cause and effect,* seventh dimension. What goes around comes around. This is the law that gets forgotten by black magic or is not taught. If you send out negative energy, it will affect you negatively as well.
8. *Law of compensation,* also called fair energy exchange. We must give to receive. I will never understand why the wealthiest people believe they deserve everything for free. Traditionally, they are the worst tippers and expect free services just because of who they are. That is not a fair energy exchange.
9. *Law of relativity.* Earth is middle Earth. We are the creation of the average of all events. When we become judgment free, we see it's all relative or based on one's perspective.

10. *Law of polarity*. Life has opposites; light and dark, male and female, positive and negative. We have to understand this is not good versus bad. Things just are. The yin-yang symbol is the best explanation of this. Polarity is not duality when we think of male/female or shadow/light. Polarity unifies like living as an angel in human form. Duality divides.

11. *Law of rhythm*. The medicine wheel, the four seasons, and the cycles of life itself teach us this law. Mother Earth has its rhythm, as do the stars in the sky. Cycles are seen in sacred geometry, the flower of life, Metatron's cube.

12. *Law of fair exchange*. Money does not exist outside of planet Earth, but exchange does. When healing work is done by a professional, the professional should get paid. If you cannot pay with cash, then you can repay the energy they gave and the time they took to pray or lay their hands on you another way, like doing a chore, picking up something, or making them something. We have to be divine love to be a farmer, to love the ground, and to enable our fruits or vegetables to sprout. We also must feed plants for them to produce. You give the plant water, and it will give you fruit or flowers.

I have read up to eighteen universal laws. The additional laws either repeat a law in a different form or add Earth laws. Money and gender do not exist outside of Earth. To talk about the law of abundance or the law of gender, you are limiting yourself to Earth rules, not universal law. Beings of light have no gender. Nor do they understand money or financial worries. If universal laws are to be *universal*, then they must apply to beings of light and otherworldly beings as well. Mother Nature also has beings on this planet that do not have gender. Look at the whiptail lizard. This species does not have a male version.

As you can guess, I have experienced all the universal laws. For example, take the one that says what we send out is what we get back, fair energy exchange. The universe, *ALL*, and the beings of light do not understand good, bad, or "no." They only understand where we put our energy. When we put our energy into fearful things, like worrying about debt, that's what we get. This is the law of attraction. Once, I was using the example of a Gucci purse and how it does not bring you happiness. I must have said Gucci purse in my conversations fifty times because, within two weeks, I was gifted a Gucci purse. Again, I had said, "You do not need a Gucci purse. Gucci purses are overpriced." I was judging them. Yet, *ALL* heard was "Gucci purse,". Thank you, dad, for my Gucci purse! Stepping out of judgement, I know carrying the Gucci purse I was gifted with did help me get my dream job.

I learned about all the universal laws and common sense in New Orleans. That's why I say I was born in the plains, in the Midwest; raised in the South; and became an adult in the West. New Orleans taught me the most lessons, only because it was the city I lived in longest.

I think back to New Orleans in the mid-nineties, I had become friends with a local tour guide the high priestess, Bloody Mary. She and I worked together creating tours. Tours highlighted New Orleans blues music with its twisted history. I had been on many explorations of New Orleans with Mary; she is a great teacher. I had a supercool insight into French Quarter & cemeteries history. It was here, listening to stories from the iconography of the markers to pointing out special mausoleums with Bloody Mary I began to really understand the universal laws. In her books, the hauntings, or stories she tells all boil down to universal laws. Check out her books to get more stories.

Since I do believe it's all about your perspective, by looking at other perspectives of a story, you could find more understanding of universal laws. None of the laws teach right versus wrong, just how you choose to understand life.

Divine Chaos

By June 2020, I had gone crazy being locked in my house, afraid of getting COVID-19 again. Lack of money, eggs, and toilet paper pushed me to drive to see my parents in Arizona. I thought maybe just a moment of family would change my luck. My mission was to find a vortex in Sedona to undo what had been done. The stupa in Sedona always brought great peace and understanding to me. It was closed due to the pandemic rules as were many locations. I had to settle for a forgotten medicine wheel, located near the parking lot of the tiny airport.

Even though the signs said do not cross and close, I was desperate for help. I snuck past the signs, over the broken barbed wire fence to a small opening. In a small clearing was the old wheel. Before I entered, I cried. I begged for help. As I walked around it, I let it all out. I eventually entered humbly from the east. A weight lifted off me, clarity shimmered inside of me.

I felt like the wheel did its job as I drove back to my parents' house. I have great respect for my family so I would never smoke cannabis or eat gummies around them. They knew I enjoyed smoking. Neither of my husband's hid their passion for the flower.

The morning I was going to leave, it took me by surprise when my mother accused me of smoking in the house. I got very defensive at the implications. I had been there for a month dodging the broadcast news of fear. I was focused on learning the actions of love. I wanted to live judgment free. I'd worked from a place of love, rubbing my dad's shoulders, making coffee, and taking out the trash. I would listen to my parents complain about me. They noted my choices in careers and past partners. They told me things I did not want to hear. I'd given my mom the new hat off my head. I was doing my best actions of love. I'd allowed their beliefs to be theirs and not mine. I had to allow the crazy information to flow through me instead of irritating me. Why would I now light up a fatty in their conservative home and disrespect them now?

She was right, there was a very potent smell in the house. The sun was just peaking up as the smell emanated from the guest room. The smell filled the entire house. One could almost feel the smoke in the air. Yet there was no smoke. Offerings of sweetgrass, pine, and tobacco hung in the air as if we were in a sweat lodge. I knew the smells were not the skunky odor of cannabis. The sweet smell was that of traditional offerings in sweat lodges.

That morning, I had completed a three-day prayer with offerings to connect with indigenous guides. I had been requesting for an indigenous American chief or healer for years with pray. I had begged for guidance, a new perspective, someone who loved the land.

He came in full garb, and his presence wasn't felt by just me. The entire house smelled of tobacco, sage, pine, and sweetgrass. It was palpable, even to my mother. My prayers had been answered. I was in a divine state. I asked humbly, "What is your name?" I was surrounded by beautiful paintings by Donn Clark. He is of the Diné (Navajo) and Chiricahua Apache tribes. I thought maybe it was one of his paintings.

It was not one of the beautiful paintings. He clearly said, "Chief Standing Bear."

Knowing a small portion of Nebraskan history, Standing Bear is known to have been a civil rights leader. In 1879, he won his case in Omaha, Nebraska, my place of birth. He and his tribe were, by law, "persons". They were given freedom and some land back. It still makes me sick to my stomach that he even had to go to court to prove he was human. It shows how backward this country began, and maybe still is.

He told me he'd come to guide me home. He also came to help me be released. I was finally going to be freed from the intestines of the ancient man of the maze. For years I digested pain and suffering. I had lost everything again! This would be the third time I had my livelihood, my store, my money, my lifestyle, my way of living, and even my health taken away. This time I also lost judgment. I had come to Sedona to find my peace. What medicine was I to learn? What mistakes did I keep making? My confusion was at its peak, and I could not feel what it was I needed to be doing.

For now, it was 8:08 a.m. It was time to start my drive back to Palm Springs with my poodle, Standing Bear and Waze app guiding me.

I felt a new confidence as I buckled myself in—the ride was going to be all downhill from here! I plugged in my trusty electronic guide and asked Chief Standing Bear to use it to communicate with me. The fem bot immediately said, "Let's go," in a proactive, positive way. We were off to go home. I was going to plan a new future. I wasn't aware I had one more obstacle to go through.

Chief Standing Bear sat next to me in my white RAV4 as I waved goodbye to my parents. I felt more love from them than ever before. I felt all my childhood issues, the walls I'd created were gone. Even when things were said I would never repeat, I knew it was just egew talking and knew they had true love for me. I thanked Chief Standing Bear for showing up, as I had always asked for a Native American guide to be with me.

He said, "I don't understand."

I said, "I have prayed for a Native American guide to help teach me more about the medicine wheel and medicine animals. As a child, I would dream of being Native American."

He said, "I do not understand. Your parents were born in America?"

"Yes," I said anxiously.

"You were born in America?" he said with much conviction.

"Yes," I said, confused by his question.

"Then you are native to America. You are Native American," he said with a chuckle.

I could not say anything back. I was stunned. He said this while he was laughing at me. Now I try to use the term *indigenous people*. Words do carry many different meanings.

With profound faith in my guide, I took a different path home than the one I normally took. I felt the fem bot map app was empowered by the chief, so it must be a safer and quicker way for me to travel. The start of the drive took me down the two-lane highway. I went through a blooming Saguaro National Park. This was a beauty I was meant to see. The prickly giants with floral wreaths were so unusual. It was an awesome sight to see all of them in bloom! With so much beauty everywhere I looked, magic was everywhere.

I was growing confident this drive was going to be graceful. We continued our talk. I asked questions I had built up in my heart about medicine animals and the medicine wheel. Standing Bear spoke of respect. A respect for our elders that was fading in our daily lives. A respect for all life, not one color or gender. The equality of humans and animals. He cried tears as he told a story of his daughters being lost in modern systems. Being forgotten and slaughtered by man's greed. He mourned for all the lost children and taken women. Those who were used as objects, tossed aside not respected. He still does not understand the speed the white man has to have for everything. Or why everything must be so fast, why are we in such a hurry? Why does life have to be so controlled? Standing Bear's heart ached for our disconnection from the Great Mother. People got lost in the myths created by European history. Had humankind has forgotten its connection to each other?

I was coming up on a small town, the last stop for gas until Quartzite. The town was Hope. I asked my companion through my heart, Should I stop here? Chief very clearly said, "No. No time to stop for Hope." I kept driving past the few buildings labeled Hope. I was steady on the two-lane highway. I noticed the wide-open space of desert was strangely still and hazy. Then I saw it a few miles ahead of me, a haboob!

It happened in an instant! From clear driving then, without any warning, I drove straight into a wall of wind and blowing sand. It was larger than any dust devil or tornado I had seen. From a distance, it looked a mile wide, stretching from the low hills out to nothingness. Sophie, my poodle, looked up. She sighed and laid back down. Several cartoonlike tumbleweeds flew past my car, and I could hear the sand and wind pounding against the car.

My hands were glued to the steering wheel, the headlights were on, and it was worse than any snowstorm I had driven in. I could not see more than five feet in front of me. I thought I should pull over and let it pass. The radio went out, and a silence covered the car. Sophie sat up and barked. Her tail started wagging.

"No!" I heard a loud voice next to me. Chief was sitting in the passenger seat looking forward calmly. He said other cars and big trucks could not see me either. They could easily hit me. He also said, "We don't know what's on the side of the road. It could make the tires go bang! Stay forward."

"Do I slow down?"

"No. Go the speed you came in. Stay at the same rate."

I was going fifty-five miles per hour on a fifty-five miles per hour highway. The cruise control was set, and I hadn't touched it since Hope. I could see the wind flying across the road, tree parts, and plants flying across the road.

What do I need to do? I was trying not to panic or pull the steering wheel off the column.

"Keep driving. You are protected. All you have to do is go straight through the chaos. Ask your dragon to carry you through."

I did as I was told. I called in the gamma ray beings, the highest order of angels. Like ancient Chinese dragons, they are long, colorful, and burning with compassionate love. They circled the car. I called for them to come with a Lemurian mantra. Nine times, I said it out loud. Sophie laid back down.

The skies got darker and heavier, not lighter. I had been in the haboob for fifteen minutes, tight grip on the steering wheel. The once light brown, fuzzy, hazy sky was now pitch-black. I could see less of the road than before. Then I noticed the strangest thing. I could see rocks, trees, and plants rolling across the road right in front of the car. I realized I no longer heard the rocks or the sand pounding the car. The car was no longer vibrating or pulling me off the road. Were we floating down the road? Was the car levitating, the heavy wind just lifting us up?

The speedometer still read fifty-five miles per hour. A calmness came over me. The chief's words echoed in my ears and heart. *You are protected from the chaos.* I felt it. My guardian angels, the dragon angels had put a shield over my car. For about twenty minutes, I drove in a daze, holding tightly onto the steering wheel, looking out the side of my eye to see Chief just staring ahead. It was the strangest feeling, really understanding. My grip loosened. I was still in the haboob. I was still on the road. I was now headed forward at sixty miles per hour. I was no longer afraid of what lay ahead.

Sophie went back to sleep; the ride now lulled her into a peaceful state. Standing Bear still sat next to me. He was enjoying the ride. Said it was much different than a horse or the train. The more confident I became, the more he started fading away. In a silent state, I calmly drove forward as the dark brown sky became lighter. Still no cars passed me or were near me. To the best of my knowledge, I was alone on the road.

Almost thirty minutes had passed, and now I was used to driving in madness. I was calm and in control. The chaos did not make me nervous anymore. I understood my lesson. I got the medicine from the jungle maze, and it all came back together for me. I looked up into the gray sky and saw two bald eagles circling above the rising dust. They led me out of the terrible storm, back to turquoise skies. Within seconds, I was back on the open road. There were no cars and no sign of what I had just gone through. I saw a sign announcing I was about to enter Quartzite. Standing Bear was no longer sitting next to me. He had found his way back into my heart.

All was good. I believed in myself. I listened to my guide. I took the medicine (I learned my lesson) and was led out into a wide-open space of unlimited possibilities. It was such a great moment of triumph and an inner balance of peace. When I made it back to Palm Springs, upon inspection of the car, I found that nothing had happened—not one scratch and not one dent could be seen. My only witness was sleeping most of the drive, not that Sophie could have told the tale. She just ran out like it had been nothing but a drive through a park.

My being changed after that trip. Conscious light flowed down my spine. I understood balance, being judgment free, and believing in a higher power. Standing Bear still answers me in meditation and sings in my heart. I know, when I need him, I just need to ask for him. He has always guided me. He led me to CeCe Stevens at the 2012 International Astrology Convention in New Orleans. He put me in front of her. She is my medicine woman and teacher. She teaches in a contemporary way on ancient topics. She takes forgotten methods and brings them into reality. Her lessons are timeless. Standing Bear is not a mythical connection. He is an elder guide I honor in my high heart chakra.

The escape from the Mayan maze was in my sight! I had been digested, taught lessons, and came out in an oversize fart of dirty air. I was pushed forward into the now moment of love.

It was chaos that surrounded me, yet divine love drove me, protected me, and led me to myself. I giggled as I bathed in almond milk, honey, and ylang-ylang oil. I washed off the old ways. Soaked in divine love. In my bathroom in my own vortex. The sunset lighting perfectly luminating my bath. I am Rachel.

I know who I am. I understand the meaning of life. I am a healer. I am a space holder. I am a worker bee. I am the ant who can carry triple its weight. I have access to unlimited divine love and conscious knowledge. *I am you*, I thought as I giggled in my bathtub after a long dusty drive through the intestines of life.

Hope Is a Four-Letter Word

Hope is a four-letter word.
It carries old energy of wanting change, of desiring better outcomes.
It is a word that movies are made of, hope the good will defeat the bad.
Storybooks hold the secrets of hope, for the knight in shining armor to bring justice.
Hope it will get better. Hope you make it.

Hope someone will come and change the situation.

Hope for a better tomorrow.

Hope is outside of our control.

Hope is what fear wants us to do.

Fuck is a four-letter word.

Fuck has more power than hope.

Fuck releases the feelings, the inner thoughts of our being.

Fuck gives the control back to the person.

Fuck gives power to the person to let go of hope and take control.

Hope gives power to an outside source, handing over its power.

Know is a four-letter word.

An angelic being said to me "give up hope,"

For to hope things will get better is giving up your power to an outside source.

They said to Know things will get better.

Be the cocreator you are. Create, do not hope. Know.

To know is to take action,

To know you are in control of you,

To know only you can change what is around you,

To know a Source far greater than you,

I know I am loved.

I know I am a co-creator.

I know I am.

Hope is a four-letter word.

Chakras Expanded

I would like to expand into two levels or layers of chakras. Let's take traditional chakras one step further to examine each a little more. We can better understand three parts or layers of a chakra: main, high, and gemstone chakra sections. A quick recap, the high chakras are the front area or top layer of each main chakra. The gemstone chakra layers are located behind the main chakras. These are areas where we can directly receive help from nature, angels, and otherworldly beings. The high chakras connect to beings of light and gauge how your individual love energy is given out on Earth. The gemstone chakras are like perfect sacred geometry cut crystals and gemstones that connect us to all kinds of guides. This is a whole new area of chakra energy that is being explored. I understand there are more layers of each chakra, but for this book we will only go into three layers.

To be honest, gemstones chakras are something I made up. As I quote Thor from *The Avengers* "All words are made up." This is my personal expression of unexplored layers of chakra energies. The main chakras are directly connected to our physical body. Where the gemstone and higher chakras are used when we ask for help or healing. When you pray or say a mantra or light a candle to make a wish, you unknowingly open one of these chakras' layers.

The gemstone chakras are like sacred geometry- full of knowledge and history. Like real gemstones, they are created over lifetimes. To me they feel like they are located at back of the chakra, connected to the spine. It makes sense it would be connected to spine since this is where it is theorized the conscious light flows from the crown down the spine. From the bottom of the spine in the case of the root chakra, to the zenith chakra at the brain stem the gemstone chakra layers deliver conscious wisdom. In the Higher Chakras, you can build love energy toward an amazing future of your own creation, for the highest good of all beings.

Through meditation the new chakras layers can be best understood. Try in meditation to think about a chakra like a plant. Start with the heart chakra and use the example of rosebush. Starting with roots of a rosebush. Think about how roots are grounded deeply in Mother Earth. The roots of rose bush drink up the water. Water is a connection to other plants as well as the entire eco system. Water is known to carry information to the rosebush. We can think of the root system of the rosebush like the gemstone chakra and water is the divine love.

The gemstone layer of the chakras is a connection to all your guides and Ascended Master. This spiritual root system is fed by millions of guides and absorbs the "water of life". The infinite space creates infinite roots for unlimited help.

Back to the rosebush example, from the roots comes the green stems. The green leaves and stems of the rosebush symbolize the main heart chakra. This is the traditional chakra known for being green and the center point of the seven main chakras.

The rosebud or flower is the high heart chakra. The bloom of the rose or also you could imagine a lotus, is a visual of the high heart chakra. The pink morganite or rose quartz energy of unlimited love. This gives unlimited potential. The energy or light is absorbed allowing the roses to bloom. Divine love is energy that makes the rosebush bloom. Doing a meditation and feeling the three chakra energies will help you understand how to connect. When you need advice, you go to the gemstone chakras for guidance. When you need physical healing or help you go to the main or traditional chakras. When you need assistance for future events or situations, go to the higher chakras.

The higher chakras could be called the divine love chakras where the gemstone chakras carry the energy of divine consciousness. Both align with the prismatic colors of the rainbow. They are ultra colors with matching sound waves. The center of both sets of chakras is the heart. This is the most connective space for divine love from the universe.

I keep saying divine love but haven't given you a full definition. Divine love, or true love as Yvette Kinchen explains in her book, *True Love not Like in the Movies*. She gives a great definition of divine love. The following is an excerpt from her book. She picked out this section just for you:

> *Love heals and restores things to their divine nature.*
> *Loving something is an ace of magic. It opens and holds a*
> *high-frequency space for a higher expression and possibility.*
> *It believes in its higher nature: it encourages it and calls*
> *it forth. Love recognizes itself and joins in strength,*
> *harmony, and union. It is our disbelief in love and in*
> *being loved that keeps us separate and at odds with the*
> *natural forces around us … Embodying your true love is*
> *taking you power back and returning your magic to you.*

Her words allow you to see, feel, and be one with you and love. For me the higher layers of the chakras really teach us this divine love and how it connects to everything. It is not just of the heart; it is of our entire being.

These newer chakra layers are being discussed in new books, podcasts, and blogs. This is a key factor to our future. Connecting to this space of divine love energy gives an unlimited future of balance. Thinking with our hearts, we can accomplish anything. With the help of a higher connection, guidance from beings of pure love will produce a life of love. It's the trickle-down theory that American politics invented. When we get love from the highest guiding us, our everyday actions become loving.

In human history we can look at the Egyptians for earliest understanding of this. They thought the brain was in our physical heart. Their understanding was the heart did more than pump life-giving blood. These early physicians thought the heart was part of the central nervous system. In 1991, scientists proved what the Egyptians already knew. The "intrinsic cardiac nervous system" was announced as the official title of the heart-brain connection.

Research went on to explain the larger connection. The gut or stomach area also hosts brain cells. This is responsible for what is called your "gut feeling" or intuition. It is also a part of your subconscious, your inner child. Your high heart is an awesome area to explore. Here you can reenergize or fall back in love with yourself. Can you feel your high heart? Can you feel unlimited love here?

I suggest experiencing any one of layers of the chakras at one a time. They are so full of knowledge and energy you could spend a week in each area. This is a new area for all of us to explore. I do not know what rules apply to these new energies. Go into your meditative state and experience them. Work on unblocking your ideal future or amplifying a chakra for your personal healing.

Without getting too philosophical, I kept it simple. It is up to you to explore what personal guides you have for each area. Only entities that are for your highest good can help you. It's a safe place to explore your own personal connections.

Higher Chakras & Gemstone Chakra Layers

Earth Star / Soul Seed Chakra

The Earth star or soul seed chakra marks you are from Earth. Just in case you ever find yourself in a position in the cosmos and you must prove you are from Earth. It's an energy that is not found only at the bottom of your feet but also in your DNA. In science it is called the Eve gene; it is the one common gene we all share—our soul seed that marks us as *made on Earth.*

This is your personal link directly to Mother Earth. It is the golden slide or golden silver cord seen in meditation. Like the crown chakra, it is not read or interpreted. This chakra cannot be blocked, even by our own doing. We may not be connected strongly here, but we all have this connection. You cannot, in any way whatsoever, be disconnected permanently from this energy or any of the chakras. Through meditation, we can travel to the soul seed chakra. It's a portal as well. It carries energy from the Earth.

In meditation, you will see your rose gold / silver cord, thread like coming out of the soul seed through your body. It is like a true root that is always there. The Earth seed anchors you to Earth no matter where you travel, both physically and in astral realms. When grounding, we connect to Earth's energy. This is the Vesica Piscis (the actual seed shape), previously discussed, across our entire energy system. It is the connection to consciousness in the physical realm and the astral planes.

The color of this chakra is surrounded in golden, white, silver light. The insides luminate with every color of all the chakras. Physically, it's directly connected to your spine. Spiritually, it is in alignment with the kundalini energy from the crown of your head. Through yoga, we got our first introduction in the Western world to the chakras, and it remains one of the greatest systems in which to learn and feel them. Now, we are expanding our understanding to more of a universal than a third dimensional Earth understanding.

We can feel Mother Earth's pain through this chakra—not just women or male gurus or highly intuitive people, all of us. Every animal, plant, rock, and human being has this connection to Earth. Starting here, you feel the immediate connection, a security to go into higher realms and do deeper healings. This is the best place to start.

Great meditation for this is Vanessa de Luna's "Vanessa Meditation," accessible on Vimeo at https://vimeo.com/704387823

High Sacral / Orange Sapphire Chakra

This was a chakra I introduced to during a surgery in the spring of 2023. It is a connection to alchemist, horticulturist, and artists of all kinds. This cluster of astral quartz is like a support group. If you are having a mental block on a project or need an idea to move anything forward from work to creative projects, this is the area you mentally step into and ask for help. Seeking advice from within instead of on your phone! Try it some time when you want expert advice from your own guides.

High Solar Plex / Golden Citrine Chakra

Happiness and divine masculine energy is found in the high solar plex. Here is where one feels and sees Metatron's cube connects you through the Christed light. This is the area where consciousness flows. A gemstone version can be found behind each of the main chakras; the energy and connection emulate the heart chakra. They are in the shape of a diamond or other sacred geometry forms.

These layers are the connection to inner child and middle self. It is where we feel our intuition. Ever get a bad feeling in your stomach before you do something wrong? That was your younger self trying to warn you not to do it. Here we can also find great confidence to do what our mission is or get done what needs to be done with ease and grace.

High Heart / Emerald Chakra

In meditation, you may feel like you are crawling through a tunnel in the back of your heart. The emerald chakra first appears to be a very dark, hidden, forgotten space. This is the space where people get "knifed in the back" or "double crossed." We can get cut off from receiving universal divine love. Here in these chakras, we can pull out the "knife in our back."

This chakra is like the roots of a plant, drawing up nutrients; this space enables us to receive not just universal love but also universal knowledge. This chakra, to me, looks like an infinite honeycomb or walls of sacred geometry that, in each of the little spaces, holds a guide or Ascended Masters.

This is our connection to the billions of guides, Ascended Masters, and past loved ones. These guides have information to help guide you in your daily life. Whatever questions you may have, you can find answers. You can find a guide or teacher or an attorney who is no longer on the third-dimensional plane or whoever you need willing to help answer your questions. Just ask for help.

I will say, in this chakra, it is one of the times when it's important to be very specific about what your question is. For example, if you have a legal contract, you must sign but do not understand the language or you have a limited time to sign it, go into this chakra for help. You will need to clearly ask for modern guidance, including the current year. You really do not want a lawyer from 1890 to help. When looking to guides, always ask for the highest good. If you speak to a guide who knows cooking instead of law, you are not going to get the right help. Always be clear in requesting the proper guidance.

High Throat / Lapis Lazuli Chakra

Of course, I have several stories around the high and gemstone layers of the communication chakra. I just don't know where to start. I will say these layers hold huge information in how you communicate with everything-from your mother to your car. The more you expand these layers the more you can hear what people are really saying. You also can express yourself without anger or fear.

High Third Eye / Star Sapphire Chakra

This is the connection to your soul self. Since the inner child is connected in the golden citrine chakra, here is where you find your higher self and oversoul. In my experiences the higher self never really speaks to me. She just shows me things or places. She is me, the perfect me, ageless, great hair, and green eyes. Higher-self Rachel never wants for anything, nor does she have me do tasks. She is just there when I am looking for higher guidance within myself.

The oversoul or monad soul is the part of me that is infinite. It is the oversoul who has the memory of the beginning of time. I asked once what is your name- it gave me a high pitch tone I can't every express. It is this being that drank the elixir to come to Earth and experience love. It is this energy that is known as "Sparkles" or creation dust. I go to "Sparkles" my highest guides when I need the most help or inspiration. It was Sparkles who showed me the gemstone chakras. It was Sparkles who taught me the gemstone chakras are divine wisdom from physical beings of the past, where the higher chakras are energies of divine love from beings of light to help with creating the future.

High Crown / Zenith Chakra

The zenith chakra is gemstone chakra. The zenith chakra connects your heart to your brain. This allows love to rule your thoughts and actions. The zenith chakra is physically located in your brain stem.

The high crown chakra is called the Transcended Chakra. It is located above your head. The high heart chakra is connected to the high crown chakra. This is where the Divine Love flows from all directions. This is how divine love can guide your thoughts.

Keep your brainstem healthy and clear! Call for your highest guides for divine consciousness. I really have a lot to say here but I need to have something to write about in a second book. These layers are all about divine consciousness as I have mentioned earlier. This is where Enlightenment begins.

CHAPTER 9

---

*The nineth dimension is infinite energy of
ALL, where Universal Laws are upheld.*

The ninth dimension was thought to be where *ALL* or God lives. This was thought to be the space of our light body or soul. This is not *ALL's* home. Nor is it even the home of the beings of light. Rather, it is a space where the God spark inside us is felt and where the soul travels from heavens to other physical realms. It's where the beings of light do their work with our requests. It is where our soul or light body expands into oneness.

When looking at universal laws as noted in the eighth dimension, we can begin to comprehend the ninth dimension as further expansion of *ALL*. When we give *ALL* human characteristics, we limit our understanding and give our personal power to those who "know more than we do."

I can't even fully describe this dimension because I do not have the full capacity to express it with words. *ALL* is really a concept that we only have a small understanding of—kind of like the belief that we only use ten percent of our brains or that we are either right-brained or left-brained. These are not truths; rather, they're ideas based on an old matrix of thought embedded in our psyche from the past hundred years. For me to say I completely understand *ALL* and I have all the truths is not even possible. Here is where we see that we are just another cog in the wheel of life. Here, we are at the "tip of the iceberg" of understanding *ALL*. We are like bacteria only visible under a microscope.

In the ninth dimension, we get to step outside of what we believe or how we understand our beliefs on Earth. For some people, it is way too hard to step outside of their own beliefs, to understand that the constant is change, that love is the only energy, and that we are vibrating in multiple dimensions at one time. It is here when I understood middle Earth is not a fictional place. Instead, literally the Earth we live on is the middle of all possible events. Not middle Earth as described in literature, but literally the average or middle of all possibilities. In astral traveling, middle Earth is the perfect Earth of ALL's will, that clearly does not exist in our reality.

In meditation, I go into the ninth dimension and always come out humbled. Sometimes, I'm even saddened about humanity's ignorance of all that is and can be. The simplest understanding, I have of this place is that we are all beings of light. We are all part of Creative Source, *ALL*.

What Goes Around Comes Around

Ten years after my first trip to Mexico in 2021 I was given another free trip to Mexico. This time was for my hard work of helping my family move from the Sedona area to Nebraska. My months of labors of love paid off in the form of a vacation with Shane. We ended up in Playa del Carmen, in the Yucatan Peninsula of Mexico. This was our dream trip of snorkeling and seeing the starfish. It was during the second summer of the pandemic.

Like my other trip to Mexico, we were treated like kings and queens at a timeshare—a beautiful all-inclusive, resort. This time, I did not have to attend meetings. Instead, it was my time to relax, explore, and be in a fully conscious state of the beauty around me. Included with the resort was a free tour of Ek' Balam, both the ruins and the cenote. I was incredibly excited for this trip; I was a different person than I had been on my first visit to Mexico. I had driven the haboob of western Arizona with all my trust in my guides. I had become balanced, full of divine love, and comfortable with who I am. The years of transition, studying mystic arts and spirituality to this point had been my Earth walk, my experiences of living my individual life.

As we prepared for our last excursion of our glamorous vacation, once again, my travel partner, this time my new husband, got woozy. He got sick on the way to the ruins. This was a different sickness than the one my first husband had experienced.

As the van ride continued, something felt the same to me. I got more curious when I realized the tour guide *was the same tour guide* from years ago! Not his cousin, the same exact person just ten years older. The resort we were staying at was owned by the same resort company I'd stayed in ten years earlier. Immediately, I started tingling when he told the same stories I'd heard a decade earlier.

When the van finally stopped and we reached our first destination, I was completely lit up! Shane dragged himself out of the van to see where we had stopped. He told me he had no intention of exploring and that I was on my own. After we got our passes from the information center he sat down. Walking towards the ruins, I snapped a shot on my iPhone. The photo showed the rainbow vortex. I stepped through the vortex and into Ek' Balam.

The familiar tour guide told stories of the unearthing of these ruins and possible histories as he guided us into the main square. He pointed out statues and living quarters and told us what his thoughts were on this ancient city. I heard nothing of what he said or pointed out. I had stepped not just into a physical vortex but also into an actual portal, as my third eye was now seeing a thriving village, not in decay or ruin.

This was a city of the divine feminine. Its name translated to "bright star jaguar". When you read the archaeological history of ruins you can find more mystical meanings than black cats. Here, we could find hieroglyphic serpents and images with wings that resembled Western depictions of angels. The area where it was located was sacred geometry with its twelve-by-twelve-kilometer main wall encircling smaller walls, down to the one-by-one-kilometer wall in the center of the city. Archaeologists knew this was a place of culture, invention, and a creativeness that we often align with divine feminine energy.

As the laws of the universe applied, there were polarities. Chichén Itzá was divine masculine. It was about control, sporting events, and sacrifice. Ek'Balam was the "polar opposite". It was the capital city, hidden among the trees. It was a place where one could feel the presence of divine love, a place of empathy.

The tour guide led us around the ruins. I did not see what my camera did. I saw people living and working. It looked like almost all women and children. This was a religious place, where people wore white skirts with colorful beads or adornments. It felt as though they all took care of one another, like the whole city was more like a college or convent. No homelessness or markets were present; even the popular game area was only a third of the size of other courts I had seen. This was a learning center, a place where women and men were treated equally and where the priests and priestesses were not above the people but, instead, worked with them.

I was drawn to the center temple, where I could see the jaguar temples—the teeth and very intricate designs to honor this sky god. Like a curious tourist, I began to climb this huge temple. As I did so, I looked at the levels of different uncovered codices or hieroglyphs of the Mayans. Farther up I went to reach Father Sky. I climbed up the historical steps, envisioning high priestesses going up to make offerings.

At the top, I was neither exhausted from the climb nor exhilarated by the scenery that surrounded me. Instead, I heard a very clear, conscious voice calling to me, "Get down from there! You do not need to be up there. You are not being born. Nor is this your death. This is not a place for you."

Who is speaking to me? I asked, while other tourists began their climb down.

"I am Mother Creatrix. Now, remove yourself from this temple and come pay your homage to me."

I did exactly what I was told. In my experience, when a crystal-clear message comes to you, you must take immediate action. Slowly, I began my descent down the great temple as a swarm of butterflies surrounded me. Mother Creatrix knew I had roses in my pocket from the lovely resort I was staying in and fresh water to give as an offering.

In the center of the city was the largest ceiba tree I had ever seen. She was calling me. It was the tree the Mayans who first called it the most sacred tree, their tree of life. I gave her my offerings and apologized for being an ignorant human. She showed me great love and shared stories of the city. She allowed me to feel the great compassion of this capital city when it was thriving and to see how the Spanish conquistadors had destroyed her looking for riches. They set the city on fire, disappointed not to find a golden city, no treasures of gemstones and gold. The treasures here were the people, the oneness, the self-governance, the higher knowledge of the connection of all things.

I saw the beginning and the end of this great city through the eyes of Mother Creatrix. She was stronger than ever in her green state of divine love and gave me an insight into how, over the past ten years, I had completely changed myself. I saw that I, too, had been born perfect and had been jaded by my surroundings. How my community had taught me polarity in a way of good versus bad and that money would answer all my problems. I saw that human love was controlled with sex and violence. My perfect soul had been confused by drugs, alcohol, processed food, and by feeling I always needed to be entertained. I saw that I hated my body, condemned myself, allowed myself to be controlled by collective thought, and hid in a world of people pleasing to give myself a pat on the back.

This was not who I was anymore. I thought to myself, *I could no longer hide in conspiracy or eat the lies of the wealthy.* I had studied reiki, meditation, and shamanism for the past ten years instead of working a normal job. The lessons of discernment came from Mother Mary and my evangelical aunt. They both emphasized how to take care of myself. I learned I am a cocreator in this world. I am perfect, just as I am at this moment, not because of surgery or expensive trips or classes. I am the perfect Rachel, because I can feel my God spark, and I understand the meaning of life is just to experience joy.

Mother Creatrix was happy for my ten-year journey, for my belief in myself and *ALL*. She was pleased I had gained the understanding that I can't please anyone but myself. She knows that, when we step out of our own fears, great things happen because we free our energy to love. She reminded me that not that long ago I was unable to sit still and now I can teach others how to meditate. She even acknowledged how I'd healed myself with divine love. She recounted the story that I'd had my ovaries removed in 2002 in New Orleans, only for doctors in California in 2017 show me ultrasounds that I had two fully functioning ovaries.

The full circle did not end with Mother Creatrix, as she told me to do a final clearing at the cenote or the oasis of Ek' Balam. The cenote was a pristine cave, a hidden water source. This was where they got their fresh water, where they bathed and swam for fun. The cycle would be completed as I dipped into the bright blue waters and swam with the ancient black catfish. The black catfish in the water made me think of the name of the city, black jaguar. This led me into a vision of myself as one of the Lyrians, the cat people of the sky, coming to Earth as Bast or Baste. My oversoul may have planted Mother Creatrix, sparking this divine city that is dedicated to love.

I had stepped out of the ten-year cycle, the ten years of confusion of spirituality, my search for divine love and my acceptance of *ALL*'s will. Was this the end of my Earth walk? No. It was just another level of understanding that I can share with you. Life goes on.

Meditation: Initiation to Divine Healing

Before jumping in, read this section a few times. The first time, you may feel fuzzy. You may even want to record yourself reading the meditation out loud for your personal use. I also recommend that, for this initiation, you either lie down flat or, if you like to meditate in lotus, sit straight up. Ideally, your back will be aligned in either position. Using any device like a chair or wall to lean against is perfect. Do find what is comfortable.

Next, clear the space you will be doing this in. If you're indoors and you can, black out the space. Hold your favorite tool or crystal. You can even do this in the bathtub! Or you can go outside and be in the bright sunshine. Find a shady spot so you don't burn. Do it under the moon or in full view of the Milky Way. Use whatever space works best for you. Set it up so you know the limits of the outside stimulus that you can handle in meditation. Prepare the space by clearing it, giving it offerings, and saying thanks.

There was a time in the past when ritual was preeminent. If I had guided you then, I would have told you the opposite of all that. Instead, you had to go into complete darkness, with only the light of one white candle. You could not have alcohol, meat, or sex for thirty days before and up to seventy-two hours after the ceremony. You needed to pray on certain days toward specific directions, wearing specific colors. Rituals used to carry heavy meaning and sometimes violent ways. Today, we are no longer limited to the scenes and grandeur of spirituality. We design our own path of what feels good and right to us individually. If you want a room full of roses and altars, then build it. If you just want to sit by the edge of water while the children laugh around you, enjoy the sounds!

All you need to do is find yourself a comfortable space as you do the meditation. Start by finding your own meditative state.

Whoever reads this, allow the energy of *ALL*/Source to be for the highest good of all humankind, all sentient beings, all plants, all animals, all the water, all our food, and all the air we breathe. Let the energy be for the good of the ground, Mother Earth, and all her inhabitants. Please allow this to be of the highest good for the planet, for everyone. Allow divine love and divine consciousness to guide me. To start the meditation, say aloud:

I humbly call upon the creator of all beings. (Say this three times.)I request divine love and divine consciousness to guide me into the highest compassionate good and wisdom of ALL. (Repeat three times.)

Begin to imagine yourself as if you are stepping out of your body. Imagine that you are walking into a cave. It's a silvery, dark red cave that leads you to an oval opening. There is a golden-silver-white slide you go down to reach the core of Mother Earth, where you see a huge, pulsing, golden seed emulating rainbow colors. It is the shape that occurs when the rainbow spheres of divine love and divine consciousness meet. You see the golden slide is your golden thread to Mother Earth. This golden-silver thread goes up your spine, reaching that crystal oil, opening your crown to divine consciousness and divine love. Imagine you are sliding down your golden thread of life to the center of a huge heart quartz in the middle of Earth.

As you are connecting to Mother Earth say aloud or to yourself:

I humbly call upon the east, element of wind with the being of light Raphael. Please be here with me. I call upon the south, element of fire, the electric blue energy rays of Archangel Michael. Please be here with me. I request the west be present, element the water Archangel Gabriel with your crystal white light, please be here with me. I call in the north, element of stone and the Archangel Uriel with your ruby red light. Please be with me. I humbly call upon divine love of (pick who you identify with) Isis, Inanna, Holy Mother Mary, Mary Magdalen. Please be here with me. I call upon divine consciousness (pick who you feel comfortable with) Buddha, Christ, Krishna, Muhammad, or Abraham. I humbly ask for my personal guided ascended masters. I open my crown to Archangel Metatron. Please come down with ultraviolet light, the universal energy that flows through everything. (Imagine this is the Holy Spirit, the chi, St. Germaine Light) Allow the ultraviolet energy to flow through me and into every part of my future energy.

In an unassuming state say, I [state your legal name three times] humbly ask for divine love healing. I request the following of myself in all times, in all space, throughout all dimensions and to self-initiate into the trinity of oneness: divine love, divine consciousness, and divine temples.

Feel how the guides have opened your crown chakra, for the divine consciousness flows through. Feel it flow.

Divine love expands out from your heart chakra. Feel divine love going in and out of the heart chakra, the emerald chakra, and the high heart chakra.

When you are ready, ask for the rainbow golden healers from all time and dimensions to come to help you expand for your highest good and for ALL.

You are divine love. Ask that compassion and understanding flow through you for eternity or until it is no longer necessary.

Next imagine floating to your golden thread of life. Ascend the golden-silver cord. Imagine you're in a prismatic cave, feeling the new divine love energies of the first chakra.

Float up into the divine womb, feeling divine love in every cell of your being. Become a ray of light from the central sun, God's light, filling you with rose gold divine love.

Gently fly down to the valley of divine love with lush green plants. Feel divine love and divine consciousness in all the beauty of the greenery around you. Become one of the green plants and bloom into infinite, pure divine love. Feel the high heart chakra fill with unlimited divine compassion.

You have dark green roots growing into the mystic emerald layer of the chakra of unlimited divine wisdom. This is where your teachers, guides and Ascended Masters connect to you.

Follow your roots into the great body of water. Float off into the lapis lazuli water as you begin to experience the vibration of the Om into the turquoise-indigo divine temples.

Feel your spirit going into divine consciousness ultraviolet light, cocooning you as you go up, up, up. The prismatic light begins to change as it takes its final launch into the vortex. As you step out of the ultraviolet cocoon, you step into the most magnificent of all the heavens. It hosts the most fantastical plants, magical creatures, and more flowers than you have ever seen. The colors, vibrations, and feelings of joy are amazing. You are divine love.

Two big, beaming divine beings, divine love and divine consciousness embrace your angelic being. All your initiations, new connections, and information is retained. Your angelic energy body travels with you, throughout all dimensions and space.

The golden-white light transitions into ultraviolet light as, once again, it cocoons around you. You enter the indigo womb of the universe to the oneness vibration of the Om that flows into the lapis lazuli waters. You reach the green valley of divine love that radiates out the central Sun or God Sun. As you walk into the divine womb, you slide down your golden thread of life back onto Mother Earth.

You walk through the vortex and step back into your body. Settle back into this present moment. Take three deep breaths and pull yourself into your physical self. Feel your new divine energy in you. Your new knowledge will all comfortably fit back into your being. Gently wiggle your way into your physical body. When you are ready, state one final time, "I am present" and include your exact location.

Give thanks to all the angels, guides, and Ascended Masters who helped you.

A Channeled Message about Mother Creatrix by www.Marigoldslove.com

I can feel her in my bones. She is the bones collector. She is the collector of the women's souls who were fragmented and lost and couldn't find their way out of the city in time before the fire. Her sweet cold bark welcomed them home, into her home, into her roots and her branches and into the cold dark Earth under her roots. She beckoned them to come to her, to find refuge in a world that was not very welcoming to them. They came in droves. Sometimes they would come and pray at her feet and offer her all of their sorrows and their worries. Sometimes they would bring her presents. Sometimes they would come after their physical bodies had been left behind and come to be a part of their soul's resting place before transitioning to another, freer existence. She took care of them. She talked to them. She let them know they were safe in her arms. She offered them wisdom and beauty and told them stories that soothed them, stories that a mother might tell a daughter to make her feel strong, brave, and confident. She could not save them all. She has been here and seen too many strife, wars, and conflicts to count. But she has also seen the beauty in the aftermath of strife, wars, and conflicts. She cannot change how the humans interact with one another, but she has seen how the daughters of those she has comforted have come back to thank her, to bless her, to offer gifts and laughter and song. She has witnessed women breaking down in front of her trunk, not knowing why or how they got there, but knowing, in their hearts, that this pilgrimage to see her was significant, and healing. What these daughters did not know in their consciousness was that their mothers had been saved by her, set their souls free after a lifetime of sorrow or loss or pain or servitude. These daughters, whether it be the star soul's daughter, a blood daughter, or the reincarnation of the mother born a daughter, would cry tears of joy at seeing the majestic tree's beautiful bark, her luscious leaves, and her strong base. Something inside of each of these daughters would be released upon seeing the tree, something inside would break open and set free ancestral wounds that had been stored in their tissues, their bones, but mostly inside of their hearts where the seeds of sadness had been planted long before they were born. Once these seeds had burst open and been released to the world, they would be transformed, into love, into grace, into a strength that defies boundaries. Those who were spiritually minded would often see their lineage and see why and how they got to this place. Those who were intuitive would laugh and know why and how they got to this place. And those who had trekked to the tree without either of these traits would also laugh and know why and how they got to this place. This tree had helped thousands upon thousands to transition from their earthly bodies into their ethereal bodies. She had her own feelings too. She felt the injustices of the world. She felt the sorrows of the women too. She felt rage and anger and sadness. But she also felt joy and peace and purpose. She was planted by one of the Mother Creatrix who knew that the spot in which this tree's sapling would grow would become a portal directly to the Divine Feminine, to Sophia Gaia's heart. This Mother Creatrix had outsmarted one of the less moral of the Creator Gods and swept down to plant this sapling without any of her compatriots knowing or seeing what had happened. She transplanted it from that world where there is no hurt, pain, or suffering. She infused it with Divine Love and put thorns on it to trick the Creator Gods into thinking she was one of them. But they were wrong. And this tree is a testament to how the Divine Feminine has many facets and many wiles that are represented by all of the Goddesses. We cannot change the history of our past, but we can revisit the feelings we feel, and we can change the feelings that we feel now in the present about the past. We can reframe our past. That Mother Creatrix knew what she was doing. And so do you. And so, do I. We simply have to follow our hearts and remember who we are and let no one stand in our way. So be it.

CHAPTER 10

*The tenth dimension is the connection of
everything to everything, all beings are
enlightened with Unity Consciousness.*

Many people believe the higher dimension in physics is the end of
dimensional growth. "String theory" is our closest understanding
of how we are all connected, not just with each other and Earth but also as
an intergalactic web connecting all dimensions in all the universes.

Here in the tenth dimension, all possibilities exist: all multi-universes,
all outcomes of free will, and *ALL*'s will exist. The web of life holds the
past of Earth's history. Another way to think about the tenth dimension
is "spiritual mycelium." Imagine the microscopic fungus connects all
plant matter underground. Now imagine it in outer space, or in the tenth
dimension as the web of life.

Once I was shown that everywhere I have been I leave my sparkle. Like
footprints of energy, I left a tiny thin sparkling trail. This stream of sparkle
has been deposited everywhere I have stepped, driven, or flown over. Every
sentient being leaves their own trail. Some are dark "egew" trails and others
are light. For thousands of years the dark trails have been more than the
light trails. Only in Earth's most recent history are the light trails starting
to overcome the trails of fear.

Cords are a more common spiritual term used. What I saw as trails of
light, string like, is often referred to as cords. There are many books and
theories about cords of attachment. It is called string theory in scientific
terms. When a person, place, or thing creates an attachment to you or you
to it, a cord is created. The most common understanding of such a cord is

the umbilical cord; here is where the mother is attached to the child. This is the strongest "cord of attachment."

Other types of cords of attachments come from people around you, not just friends or family. Many people say they feel like puppets and that jobs or bosses "hold their strings." When you understand string theory, you see they kind of do. You can allow cords of attachment to control your every thought, almost as if you're possessed. When too many cords get built up, people feel buried or overwhelmed by everything.

I understood cords very clearly when I was going through a divorce. The cord of attachment to a spouse or partner is in the heart, but my first husband had me in my uterus area as a mother to a child. Rather, I held him in this area by enabling him. I was able to feel his pain as a mother does that of a child. I could feel his joy, his sorrow, his knee pains. I had wrongly placed his cord of attachment to me like a mother to a child, not a spouse to a spouse or a partnership of love. He loved me, and I loved him, but not in divine love. Instead, we loved each other in an enabling way, where we supported each other's bad habits, instead of growing together.

It took several prayers to White Light Angel Michael to remove this cord and free myself from my own doing. We are the ones who allow the attachments. Therefore, we are ones who can free ourselves from them. When I finally removed the cord with help from others, Bob felt it immediately. He texted me to ask what was wrong only ten minutes after the prayer to remove it. I felt light and free from my own thoughts. I freed myself from him by removing the cord of attachment.

Another lesson to learn in this dimension is "as above so below." It is a super popular cliché in the spiritual world. Still, I have used it. People say it, but do they truly understand it? Some believe that Earth is just a battlefield of good versus bad. As I have already explained, that would not be possible in the "above" heavens since no evil exists outside of Earth. This is the above area where everything plays out just as it is. I think it is more of what is going on with the collective physically can be represented in whole Earth.

RACHEL OTTO

What Is String Theory?

An excerpt from Space.com helps to answer that question:

*String theory is the idea in theoretical physics that reality
is made up of infinitesimal vibrating strings, smaller than
atoms, electrons, or quarks. According to this theory, as
the strings vibrate, twist and fold, they produce effects in
many, tiny dimensions that humans interpret as everything
from particle physics to large-scale phenomena like gravity.*

*String theory has been held up as a possible "theory
of everything," a single framework that could unite
general relativity and quantum mechanics, two
theories that underlie almost all modern physics.*[4]

***

All possibilities play out in this dimension. A silly, yet good example of all the possibilities is from the movie series *The Avengers*. In the epic battle to stop the warlord Thanos from destroying all of creation, Dr. Strange, the mystical arts superhero, goes into meditation. In meditation, Dr. Strange goes into the tenth dimension, where he can see all possibilities. He goes through more than 14 million possibilities of actions to stop the destruction of Thanos. Of course, since it is the movies, he takes the action of the 14,550,001, where peace would ultimately be found, and the universe is saved.

How I have meditative experiences is kind of similar; well, not to the extreme of the end of the world. My years spent as a meeting planner made me cautious of all possibilities. I planned outdoor events, large conventions, and short outings I had to be conscious of all the problems that may come up. Weather was always an issue. Mother Earth's events were the worst-case scenario. Concerns of heat, cold, rain, floods, winds, hurricanes would race in my mind. I would also consider the individual attendee. What if someone had a stroke or an allergic reaction to the food? The possibilities

---

[4] Charlie Wood and Vicky Stein, "What Is String Theory," Space.com, January 20, 2022.

would play out in my mind. Eventually I would get to a place where I was fully prepared for multiple outcomes.

With all my over planning and consideration with deep contemplation, playing out each scenario in my head, nothing majorly bad ever happened. Only one time was I truly caught off guard—and by my own mistake. I had planned a huge party at the Hard Rock Café on the wrong night. I had written the wrong day for the event on the schedule. My greatest fear had come true and I faced it.

Funny enough, it seems the greatest fear is our own freedom, choice. Your free will. As you come into your own personal power, you'll face fear of what you can and can't do. Evil is going against us out of fear of our free will. Evil is only a human feeling. Tricksters, dark shadows, and voodoo are not evil. Humankind just warps them into evil out of fear. In the tenth dimension, we can see how fear plays a role in limiting free will. Evil exists for control, a desire for power or a mental issue that is so deeply imbedded in a person's psyche that 24-hour observation is necessary.

From 1984 until 2012, I was super into conspiracy theories, prophecies, and the end of time beliefs. In the nineties, I worked in a convention center in rural Nebraska, listening to militia groups who wanted to take up arms. Only 25 years later did they try to overthrow the US government on January 6th. I was lost in the human egew of fear, hate, and mistrust, alongside religious groups making claims about the end of times. I was ready for the worst of humanity. What I found instead of hate and fear was our Creator. I found the Source of all the universe inside of *me*! Crazier than finding this most perfect unconditional love within myself was knowing that everyone has it. The closer I try to live within God's will for me, the simpler and happier life has become.

Now is the great awakening. I know it's hard to see or understand as we stand in the "now" movement of it. What we as a collective are experiencing is a true transition into unconditional love and divine consciousness. I, like many, feel the anxiety and fear, the lies, the hate, and all the "isms" that have made our world what it was, not what it can be. With the current mixed messages coming from churches and governments, who knows what to believe? Not just the United States is being polarized, all parts of the world have different issues they are dealing with. I know what to believe in.

Believe in you. Believe in the God spark that connects you to everything from the fly to the plastic cup. I admit I had been concerned about the state of the United States, until one birthday. For three days, the sky hosted a huge sunbow, or a rainbow circle that followed me from Palm Springs to Sedona. It was a sign, just like the one God sent to Moses. I know this was God's promise of unconditional love and of the unlimited possibilities that await each of us. Yes, we will have earthquakes, hurricanes, and fires. But I know God loves each of us so much that, by taking our daily actions of self-love and tolerance, we will always be taken care of. God's gang of love and light only wants *your* happiness. This was a promise that we no longer needed to suffer! Life is a wheel. We're just flowing with it. The rainbow wheel shows all tribes, all colors working as one. This gives us a lesson for what we will achieve and how to get along. That's it, folks. The great mystery of life is to learn how to get along with one another. Now is the time to step into *your* happiness!

We individuals can create a peaceful world. It is not just voting or going to church that will bring peace. It is up to you to love you. It is a global reconnection of the individual to oneself. Once we start that singular point of one individual, as in string theory, the vibrations of life connect all of us. We need to have peace inside of ourselves to save the external world. The balance or the peace we feel vibrates out with the relationships we have with all things. Like a drop of water into a pond, the rings of our peace echo out into the surrounding area.

For some people, as they transition into consciousness and divine love, they go through what feels like a death process. This is a process of releasing old ways, the old you. Sometimes even physical changes happen to you. You might lose weight, have hair grow back or ulcers going away.

As we change, so does our past. Some call it karma clearing. The transition of our past is choosing to let go of old ways, forgiving ourselves and others. We need to keep growing, allowing old thoughts and anger to die off and keep transitioning forward.

We, as a collective, are in training for these higher dimensions and understanding that we still can't fully comprehend. Unity Consciousness helps the masses of people gain divine consciousness with ease and grace. There is no adverse response from healing, just a way of happiness becoming main steam instead of fearing everything.

Fear of change, fear of any kind should not deter us. Unity Consciousness is understanding everything is connected and all things are made of the same energy. It happens when we choose divine love, everyone we encounter is changed by us on some level. We are beacons of divine love and understanding. Do not worry about how we will do this or even what roles you should play. Just know that you are on the right path, and everything you do is moving toward the ultimate goal of world peace, bringing a higher consciousness to the human race.

Start getting to know astral realms within

It's good to start within when doing astral travel or astral projection. Go inside your own energy. Finding the balance of your life and your health is the goal of astral traveling. It comes from understanding from within. Traveling to other heavens or astral planes is easier. In the astral realms we can follow the "thread of life" or the connections we all have with everything. Going through the cosmic chakra system is an easy introduction to astral planes and feeling how they are all connected. Here is a basic understanding of the chakras of the cosmos. You could just go visit one area or take a trip to all of them.

Prismatic Divine Love

We start as pure love and light in the astral realms. It is a prismatic space, with no defined shape. It is brighter than we can see so it just appears as millions of rainbows. It is like sparkles of love that fill infinite space with divine love. As you go in and out of various astral locations, you will travel in with divine love in divine conscious light. When imagining this space you can think of it as a tunnel in a cave, a light tube or quartz hallway.

First Cosmic Chakra, Saturn

This is a golden platinum color. Imagine that you're walking on red ground on Saturn. Feel the land beneath your feet. Envision red rocks, like those found in Colorado or Arizona. Walk toward a huge canyon wall with a brilliant orange cave. Here is the cosmic soul star, connecting all the universe. See your golden-silver cord of life trailing behind you as you are still connected to your physical self. Imagine walking on the red planet towards the orange cave.

Second Cosmic Chakra, Sirius

Next enter the pale silver pink cosmic womb of the second cosmic chakra. In this prismatic salmon colored cosmic womb is where you find seedling ideas, creativity bouncing around, and abundant life. Here is where to go to find inspiration and creation. Feel the light codes and high energy here. When you are ready walk toward the bright yellow light at the end of the crystal cave.

Third Cosmic Chakra, Helios the Central Sun

Become one with the cosmic sun, Helios. Feel the divine energy spiral through your being as you become one with the creator you are. Here you can feel how much the world loves you. This is the center of universal happiness with swirling colors of golden orange and bright yellow gold. Become a beam of sunlight and flow into divine love.

Fourth Cosmic Chakra, Venus

As a sunbeam, you enter the most incredible pink and bright white space, almost as if you were in a gigantic rose bloom. Venus is like walking on clouds while being tickled. Feel the compassionate energy of the ascended masters of Divine Love, Holy Inanna, Isis, Quan Yin, White Tarot, Shakti, Holy Mother Mary, Mary Magdalene. Whomever you feel or whatever higher deity is drawn to you. Feel as this rose color loving energy moves into your being. Explore the valley on Venus filled with divine love goddesses. Slowly float towards the beautiful body of water.

Fifth Cosmic Chakra, Mercury

The living water of the cosmic consciousness is light blues with golden silver undertones. This is no ordinary body of water. Instead, this is pure love energy; it is the healing love energy fluid that will heal and clear. Communicate with higher beings in this space. Speak your truths and hear what others are trying to tell you. Float into the Great Eye of *ALL*.

Sixth Cosmic Chakra, Jupiter

As you enter Jupiter, the universal third eye, you are seeing out of the eyes of your highest self. Here, you can freely fly throughout the cosmos. Gain new spiritual gifts and insights in this golden silver ultraviolet pink space. This infinite, unlimited space opens all pathways to universal knowledge instantly. Become part of the cosmos and fly through all universes, past stars, suns, planets like a meteor traveling space.

Seventh Cosmic Chakra, Uranus

On Uranus a lime green silver light of divine consciousness and divine wisdom fill your being. Divine leaders of wisdom guided by love are Noah, Jesus Christ, Osiris, Buddha, Shiva, or whomever you feel drawn to. Allow this new energy to flow down your crown into your brain stem and down your spine. Feel as it energizes your spine to completion by connecting into all the cosmic chakras, expanding you. Here you become one with *ALL*. Become the conscious light itself, feel the highest vibration of divine consciousness.

To expand your experience, check out "Cosmos Chakra Meditation" on Vimeo, a guided meditation for the cosmos chakra experience found at https://vimeo.com/697818846

When Asked

When asked to taste your happiness,
It was delectable—creamy sweet and savory all in one bite.
When asked to see your happiness,
It was you looking out at your backyard,
A happy place, a proud space of yours.
When asked to hear your happiness.
It was a child's giggle.

A laugh so contagious it made you smile.
The child was you.
When asked to feel your happiness.
It was a dreamy state of cheers to you.
A feeling of achieving your desires.
When you wanted happiness, you couldn't feel it,
When you wanted God, you asked others where it was.
You want yourself to be happy, to be safe.
Neither of those are outside of you.
Both of these are already in you.
You just forgot.
ALL is within you!
The myth of separation came true.
Take a breath and find that one space inside you.
Find divine love and let it transform you.
Love is not on the outside.
ALL is within you.
It's the internal that grows from you.
It's the conscious light that connects *ALL*.
Your happiness is you!
Your dreams get to come true!
Love is you!
You are love!
You are *ALL!*
ALL is within you.

CHAPTER 11

The eleventh dimension is Helios which hosts the Akashic records. A library of everything that has ever existed.

Helios is the name for the great central sun. It is the home of beings of light and hosts the Akashic records in the eleventh dimension. In this dimension, beings take account and keep an unbiased record of past lives. Here in the Akashic records is also where you can find your individual contract with *ALL*. This contract tells of what lessons you must learn during your lifetime. It is also a place to where oversouls get ready for their next journey back to Earth for their next life.

Helios is what I call "highest of the heavens". The higher realms of beings of light and ascended masters exist here. This is where we can find the realms of the Orishas and other deities like Ganesh, White Tara, and Buddha. There are other heavenly dimensions from the seventh to the ninth. Here are the highest heaven or realms for otherworldly beings too, like the Sirus and Pleiadeans.

As I understand, before an oversoul enters a physical form on planet Earth they must wipe out the memories of the thousands upon thousands of lives the oversoul lived or experienced. It makes sense, at three years old, to know how to speak a hundred different languages may be confusing. Or have psychologists diagnose you with multiple personality disorder by age five. It would become too chaotic, too overwhelming to know everything as a child. One would go mad hearing different thoughts and being tied to old perspectives, instead of having a unique experience.

When I say "drank the Kool-Aid" to forget past lives, it doesn't mean those memories are inaccessible. In this case "Kool-Aid" is the reference to a magical elixir that is taken by the oversoul before it enters an Earth avatar. Our physical body can be thought of like a car. The oversoul comes down from heaven into a shiny brand-new car. It is up to the oversoul, or the new Earth soul to take care of the car. Just like our physical body, the car needs a driver, the oversoul, gas to make it work, food and water, and maintenance, taking care of the body.

My earliest childhood memories were when I was about two or three years old. My nana and papa lived on a farm in Orchard, Nebraska. They had a really old swing set. I remember very clearly it had one rusty swing, one broken trapeze bar, and a plastic horse on the red triangle stand.

I thought that the horse was real. It was so real in my world that I ran inside to fetch my Aunt Cathy and Aunt Nettie. "Look! Look at what the horse did. It went poo-poo!" I said gleefully as I proudly showed them how this plastic horse was able to take a little poop right below itself.

My aunts didn't believe me that the plastic swinging horse had come to life to poop. To this day, I swear I stepped into the fourth dimension, and that the constipated plastic horse finally let out all it was holding onto. I remember being scolded about being a lady. Just because we lived on a farm didn't mean I could act that way. I was supposed to be a young lady in my yellow sunflower dress.

This event triggered a memory in me. About that time, I was picking up words right and left. I was very chatty for a three-year-old. I went back outside the barn to go play with Aunt Cathy and Aunt Nettie. I remember standing up in the middle of the field, suddenly feeling completely panicked. The rest I don't remember, as I blacked out. It was my Aunt Cathy who recited the story to me years later. She said I looked her directly in the eyes and started speaking with a very thick accent. She said it might have been French or a Caribbean dialect. She could only understand a few words I was saying because I was talking in broken English. I kept asking her if my children were OK. "Are my children safe? Where are my children?"

It terrified my aunts that, out of this tiny body came this dramatic speech in a clear voice. A voice not of a sweet little girl. Apparently, I gave details about who I was, where I was from, and what I was looking for. I demanded to know where my children were and what had become of them. She did not know what to say or how to answer me.

In fact, my aunt only whispered the story to me back when I was in high school and once again after college. It was not to be spoken about out loud. No one wanted the first grandchild to be put into a mental institution by age three. Then there was another event that was never explained, and the only one who could explain it to me is no longer alive on this plane.

This was one of my past lives, a piece of my oversoul's history, coming through that was never discussed or truly explained to me as a child. Somehow in that early time of my life, parts of my oversouls memory broke through. Apparently, the elixir memory wipe didn't completely take. Parts of my memory and my spiritual energies started flooding in. My higher self realized this was not the time to figure out the karma of my past lives. Nor was it the right age to have spiritual gifts given to me. Instead, it was the time to learn what being a human child in the 1970s was like. This was when I "capped" myself or my highest self collaborated with my oversoul, to hold back the knowledge until I went searching for it.

Years later, I would meet a healing shaman named Rebecca Green. She is a wonderful and insightful teacher. Rebecca introduced me to different forms of meditation. She opened doors to questions I had about myself and past lives I had memories of. Her techniques are gentle, yet so powerful that the lessons are still at the top of my mind. Rebecca helped me see the whole story of the woman who had shown herself to my aunts. In this lifetime I ran the household on a Caribbean plantation. I was in-charge of the house slaves. After an uncontrollable event happened, my eldest son sold me into slavery to be sent away from the island. I died in Mississippi alone. The memories came flooding back to me bringing me to tears.

Rebecca helped me clear this past karma. Other seers and healers told me the same story of this life. They would describe it in different ways. Yet all saw the same details, like the black cast iron pot I would cook in every night and the story always ended the same way with me dying alone in slavery in a distant land.

I even met up with one of the children from this past life. While having lunch with a client, we both spiritually stepped into the memory. It was like a scene in a movie. At one point, we were physically eating in a fancy restaurant in Jackson Square. The next, she was running to me. It was a beautiful island plantation. I could clearly see my cooking pot and what I was making for dinner. We would have stayed in this memory together if the waiter had not come to the table with a check to kick us out. He was weirded out that we'd sat for twenty minutes just staring into each other's eyes, not saying a word.

The area where anyone can find information on their past lives is held within the Akashic records. This is the ultimate, galactic library of everything that ever happened. Really, a complete unbiased recording of *every second* of Earth's and the entire universe's existence. It is a galactic library bigger than Earth itself. The Akashic records contain the history of everything created *everything*. It has the record of *ALL*'s creations.

This is bigger than any library we can imagine. The technology that holds these images, these memories is beyond what science can explain. It is organized by your legal name at birth, similar to governments' ways of keeping records. Instead of a social security number, we are arranged by our birthdate, birth time, birth year and city, state, and country of birth.

When someone says they can time travel, they most likely have entered into these realms. It does feel like a movie for some readers of the records. Once, I had a friend open the records for me as I was sitting next to her. Before she could tell me what she saw, I saw it playing out like a security video. I was able to see myself as an Egyptian high priestess doing a ceremony. Another Egyptian priest stepped behind me and stabbed me in the back of heart on my altar. I sat and watched the priest and his followers collect my blood. I had been doubled-crossed by my own people.

I have had others go into my records to clear me, and none was as vivid as this incident. This was when I recognized that time travel is not what we thought it was. Here in the records, you can only watch and feel what happened; you can't change the actual events. What you can change is how it affects you in the present moment. We have the ability to forgive ourselves and others who have cursed or accused us. This is what is called clearing your karma or clearing your records. This has been confused with time travel. You can see the past here, but it's like you are a fly just observing. Only forgiving it can heal the past. We can only make things better for ourselves, not worse. We can only change our past with divine love. By forgiving our past mistakes or regressions we can clear the record. It is called clearing your karma. Forgive yourself for your past mistakes.

It is here in the eleventh dimension where the Akashic records are kept. You can access them through the sixth dimension's portals, but they "exist" in the eleventh dimension. This is where *ALL* can experience everything you have. This is where joy was to be built up for *ALL* to experience.

I know amazing Akashic readers, like Cindy Hamilton. She can help you clear your past lives. Clearing at this level takes place outside the physical body. By letting go of traumas, contracts to self, and old karma, you can heal your body, break habits, or find a peace that was missing.

With love and kindness Cindy can release you from what you don't know is holding you back. Even stepping on her land can clear away guilt causing pain within your body. Cindy is the greatest healer I have personally experienced. Her ability to love unconditionally and her connection to *ALL* is, well I can't even properly express it. I can't even compare her to another person on this planet. Cindy can help you understand what blocks you have in your life. Other Akashic readers have tapped my blocks or curses from past lives out of my feet. Yet Cindy was able to explain my issues not just claim to remove them.

We must come to an understanding that we can no longer allow fear and guilt of the collective consciousness to control us. We need to let go of the past, clear the Akashic records of what no longer serves us. My records are constantly being cleared on higher levels. Cindy still clears out negative creeps that come into my physical body. I have no desire to investigate my oversouls past. Many questions for me have already been answered. When I need advice or help, I investigate my own chakras and figure out who to ask for help. I believe our excitement and thoughts should go towards a future of divine love. Getting stuck in the past doesn't allow for any forward growth or movement.

If understanding your past is of interest to you, it is worth going to a professional like Cindy or Rebecca. For me, it's brought closure to my old habits. Helped me be who I am at this moment. People can get lost in the past. They may try to make their current lives emulate their past lives. That is not the purpose of reading your records. It is to learn how to be better in this lifetime. Stick with a professional, just like you would not go see a college student for heart surgery.

Meditation: Dragons Breath

This is a healing breath that can be used anytime, anywhere. Call up the angelic dragon inside you. This is a technique that came to me naturally and has a great healing energy. I call it dragon's breath referring to their dragon like form.

I have found it is very close to ujjayi or victorious breathing in the yoga tradition, just adding more power behind it. To understand the mechanics behind this breath, watch one or both of these videos on YouTube— "Ujjayi/Victorious Breathing" by Ekhart Yoga (https://www.youtube.com/watch?v=kQA_VQcJLv4) or "Ujjayi Breathing" by Yoga with Adriene (https://www.youtube.com/watch?v=IQrsJ-yZWV8).

The difference between ujjayi breath and cosmic dragons' breath is the universal healing energy. This breath is used to clear out blocks in chakras, to remove possessions, to clear karma, and to release people from fear. It can be used in the present moment or can be used in guided meditation. It can be used on others or on yourself.

It is very simple to use. When you are ready to try dragons' breath, first, as always, make sure you are grounded. As the above videos describe, it doesn't matter if you are standing or sitting, but what does matter is that your spine is straight!

Breathe in through your nose and out your mouth with no sound when you first start. Feel the energy build in your hara or chi point (which is two fingers below your belly button, inside of you). We want to build our energy here; focus on divine love, the conscious light flowing.

You may even call upon a specific being of light to come through your breath. You can call upon the color or the healing energy of your personal beliefs, your guides. It is not limited in anyway; you can just call for a guide for the highest good or healing.

After a few breaths, or once you feel the power has built up in your hara, on your next exhale, let it flow out of the back of your throat. Feel the heat, the energy as you exhale out with power.

Allow the energy to flow out. Don't force anything. Allow the energy to come out and do what is needed. Let the fiery breath clear, energize, and rejuvenate you.

Sound may follow with the breath out. Feel as though you are breathing colored, conscious, love energy light—like a fire-breathing dragon.

Sit with it in meditation and feel your own energy build. It is possible to send this without sound or drama of any kind. I tend to make a loud sound as the energy flows out with great love. You do what feels right to you, just try it!

Cosmic Dragons' Message

New cosmic dragon portals have opened on Earth! Thousands of these beautiful, open light beings have come here. The fourth, the fifth, and the amazing third dimensional dragons are here too. Remember, these are *spiritual dragons*!

Cosmic dragons are ancient, wise, and ethereal. Openhearted beings from the angelic kingdoms, they reside alongside guardian angels and unicorns. They exist on waves of light vibrations of love. They work together for the highest good of *ALL*. Angelic dragons do not have free will like we humans do. Their only desire is to serve *ALL* to spread divine love, wisdom, and light wherever they go.

Light and love radiate from the hearts of the cosmic dragons forming their etheric wings. They are like bolts of electricity radiating high energy. The center of their crown is so developed that, at times, it seems as if they have more than one head. They are the gamma ray angels of the highest ranks. The gamma ray beings radiate divine love that is unimaginable to us and creates a shining aura resembling six imposing wings. *ALL* has given the spiritual dragons a gift that they can deconstruct and create.

The angels maintain the vision, while the dragons manifest it. They can even create physical objects! Amazingly the cosmic dragons vibrate in all dimensions. Most of the people on Earth live in a third dimensional, material world with a closed heart. When people begin to enter the fourth dimension as they learn to open their hearts to love. Third dimensional people can experience a fourth dimensional world when they have a joyful moment of love. But alas, the people then close their hearts and return to the third dimensional world, and the dragon energy disappears.

The cosmic dragons are incredible because, unlike other heavenly creatures, they can travel effortlessly between dimensions by adjusting their vibrations. *ALL* has given them a long and slender reptilian-like body that allows them to pierce dimensions and glide easily through space. They can plunge into spaces that other beings of light cannot enter. The cosmic dragons can exhale ethereal fire, purifying, and transforming dense energies into love.

Cosmic dragons are masters of purification. When you need to travel through dimensions while meditating or sleeping, ask a cosmic dragon to take you there. Travel safely under its wings. The cosmic dragons have been released!

CHAPTER 12

The twelfth dimension is knowing your absolute self, you are ALL and home to the grand cosmic council of ALL.

W hen I thought about writing this book, the nineth dimension felt like that was enough to explore. Then quantum physics opened a higher understanding of dimensions. For example, it is like using the String Theory to understand the tenth dimension as the web of life. All of this was a new understanding for me. The eleventh dimension is Helios and with some places best left for those trained in akashic records. I had been taught that as a light worker I did not need to go any higher than the nineth dimension to help humanity. Then two events changed my mind on higher dimensional work.

One conversation with a very well-known channeler of Archangel Gabriel piqued my curiosity. On a sunny afternoon in Palm Desert, Gabriel began to speak directly to me. I was open to receiving messages. After what I'd experienced in Los Angeles with the refrigerator experience, I felt comfortable talking with any object or spirit. In this conversation, I was told and shown my soul's age. I understood a larger perspective of *ALL* than I ever had.

Archangel Gabriel told me of my memories from the beginning of time were real. This was not something most people had or could access. The being of light explained what I'd thought was a dream of myself in a perfect state with *ALL* was not a dream. Rather, it was a glimpse of my oversoul. My oversoul is linked to the cosmic creation dust. It is a small sparkle from every planet, moon, star, sun in all the universe. On Earth, I can see, feel, and understand my connection to stars and planets. I can trace my soul lineage deep into the unknown before the stars were even formed.

I remembered about age five trying to understand gravity. I could not figure out why we needed beds. I also struggled to understand why we were not floating. For years in my youth, I would dream of floating in the great void to make me feel comfortable.

In my late forties, I remembered being in my oversoul's natural state. This memory was of incredible energy of *ALL*'s unconditional love energy shooting out of my head. The power of a million supernovas emulated from me. I was holding the beautiful, prismatic void or womb space for all the universes with a few other beings. We held the space while They Who Have No Name was creating galaxies, stars, and planets.

It was in this personal conversation that was not in my head, my thoughts were confirmed. A third dimensional conversation with the being of light Gabriel, speaking directly to me. The angel told me that I existed in the twelfth dimension. They told me I was older than them. Gabriel went on saying that I have a soul lineage that goes back to the beginning of time. As this information exploded through my cells, I was in awe. The confirmation of what I had been experiencing began to take shape within me. The twelfth dimension is not a glorious place to clear karma or a healing with Christ consciousness. Instead, it is the never-ending committee meeting on how *ALL*'s great plan is going. Discussing how *ALL*'s will is taking shape.

The twelfth dimension is where you will find your absolute self. Where all parts of our individual soul are completely one. It is a space where the highest of all universal beings—or, again, what may be called aliens or beings of light, entities we do not fully understand—also find their perfect oneness.

In this highest of heavens, they gather to keep the entire universe, all its galaxies, and all its constituents in the flow of divine love. Basically, it's like a 24-7 United Nations conference that never ends.

I never felt any fight for power in these meetings. Unlike in human meetings, where people struggle for power, here, everyone was equal. They truly existed for the highest good of *ALL*. They are *ALL*'s appendages. Before I had seen *ALL* or the Creative Source as living water of high energy of love, this dimension was the most physical reality of *ALL*.

As I told my friend Vanessa about this place, she knew exactly what I was talking about. From her perspective, it was a very special temple that she could see into but did not enter. It looked like twelve beings whose faces you could not see, as if they were looking into the void. They stood around Metatron's cube in astral form as discussion went on in their mind space, not using voices. She knew these were part of a high council, not here to judge but, instead, to guide for the highest good of *ALL*. That was the important part both she and I understood. These were not judges. Nor were they just creator or destroyer beings. Rather, they were the representatives of the major entities of the universes. I think she saw no faces because they each had different representative circulates in and out as needed. They were not one singular being but, instead, a collective consciousness of different entities. I saw more than twelve. I do not think the exact number matters. What we both understood was this was where *ALL*'s will for the highest good moves forward guided by divine love.

These colossal beings were all the souls, all the entities, all the stars and planets of the universe, and of all dimensions—everything. It was a oneness with *ALL*, not a division or hierarchy.

I have heard others say it was like being in the mouth of the greatest crystalline dragon. The highest of the gamma rays in their natural habitat. The great beast would swirl and consume what was surrounding it to transform it for the highest good of *ALL*. There is no "I" in this space. A place of transformation to the perfection of what we can be. This makes sense to me, since I wasn't even aware I was traveling in this dimension.

I still do not fully comprehend this level of consciousness of the twelfth dimension. It is beyond any image, sound, or vibration on our plane. It is not of conflict or of control. It is true compassion and a forward way of being I can't express. It's like that first thrill of a roller-coaster ride, that first second that is expansive from within. It's where the highest deities, the ascended masters convene. It is everything. It is the beginning and the end. It is infinite.

The twelfth dimension is a space my words can hardly describe. No words are spoken there, not even light language. It is pure sound that is a singular vibration. Colors, feelings, music, and movement beyond our dreams. It is not the past, present, or future. It is and will always be the space of the *now* moment.

The closest way I can help you feel and comprehend this dimension is only with sound. Digital images and videos work for eleventh and lower dimensions. We can grasp an understanding with our eyes. Here in the twelfth, it is as though we are experiencing all of our physical senses at once. Movement and music can give us this feeling. There are several cosmic musicians who can bring you to this state. Tom Kenyon's was the first sound that took me out into the sixth dimension. Dr. Todd's Lemurian Choir not only takes you to a higher dimension but also helps you download higher knowledge that can truly expand your astral traveling.

This is also an area you may not completely experience on your first journey or any journey. The twelfth dimension requires balance and a desire to expand. You need to clean yourself karmically before the doors open to you. You have to be free of your ego here. Free yourself from worries. Know with confidence that you are a cocreator. You must be willing to let go of everything. Openly and humbly walk into the void with only divine love in your heart. In plain English, you must achieve self-love.

The second experience that opened me to the twelfth dimension was an emergency hysterectomy. My uterus had been compromised. Polyps, fibroids, cysts, and a tumor had invaded my womb space. This was not the first time I had to medically deal with my reproductive organs. For my thirty birthday I had a small watermelon sized tumor on my right ovary. The mature teratomas had to be completely removed, ovary and all. Since we did not know if it was cancerous or not, a section of the left ovary was also removed. I was so grateful for it not being cancerous. In the process, I lost my right ovary.

From 2017 until 2023 I was in the emergency room four times dealing with uterine issues. Several doctors and professionals with high tech tools told me I had two fully functioning ovaries. They would show me photographs and on computer screens. One doctor sent me home after doing an ultrasound. She said I had a perfectly normal uterus with two normal ovaries. The doctors did not think I needed a hysterectomy in 2017 after an ectopic pregnancy where I almost bleed to death.

It was a true miracle that I had grown back the right ovary. In June 2023, I was told that the miracle of my growing back my right ovary needed to be removed. I was crushed to lose what I had worked so hard to regain.

With only a week notice before surgery, I began to meditate to let go of the injured organs. I sent healing energy to my future self. I cried for the loss, the death of my uterus and ovaries. In the first message I received, I was told that growing back my right ovary was not a miracle. We are the miracle- living on Earth is the miracle. Each day we are given is a miracle.

To her great surprise, my surgeon told me after the surgery that she only found one ovary. The surgical photographs of my organs showed only the left ovary. She was confused by this as she was one of the doctors who had shown me on the big screen that I had two ovaries. My personal theory is that I had energetically created a right ovary with my Rainbow Reiki training.

After the surgery I was lost in pain and confusion. I could not meditate. I felt completely disconnected from everything. I was fortunate to have healers work on me daily. They would clear out the machines' energies in me: from the tube down my throat to the laparoscopic robotic arms inside my body. I purged out the anesthesia for days after. It would take several healers to clear out the gunk from the surgery.

I tried to go to healing temples in meditation. Places I normally could visit in the blink of an eye would not allow me to enter. I could not get into any healing environments. A week after the surgery, I was still not healing. I got shingles, a bladder infection and horrible headaches from the CO_2 gas used. I was doing my best to heal yet felt nothing. No fuzzy feeling of energy, no joy in my heart, no divine love, just sleeplessness, numbness, and pain.

Then one night as I tried to get into a healing state, the guides took me somewhere else. I felt myself being water, all night long. In my dream state, I started out as a drop of water falling from the sky. I joined other drops in a small stream down a mountain. For a moment I froze and turned into ice. As the sun melted the ice, the stream became a waterfall, then a raging river. I was swallowed and released by several animals along the way. I kept moving forward into the lands and into the ocean. This was not the end as I evaporated back into clouds to do it all over again! My understanding of water has since changed. It no longer means to me stay in the flow, instead it means to be flexible. To be transformative like water, which exists in all forms- liquid, solid and gas.

The next evening, I became air. I was air in lungs of animals, a cool breeze, a tornado, and a haboob. This experience taught me the power of spiral breath and how to be open. I learned how to flow with the ups and downs of life, not to go against but to flow forward. The third night, I became Earth. Not heavy mountains, but the underground mycelium and crystal caves. I became the foundation of all reality, a cornerstone of future buildings. The fourth night, I was light, fire energy. I felt the colors of life as a rainbow. I felt the process of photosynthesis. I was a beam of sunlight to being absorbed by a flower, then was eaten by an animal to give them energy. On the fifth night, I was sound. At first it made me nauseous. It was a high and low vibration all at once. With the lessons I had learned from air and water, I was able to let go of physical reality and flow with sound. I traveled with OM from its present point back to Source.

The next day would be the summer solstice. I knew it could have the energy to help me complete my healing cycle. Unknowingly I ate no meat for two days, had no alcohol for months, even stopped cannabis use. For the first time in years, I did not join up with a group or do an international group mediation to help open a portal or invite in the summer energy. Instead, a lovely friend sent me a guided meditation to invite the energy back into myself.

After the meditation I sat outside. Soon my backyard was full of birds. The two hummingbirds who lived there did a dance for me. A prairie falcon flew in to check in on me. A roadrunner stopped by to say hello and reminded me I was not alone. Then a northern cardinal came to tell me what I needed to do next. He very loudly sang to me about my spiritual umbilical cord that was just floating out into nowhere. He explained how I was cut with a knife, not just physically but also spiritually. I was disconnected at my bellybutton. At first, I thought he meant connect to my mom. I did not feel right to connect to her. Then I thought he meant Mother Earth. As I energetically reached out, that was not it either.

I became frustrated. I knew I was disconnected. Then the cardinal swooped down to get my attention. Finally, I understood. The crimson red bird flew in an ankh form. I needed to connect back to myself! Using my imagination, I grabbed the free flowing energetical umbilical cord. I pulled it into a loop and inserted it into my new space. Like a lightning bolt, I could feel it again. I felt happy, I felt joy, I felt the fuzzy feeling of healing! My womb space could begin to heal.

This clearing time for me opened me up to a new comprehension of the twelfth dimension. The next meditation put me in the great council. My womb changed from organs to an astral crystal vortex. A different kind of creation space- the great void was not just in the cells of my body, but now had its own space. It would take me months to totally digest this new me.

Our politics are all made up of crisis. Media of all kinds, religions, all structures of humankind is all worthless outside of Earth. These systems have turned us against each other, created caste systems, built false hierarchies. None of our collective priorities are even real. We have gone away from the original meaning of this place we call Earth. We are here to learn how to get along with one another. So far it feels as though we are failing.

Yet in the great council they do not see failure. They do not see the war or the devastation of the land. They see forward movement. They do not judge us, nor do they want to help; they just observe. They are recording the expression of a place of free will.

The twelfth dimension is for those on paths to enlightenment or pure of heart. You do not get let in on drugs or with the help of plant medicine. Certain plant medicines can get you up to the eleventh dimension. However, they can't hold lessons. Plant or manmade medicines are not allowed in the space of the twelfth dimension or beyond. This is truly a place that comes with experience and balance from within. It is not a place for wishes or creation. Rather, it is a place where one's soul mind brings a completion of *ALL*'s will.

As with any special place you must be prepared in advance. Fasting or going on a vegetarian diet are good ways to prepare. Also do not eat processed foods, drink alcohol, caffeine, or tobacco. Be in good health overall. These simple steps lead to a far greater experience with any meditation. All of that is required to get into twelfth dimension.

Please know I am not recommending that you become a vegetarian or vegan. I cannot be vegetarian, or a vegan based on my blood type. A strictly vegetarian diet does not allow me to function at my highest level. For thirty days, with proper supplements, I can do a vegan diet. That will clean my liver and my gut. It also helps me get into higher states of consciousness.

Eating raw vegetables, ancient grains, and fruits clears out the toxins in our physical body. It is true that the more in tune you are with your body, the more you can experience.

If you really want to go all the way into the intergalactic high council, into the home of the great gamma ray beings, then prepare yourself. Do your shadow work, forgive yourself, and love yourself. Find your balance. Eat healthfully. Respect your body, your being. Believe in the future and fly. Let go of all your earthly possessions just for a moment. It is totally achievable. Who knows how high you can go? There are no limits to any of the dimensions, and I am pretty sure it continues past earthly knowledge.

I recorded a simple guided meditation that can help you experience this expansive oneness to start your own exploration of this dimension. To help you to experience this dimension, listen here to a guided meditation on my website, www.waychilllife.com

Daily Practice: Divine Stretch

Since the pandemic I have created my own daily ritual. It helps me feel the love and connect with guides every day. Getting help from guides is no longer limited to prayer or meditation. Instead, we can live in appreciative gratitude and in a constant connection to all things through divine love and divine consciousness. By doing the divine stretch daily, my life is happier.

The divine stretch can take place anywhere at any time. It's just something that I do first thing every morning. A simple practice of saying thank you and connecting in with everything for the day and then clearing off the day at night. The divine morning stretch connects you to guides, love and your Godspark. I love to do it outside facing the morning sun. In the evening, the divine evening stretch is a release from the day's drama. I do outside but both could be done anywhere inside as well.

To begin, start by touching the ground and say, "Thank You." A symbolic gesture to connect to Mother Earth. If you can touch your toes, or what feels good and hold it in a stretch for just a moment. Or you could do a pendulum swing by letting your arms hang down while having a flat back in tabletop position. Let your arms swing with the rhythm of the Earth.

Then say, "Thank You" with prayer hands at your heart level. Imagine that you are plugging into your heart chakra. Again, just holding for a few seconds to feel the flow of love energy.

Then lift your hands to your third eye, saying a third "thank you" to Father Sky. Do this three times and end by lifting your arms up to the sky. Next, slowly move your arms backwards making large circles.

As you are doing giant arm circles counterclockwise imagine you have roots coming out of your feet. Imagine your new roots are pulling up the energy of Mother Earth. Feel the connection to roots of other plants and trees by connecting to the mycelium beneath your feet. Do three to nine arm circles while pulling up divine love from Mother Earth.

Next, request that Father Sky come connect with you and bring in the divine consciousness. For this I do three to nine arm circles forward or clockwise. Open the crown of your head and invite in the divine consciousness.

After the arm circles of connection, open your heart to be guided by love. Do this by opening your arms out in front of you. At heart level do this action three to nine times. Intentionally ask to be guided by divine love and take actions of love.

After completing the heart to love, open the back of your heart to receive the guidance. Three to nine times, do the reverse, cross your arms across your chest. It is a self-hug. As you hug yourself putting a different arm in front each time, think "please allow all my ancestors and those who came before me to help guide me along my day".

After that first stretch and connection, I do my own version of tapping. Tapping or emotional freedom techniques can release a lot of anxiety. There are hundreds of YouTube videos of people doing EFT or tapping techniques. Check it out to learn what is best for you. I tap each side of my hand nine times, then I tap my crown nine times. When I do this, I think about how grateful I am for what I have now and what I want in the future.

After the crown I tap third eye nine times, under each eye nine times, under nose nine times, my chin nine times, my thyroid nine times at base of shoulder and finally under my arms nine times. I focus on gratitude for the now and what I would like to feel like in the future. After the tapping I do a shimmy to get the blood flowing.

During the day, take actions of love, step forward and choose love. Change your perspective. Change your story. Feel the medicine wheel of life daily. Acknowledge if it's a down day to pamper yourself and enjoy the up days. Do additional meditation if you feel like you are caught in negative guides or have anxiety you can't explain. Reaching out for help is an action of love when you just can't find the positivity for the day. The goal is living in balance. Find the middle point between depression and rambunctiousness and live at a medium pace.

Use the divine evening stretch to clear off the day. When you do the divine evening stretch, you let go of the day's dramas, whatever judgement you may have had. If you are holding onto pain or others' pain, wipe it off! It is called the angel wing wipe in some reiki practices. Literally, you're brushing off what you no longer need. Brush your arms together swiping in a downward motion. You can also shake off the day.

Pat down each arm three times. Next pat down the right side of your body three times, then the left side. Do the same to your legs. Pat down the front three times and then the side three times. Patting down is a way to stimulate the lymph nodes.

Next, dry brushing or brushing off the energy in your aura. Do this across your entire body. Brush off the energy you just tapped out. Brush down so that the Earth can recycle what you no longer need. Imagine as if you are clearing off the egew and the negative creeps. Send it to Mother Earth to be recycled.

End with the three thank you's by touching the ground, going to your heart, and lifting your hands in the air.

These simple practices will help you in many ways. If we would all do this practice, we would elevate this planet. It makes for a life full of ease and grace.

The universe is awesome! We can only begin to imagine what life could be. The universe goes with the flow, the Age of Aquarius is almost here. Bring this future peace and harmony into your daily life. We have been waiting for this time of transition. We know that what comes out of this is going to be absolutely amazing. Completely awesome! The way in which things happen is up to the universe. We have been experiencing a lot of transitions since the early 1900s, and even more to come! This is part of the expansion of Earth and all that is. It's going to be a constant change. That's why life is a continuous journey. Spirituality is not a place; it's flowing with the changes with gratitude and love.

Let's take this opportunity now to step outside of ourselves, to really be conscious of nature. As I watch the sunrise every day, it is a new promise—a new beginning every day! New beginnings come not just on New Year's Day or a new moon; a new opportunity happens every instant.

It's Divine Love, Not Luck

Thank you for reading my book! We have traveled through the twelve dimensions of life with the understanding of divine love. We all have different life experiences, yet they all give the same lesson, how to have a clearer understanding of life. We learned we control our lives through love. When we allow divine love and divine consciousness to guide our lives, we become the cocreators. Filling our being every morning with gratitude while we walk in love. When we are divine love, we can resolve issues with love. Some say it's like getting your magic back. Your good luck is working for you again. Your mojo is working.

I feel like, at times, I got my wish, and I have my X-Men superpowers that I dreamed of as a child. It happened. I can send out healing energy across all time and space. I have proven it to others time and time again. Clients across the world who I have never met can feel the energy, the divine love I carry.

I may fall or take two steps backward, and forget I am part of creation. Maybe I will even feel separated from myself. That cycle of feeling happy and then beating myself up happened for years. Finally, I have broken the pattern. I do still make mistakes. I look at them as lessons learned. I forgive myself and situations regularly. What I have learned from all my downloads of light codes is divine love. It does take effort to rid yourself of fear and violence.

At one point, you understand that you are the perfect you. Once you feel that deeply in all of your being, you emit joy in every movement. Find that beat, the ever-changing favorite song that makes you shimmy in joy. Like me, you too can find that balance of joy, understanding what will be done better. Living without drama or fear will become your norm. Living in gratitude has changed so much for me.

Before you know it, you understand that all will be resolved. A new confidence will spiral out of you. You will take actions of love using divine love energy. That is the superpower. It's available to everyone, anywhere, always. It is a choice you must make deep within yourself to see the joy of life, to find the good in everything, and to understand that life is just full of lessons. We are here to learn how to be better beings and how to experience joy with every breath.

Divine love and divine consciousness work. At first, for me, it felt like a lot to do. It may take a bit longer than you think, yet it goes quickly. I struggled at first to change my morning routine to include the divine stretch. I had to break the habit of meditating in bed before sleeping. It took me a while to start new habits. Changing my diet took years. I went from pork only to no pork. I had to rebuild my gut. I did several physical cleanses and went through much stress and anxiety. Finding the right supplements was costly and took lots of research. I recommend going to a naturopathic doctor for a second opinion. This of course, in addition to your traditional Western physicians. Just a side note, I spent over $3,000 with a naturopathy doctor, only to get the same answer from my nurse practitioner.

I believe in working with both Eastern and Western practitioners that are certified. I love my chiropractor and follow holistic nutritionists. I follow what my body's needs are now, not what the trendy diet is. Even understanding your personal allergies to food or the environment is meaningful when it comes to finding balance in your life.

I now know that stress is of my own making. Imagining in my head that situations were worse than they were. I no longer needed this major habit in my life. I did not need to make drama within myself, let alone around me. Living drama-free allows for clearer, easier pathways to living in love. I have made new habits. I found ways to love myself without suffering, blaming, or punishment.

The more joy I have in my heart, the more it spreads to my whole life. When I am in public, I smile and send out love to all the people I see. I do see a response. People are nice to those who show love. I respect all those around me, and they can feel it. It is time to be kind again and to show our tolerance for each other. Let's make this a nice planet and learn our lessons from the past.

During your own transition to love, you may even inadvertently hurt yourself if you are not paying attention. Your wake-up call does not need to hurt. Choosing to forgive yourself and others takes practice. It does not need to hurt you. Removing toxins from your body, and old fears you hold onto, will feel good to release.

While we go through our transition to love, we purge out toxins and traumas we knowingly or unknowingly held onto. This may happen to you; you may find something small triggers a bigger issue as you clear out your past fears. As you clear out your past, forgive yourself, and find your deepest secret; you can find a much easier way than getting a tattoo to erase it. Find your divine love and let go of the past. Purging toxins has been a specialty of mine for decades. My body always tried to take care of itself. As a girlfriend said once to me, we keep cleaning house and yet we still have lessons to learn. We forget we also must pull out the stove and clean out the hidden gunk.

Transformation can be messy. Give yourself space and time to experience all of this crazy information. The downloads may have already started as the buzzing in your soul is loud and palpable. Waking up at the same time at night, or seeing repeating numbers are signs you are on the right path. Soon you will find your daily state of joyful gratitude, it just gets lovelier and lovelier! You will find a rhythm in your day, your actions of love, in every breath. Life is good. Let's celebrate it!

So Now What?

Go live life to the fullest. It is your time to have fun and choose joy. I gave you a simplified understanding of how everything is connected. I showed you examples that you, as an individual, are far more in control of your life than we have been taught in the past. We have examined and experienced divine love and divine consciousness in each dimension. I've shown you ways to create your own life of your balance, your love, and your happiness. Now, it is all up to you.

There is much more to be written and understood on each of these dimensions. I am to be a living example of joyful, divine love and conscious light. I do live in love every day of my life, grateful to be—grateful for all that is and all that will be. Divine consciousness allows me to be aware of my happiness and the beauty that surrounds me. This does not mean it is a perfect life; I make mistakes and uncontrollable situations are all a part of living.

Be observant of your community, your surroundings, and the present moment always. It feels like living in a fuzzy state when you are fully connected. The colors are brighter. You see animals in the distance. And life feels stronger. Look at the colors you are wearing. Do they reflect an imbalance in your chakras or are they possibly giving you strength in an area?

My only desire is for you to find your own balance, your own peace in your own way and to live the most joyful life you can. Be your own guru, learn from your inner voice.

What I would like for you to take from this book is that you are in control of your own life. You have all the knowledge of divine love and divine consciousness within every cell of your being. It is simply stated in the principles: In the now, love thyself, heal thyself, self-governance, and live judgement-free in appreciative gratitude.

You will not have to hide from anything. Face your biggest fears. When the drama is gone, the judgment-free living is easy with practice. Soon, you will see your individual dream and the bigger picture of life. Your purpose is simply to experience divine love, to be joyful. That's what *ALL* put of us here for. It's truly whatever you want. Follow your inner child's dream, your dream of your highest good. Find what makes you happy! We have come to a point where we can do anything that brings us joy without hurting anything or anyone. The Age of Aquarius will allow us to step out of fear and let love rule. This is the time that, instead of being ruled from the top down, the Aquarian Age is about community, expansion of technology for the individual, and inspiration for new ways of living. We are in a transition time. We can still experience and begin to live in this way.

Go find your fun, your happiness. Go get a wonderful job, being paid to be your happiest self. It does not matter where or what your job is, so long as you are happy doing it. The divine love that flows through you is you. Send it to others as a connection to all things. Divine conscious light connects us to all the dimensions and all beings everywhere.

We all live on the same planet. We are all made the same on the inside. It is how we treat ourselves that makes us different. We can begin to feel conscious knowledge of the rocks, understanding our alien history in our DNA. We can even speak to the plastic cup and mundane objects that are tied deeply with our daily lives. As we feel into the flow of the *now* of all things tied to us, we can understand that nothing is sacred because *it all is sacred*. We are a living miracle. Every day is a gift to be present on this planet.

This is not the end of my quest for divine love, as now it has grown into wanting the world to know about divine love. My journey is constantly changing, in that it is a segment of *ALL*'s journey, which is infinite. Mother Earth will continue to grow and change. The more unified you are with her, the less her natural disasters will affect you. Transitions are in high gear; we can change immediately with love.

I will always be a dreamer. My realistic voice says, "Not in my lifetime will love rule." But what if? What if, just for the moment, we all lived judgment free, connected to the Earth and each other, allowing divine love to rule? How different the world would be. We live in a moment when it is possible.

It is time to look at the past and learn from it! Earth is a learning planet. For thousands of years, we have not learned from our mistakes. Let's change Earth from the learning planet to the loving planet! That is the true goal and purpose for all life on Earth. We must wake up and forgive our past mistakes. Whether it was yesterday, ten years ago, or ten thousand years ago, learn your lessons. Forgive yourself, forgive others and forgive situations that created the lessons. Life is to be lived, not feared. Much is coming quickly during this great transition. Make friends with your shadow self. Flow forward.

We can dream of a world never imagined—a world of our own making, of divine love and divine consciousness. Let's get this party started on Earth. Let love rule.

It's time for you to live your life. Call it what you like, Earth walk, spiritual journey, living; it is your life. You are the director, the producer, the designer, the casting director, and the main actor. How are you called to bring in joy? Live exactly who you want to be. Remember the only limitation is whatever limits you put upon yourself. This is your time, your dream, and your life.

This book is dedicated to you—for your freedom of divine love is within you. Accept the guidance of divine consciousness. Accept the divine love and divine consciousness of *ALL's* creation. You will feel the drama and fear fade away as you dream with gratitude of what will come. Live in your future joy now. **Divine love to you.**

GLOSSARY

<u>Angels</u> see Beings of Light

<u>Ascended Master</u> are the highest of the teacher guides. From Jesus Christ to Bob Marley, they can come from Earth as well as other astral realms.

<u>Ascension Reactions</u>, also known as ascension flu, is a possible reaction to going into higher places without grounding and detoxing first. Varies from person to person as well with symptoms ranging from tiredness, putting on weight, losing weight, constant state of fuzziness to throwing up. Goes away after self-care.

<u>Astral Projection or Astral Travel</u> is a deep meditative state where your conscious middle self spirit goes to a heavenly space or to other locations including other planets.

<u>Astral Realms</u> are heavens or spaces outside of Earth's time and space.

<u>Akashic Records</u> are a collection of all universal events, thoughts, expressions, and emotions of all life forms: past through future. It is the size of a universe. Billions of stars each have a space in the akashic records that is dedicated to their oversoul's complete history. It's where your past life information is stored.

<u>Blocks</u> can be thoughts, actions or beliefs that can hold you back from the highest good.

It can come from upbringing, community, social media or brought on by your own negative thoughts. They are typically in the energy of the chakras but can be found in other places with the energetical body.

Beings of Light are high frequency energy beings that are the senses for ALL, the Creative Source, God of Gods. They are angels and cosmic dragons; their form is all things.

Chakras are part of an energy system that exists within everything. They are disc-like in shape, in every color imaginable. They stack on top of one other in a specific order. Each chakra holds a different type of energy, both receiving and giving. Seven of them are commonly used in Hindi, and yogic practices. Below is basic information.

First chakra - root chakra

- *Color*: Primary Red
- *Physical location*: Between vagina/scrotum and anus
- *Areas of interest*: Grounding, security, fight-or-flight response
- *Body*: Bones and nails
- *Stones*: Red Earth, hematite, garnet, red aventurine, smoky quartz

Second chakra - sacral chakra

- *Color*: Brilliant orange
- *Physical location*: Your index and middle fingers width below the naval
- *Areas of interest*: Creation, creativity, sexuality, reproduction, relationships
- *Body*: Blood, all body fluids, sexual organs
- *Stones*: Orange calcite, carnelian, vanadinite

Third chakra - solar plexus or sun chakra

- *Color*: Yellow
- *Physical location*: Two inches below breastbone

- *Areas of Interest*: Confidence, self-love, intellect, personal power, individuality
- *Body*: Digestive: large intestines, stomach, adrenals
- *Stones*: Yellow diamond, citrine, yellow jasper, golden calcite

Fourth chakra - heart chakra

- *Color*: Green
- *Physical location*: Imagine a line from under arm to the middle of your chest
- *Areas of Interest*: Divine love, compassion, emotional balance
- *Body:* Heart and lungs, small intestines
- *Stones*: Green aventurine, jade, watermelon tourmaline

Fifth chakra - communication chakra

- *Color*: Bright blue
- *Physical location*: In the neck area, above the collar bone
- *Areas of Interest*: Communication, self-expression
- *Body:* Larynx, skeletal musculature, thyroid, ears and throat
- *Stones*: Sodalite, anglesite, blue turquoise, blue calcite

Sixth chakra - third eye

- *Color:* Indigo
- *Physical location*: Centered between eyebrows.
- *Areas of interest*: Intuition, psychic ability, spiritual awareness, consciousness
- *Body*: Pituitary
- *Stones* : Sugilite, azurite, labradorite, Lemurian quartz

Seventh chakra - crown chakra

- *Color*: Ultraviolet
- *Physical location*: Top of the head
- *Areas of interest*: Spiritual connection with the divine enlightenment

- *Body:* Pineal gland, endocrine system
- *Stones*: Clear quartz, white calcite, amethyst

Chi / Ki ancient words for life force energy

Discernment is the ability to know what is for your highest good and what is not.

Cosmic Dragons are the highest frequency beings of light (angels) known as Gamma Ray

Beings, X Ray Beings and Ultraviolet Beings. They are called dragons because of their long wavy body with various colored light energy. They burn with compassion.

Egew is where the fear of the human ego gathers. It is a shadow like, dark oily conscious substance. It is created by the collective consciousness of all humans.

High & Gemstone Chakra Layers Basic Information

Root / Soul Seed Chakra

High & gemstone chakra of the first chakra

- Gemstone & High Color: Golden Light emulating with every color on the inside
- Gemstone & High Physical location: Beneath feet
- Gemstone Shape: Seed, the flower of life.
- Stones: Natural black sapphire, tourmaline, black rainbow obsidian, Lemurian seed crystal
- Areas of interest: Connection to Earth, balance, golden silver thread of life
- Guidance for: Healing love to Earth and physical body
- High Angelic Guides: Sandalphon, Ariel

High Sacral /Orange Sapphire

High & gemstone chakra layers of the second chakra

- Gemstone Color: Bright orange to yellow light to green
- Gemstone Location: Behind the second chakra starting at the spine going outwardly.
- Gemstone Shape: Quartz cluster
- Gemstones: Orange sapphire, sunstone, rainbow moonstone, fire opal
- Areas of interest: Guidance for creating
- High color: Peridot
- High Location: 3 cm to 33 inches in front of your second chakra
- High Angelic Guides: Archangel Gabriel & Uriel, Lailah, Omael, Johpiel

High Solar Plex / Golden Citrine

High & gemstone chakra of the third chakra

- Gemstone Color: Prismatic golden yellow to bright orange
- Gemstone Location: Behind the third chakra starting at the spine going outwardly.
- Gemstone Shape: Round, Sphere
- Gemstones: Yellow diamond, chrysoberyl, yellow sapphire, golden citrine
- Areas of Interest: Self-consciousness, knowing your response to others
- High Color: Fire orange with blue greenish flames
- High Location: 3 cm to 33 inches in front of third chakra
- High Angelic Guides: Archangel Raphael & Chamuel, Haniel, Jeremiel

High Heart / Emerald

High & gemstone chakra of the fourth chakra

- Gemstone Color: Deep emerald so green it looks black.
- Gemstone Physical Location: Back of heart chakra up to brain stem
- Gemstone Shape: Rhombohedron or diamond
- Gemstones: Emerald, black diamond, malachite, green sapphire
- Areas of interest: Connection to universal knowledge and universal divine love
- High Heart Color: Rose, cotton candy pink, pink tourmaline
- High Heart Location: 3 cm to 33 inches above your heart chakra
- High Heart Guides: Holy Inanna, Isis, Quan Yin, White Tarot, Shakti, Holy Mother Mary, Mary Magdalene

High Throat / Lapis Lazuli

High & gemstone chakra of the fifth chakra

- Gemstone Color: Deep blue to turquoise blue with gold and silver
- Gemstone Location: Back of throat chakra up to brain stem
- Gemstone: Shape: Egg or oval
- Gemstones: Lapis lazuli, azure sapphire, Lander blue, spider web turquoise or Bisbee turquoise
- Areas of interest: Help with communication-speaking to otherworldly beings, international people, people of other cultures. Understanding light language and music in new ways
- High Color: Aqua green, crystal blue
- High Location: 3 cm to 33 inches above your throat chakra
- High Angelic Guides: Archangels Gabriel and Sandalphon, Israfel

<u>High Third Eye /Star Sapphire</u>

High & gemstone chakra of the sixth chakra

- Gemstone Color: Like a super seven crystal- carries all the gemstone colors.
- Gemstone Location: Pituitary gland
- Gemstone Shape: Double terminated quartz, Vogel cut crystal.
- Gemstones: Star sapphire, dumortierite, super seven quartz
- Areas of interest: Connection to higher self and over soul
- High Color: Prismatic rainbow-like clear quartz
- High location: 3 cm to 33 inches above your third eye
- High Angelic Guides: Your guardian angel

<u>High Crown / Zenith Chakra</u>

High & gemstone chakra of the seventh chakra

- Gemstone & High Color: Ultraviolet
- Gemstone & High Physical location: Beneath feet
- Gemstone Shape: Metatron's Cube
- Stones: Nirvana quartz, amethyst, purple sapphire, clear quartz
- Areas of interest: Bring in divine consciousness, divine wisdom to be guided by divine love.
- Guidance for: Divine Consciousness Christ, Buddha, Abraham, Krishna, Muhammad
- High Angelic Guides: Archangel Metatron & Michael, Holy Spirit

<u>Grounding / grounded</u> Grounding is also called earthing. It is when are connected to the rhythm of Earth, to be in communication with nature. This is done by walking barefooted or putting your hands on the ground or imagining that roots are coming out of your feet into the Earth. Drinking salt water can help ground you as well.

<u>Hara</u> is a physical spiritual center point inside the body at the lower part of your belly.

It is your core of energy and is part of your connection to *ALL,* your Godspark.

Healing responses happen in many ways and form at different times in your life. Healing responses (or reactions) are unique to each individual and each situation. There may be feelings of euphoria, wooziness, headache, ringing in the ears, dehydration, hungry feeling, or little response to no feelings. They can last from a few minutes to a few weeks depending on the work being done.

Lemurian An ancient civilization that lived on Le Mu and existed at the same time as Atlantis. It was a chain of mountains and islands where the people were deeply tied into nature.

Light Language is the language the beings of light speak, also spoken by all other worldly beings. It is a universal language.

Light Codes are higher conscious knowledge sent by beings of light and other worldly beings in rays of sunlight or starlight. These codes help open divine wisdom in your DNA or genetic makeup. Sometimes a buzzing or high energy feeling. It can make you fatigued or unable to sleep.

Lovist is one who lives by the Principles of Divine Love and Divine Consciousness.

Principles of Divine Love and Divine Consciousness:
In the *Now,*
Love thyself,
Heal thyself,
Self-governance
Live judgment free
In appreciative gratitude.

Malas are prayer beads like a rosary used to count mantras or prayers. It has 108 beads or knots.

<u>Portals</u> are bridges that look like a matrix that are within your spiritual world and accessed in meditation or sleep. They are the rainbow bridges, and prismatic tunnels that are gateways are within our consciousness to allow us to quickly travel anywhere or to recycle what is no longer needed.

<u>Sweet Bath</u> is a bath made with any combination of milk, mylks, honey, champagne, with your favorite flowers or essences.

<u>Reiki</u> A traditional Japan's form of energetical massage using universal life energy to help with physical and mental issues.

<u>White Light Beings</u> and <u>Ultraviolet Beings</u> are known as Archangels, are part of the Long Wave beings of light. The common angel ball or group of beings of light are Raphael: East Element: Air, Greatest healer Michael: South, Element of Fire, Greatest Protector. Gabriel: West, Element of water, Sound and Transition. Uriel: North, Element of Earth, Foundation. Metatron: Above, Sacred Geometry, Provider of Divine Consciousness, Father Sky. Sandalphon: Below, Nature, Provider of Divine Love, Mother Earth.

<u>Unity Consciousness</u> is a connection deep within your heart to all things, an understanding of oneness.

<u>Vesica Piscis</u> was created when divine consciousness had the thought of divine love. This thought formed a small, round sphere. It split into two spheres. The two spheres formed the Vesica Piscis. The Vesica Piscis is the area where these two spheres overlapped. It is here where sound and light began. It is within the consciousness of the Creator and its understanding of expansion of Itself, here in this egg-like shape.

<u>Vortex</u> or vortices are physical locations that carry energy of other dimensions, places or planets on Earth.

Thank You and Recommendations

I know it's proper practice to write an individual thank you note to each person. It would be a whole chapter to include all the people who influenced this book. Friends like Jamie, who encouraged me to write about dimensions, and Leslie Schellie who did the first round of editing, for Rynda who helped me make the final payment to print the book. This book would never have been completed if it wasn't for Susie Cox. So many other people are a part of this book. I am so grateful for all the people in my life. Here are some I would like to thank and recommend:

Archangel Michael www.archangel-michael.us

Adkins, Kay, Reiki master, healer, reikikay444@gmail.com also author of great books

Adkins, Kay, Gitte Europa, and Rachel Otto. *The Prophecy Map of Nova Gaia* (Independently; Amazon, 2021).

Artists- All artists! Alison Chism, Delatorre Brothers, Ace Harper, Jamie Hayes, Sibylle Peretti, Kait Rhoads, Craig Tracy, Karen Willenbrink-Johnsen to name a few.

Avalon, Arthur, and Sir John George Woodroffe. *The Serpent Power: The Secrets of Tantric and Shaktic Yoga.* (Dover Publications, 1974).

Barton, Kanela, Rev., Watsu Water Therapy, kanwatsu@aol.com

Beyond the Desert, Rancho Mirage, California, beyondthedesert111@gmail.com

Bradley-Pecoul, Paige, Blue Heart Yoga and Wellness Gretna, LA

Brownlowe, Jeremy M, fabulous books and poems found at www.typewritertroubadour.com.

Carne, Sharon, Sound healer, www.soundwellness.com

Cox, Susie, Astrologer, awesome person and author www.susiecox.com

Channeled blog, www.marigoldslove.com

Crystal Fantasy, Palm Springs, California

De Luna, Vanessa, Healer, psychic, and awesome person, www.vanessa222.com

Deike, Levi, healer and counselor, @levi0099, LinkTree, and @dr.levideike Instagram

Dyer, Wayne W. Author, and speaker

Earth Odyssey, French Quarter, New Orleans

Emoto, Masaru. *The Hidden Messages in Water* (Beyond Words Publishing, 2004).

Elizabeth Essential oils, www.elizabethessentials.com

Enlighten World Network, Facebook, YouTube, www.enlightenedworld. online/

Gitte, Europa, healer, www.europagitte.com

Green, Rebecca, Shaman, www.soulsomatics.com

Hamilton, Cindy, Healer, akashic record reader, readingswithcindy2@ gmail.com

Hay, Louise has several instrumental books, as well as podcasts.

The Haunted Museum with Bloody Mary, www.bloodymarystours.com

Hicks, Esther, and Jerry Hicks with Abraham have many wonderful publications and podcasts.

Joan of Angels, Angelic Art, and guide, www.joanofangels.com

Judith, Anodea. *Eastern Body, Western Mind* (Berkeley: Celestial Arts, 1996).

Kinchen, Yvette. *True Love, Not Like in the Movies* (Bloomington: Balboa Press, 2022).

Kenyon, Tom, Musician sound healer, www.tomkenyon.com

Lilian, Shelton, Healer extraordinaire and author, www.awakenchange.com

Lily Dale Assembly, New York

Lübeck, Walter has several books and classes on *Rainbow Reiki*. All of Walter Lübeck's books and cards are wonderful! https://walterluebeck. com/en/

Marchesseault, Marie, 1st Dan, Rainbow Reiki master healer, www. reikirejuvenation.massageplanet.com

Marsh, Phillip, Holy Fire III Reiki master teacher, Holy Fire III karuna Reiki master teacher, founder of Kaleidoscopic Reiki, owner of Mystical Treasures Emporium in Montgomery, Alabama

Mbodj Fatimata, awakenwithfatima.com

My mom, dad, sisters, niece, nephew, brother-in-law, husband, and Sophie

National Parks in United States of America

Noble, Steve, meditations on YouTube

Ober, Clinton, Martin Zucker, and Stephen Sinatra. *Earthing: The Most Important Health Discovery Ever?* (Basic Health Publications, 2010).

Ovokaitys, Dr. Todd, Lemurian Choir and Lemurian Pineal Toning

Petter, Frank Arjava Amazing person to learn from in person and his books www.frankarjavapetter.com

Portal to Ascension, https://portaltoascension.org/

Rochester, Judith, Rev., PhD. *To Touch the Soul: How to Become a Medium* (Watermark Inc, 2016).

Rooney, Dakota, aerialist and Pilates goddess, Flying Squirrel Studios, NYC

Rosetree, Rose, *Cutting Cords of Attachment* (Women's Intuition Worldwide, LLC, 2007).

Sams, Jamie and David Carson's *Medicine Cards* and Jamie's *Shaman Cards*

Sherab, Khenehen Palden, and Khenpo Tsewang Dongyal, *Tara's Enlightened Activity* (Snow Lion Publications, Incorporated, 2007).

Stevens, Cece, Astrologer and medicine woman CeceSt@aol.com

Truth Be Told Worldwide, podcast, www.truthbetoldworldwide.com

Weiss, Anjeanne, 1st Dan master, Rainbow Reiki, and licensed counselor www.wyzeheart.com

Van der Kolk, Bessel, MD. *The Body Keeps the Score* (Viking Press, 2014).

ABOUT THE AUTHOR

Rachel Otto's goal is to teach individuals about love at the highest, purest level. Spirituality is an integral part of living a balanced life and with love everything can be achieved. Through her decades of spiritual studies and varied techniques at her disposal, she has found a way that will raise your awareness of your mind and body. Rachel is a 1st Dan Master of Rainbow Reiki, a licensed angelic teacher, as well as being certified in other energy healing modalities. She has enjoyed lecturing and teaching across the United States and has conducted more than eight thousand individual healing sessions, in addition to leading private group gatherings.